Music—Psychoanalysis—Musicology

There is a growing interest in what psychoanalytic theory brings to studying and researching music. Bringing together established scholars within the field, as well as emerging voices, this collection outlines and advances psychoanalytic approaches to our understanding of a range of musics—from the romantic and the modernist to the contemporary popular. Drawing on the work of Freud, Lacan, Jung, Žižek, Barthes, and others, it demonstrates the efficacy of psychoanalytic theories in fields such as music analysis, music and culture, and musical improvisation. It engages debates about both the methods through which music is understood and the situations in which it is experienced, including those of performance and listening. This collection is an invaluable resource for students, lecturers, researchers, and anyone else interested in the intersections between music, psychoanalysis, and musicology.

Samuel Wilson is Tutor in Music Philosophy and Aesthetics at Guildhall School of Music and Drama and Lecturer in Contextual Studies at London Contemporary Dance School. He completed his PhD in 2013 at Royal Holloway, University of London. His research explores music and subjectivity in the intellectual and material contexts of recent modernity. He has published on contemporary music and aesthetics, drawing on a range of theoretical perspectives—from psychoanalysis and Critical Theory to phenomenology and posthumanism.

Music—Psychoanalysis—Musicology

Edited by Samuel Wilson

LONDON AND NEW YORK

First published 2018
by Routledge
2 Park Square, Milton Park, Abingdon, Oxon OX14 4RN

and by Routledge
711 Third Avenue, New York, NY 10017

Routledge is an imprint of the Taylor & Francis Group, an informa business

© 2018 selection and editorial matter, Samuel Wilson; individual chapters, the contributors

The right of Samuel Wilson to be identified as the author of the editorial material, and of the authors for their individual chapters, has been asserted in accordance with sections 77 and 78 of the Copyright, Designs and Patents Act 1988.

All rights reserved. No part of this book may be reprinted or reproduced or utilised in any form or by any electronic, mechanical, or other means, now known or hereafter invented, including photocopying and recording, or in any information storage or retrieval system, without permission in writing from the publishers.

Trademark notice: Product or corporate names may be trademarks or registered trademarks, and are used only for identification and explanation without intent to infringe.

British Library Cataloguing in Publication Data
A catalogue record for this book is available from the British Library

Library of Congress Cataloging in Publication Data
Names: Wilson, Samuel
Title: Music—psychoanalysis—musicology / edited by Samuel Wilson.
Description: Abingdon, Oxon; New York, NY: Routledge, 2018. | Includes bibliographical references and index.
Identifiers: LCCN 2017032560 | ISBN 9781472485830 (hardback) | ISBN 9781315596563 (ebook)
Subjects: LCSH: Music—Psychological aspects. | Psychoanalysis and music.
Classification: LCC ML3830 .M9815 2018 | DDC 781.1/1—dc23
LC record available at https://lccn.loc.gov/2017032560

ISBN: 978-1-4724-8583-0 (hbk)
ISBN: 978-1-315-59656-3 (ebk)

Typeset in Times New Roman
by codeMantra

Printed and bound by CPI Group (UK) Ltd, Croydon, CR0 4YY

Contents

List of figures vii
List of music examples viii
Acknowledgements ix
List of Contributors x

Introduction 1
SAMUEL WILSON

PART I
Psychoanalysis, musical analysis, and method 23

1 **Speaking of the voice in psychoanalysis and music** 25
   DAVID BARD-SCHWARZ

2 **Parallels between Schoenberg and Freud** 49
   ALEXANDER CARPENTER

3 **The psychodynamics of neo-Riemannian theory** 66
   KENNETH M. SMITH

4 **Schubert, music theory, and Lacanian fantasy** 84
   CHRISTOPHER TARRANT

5 **Subjective and objective violence in Taylor Swift's 'I Knew You Were Trouble'** 100
   ALEXI VELLIANITIS

PART II
Situating music and psychoanalysis — 117

6 **Does the psychoanalysis of music have a 'subject'?** — 119
   SAMUEL WILSON

7 **Jung and the transcendent function in music therapy** — 136
   RACHEL DARNLEY-SMITH

8 **Symbolic listening: the resistance of enjoyment and the enjoyment of resistance** — 151
   JUN ZUBILLAGA-POW

9 **Masochism and sentimentality: Barthes's Schumann and Schumann's Chopin** — 164
   STEPHEN DOWNES

   Bibliography — 183
   Index — 201

Figures

1.1	Robert Schumann, "Im wunderschönen Monat Mai" from Robert Schumann's *Dichterliebe*. Dietrich-Fischer Dieskau and Gerald Moore	28
1.2	Robert Schumann, "Im wunderschönen Monat Mai" from Robert Schumann's *Dichterliebe*. Charles Panzera and Alfret Cortot	29
1.3	Representation of the Lacanian psychic apparatus	34
1.4	Screenshot of Jacques Lacan speaking the words "le sujet" from *Lacan parle* (1972)	36
1.5	Screenshot of Cathy Berberian performing "tense muttering" at the beginning of Luciano Berio's *Sequenza III*	37
1.6	Heinrich Heine, 'Ich stand in dunkeln Träuman' from *Die Heimkehr, Buch der Lieder*	40
3.1	A central nub of *c* on Hostinskŷ's Tonnetz	67
3.2	Problematic *Tonnetz* reduction of Tristan's opening progression	70
3.3	Conception of Lendvai's Axis System, based on hexatonically related C–E–G♯	71
3.4	Rotation of Axes to show the opening Tristan progression	71
3.5	Conception of Weber Space, with collapsed major & minor, and rotated 90°	72
3.6	Metaphor & metonymy and substitution and combination chord relationships	74
3.7	Richard Wagner, *Tristan & Isolde*, Prelude, bars 1–17	79
3.8	Richard Wagner, *Tristan & Isolde*, Prelude, table of rotations, bars 44–77	79
4.1	Quartet in G major, D. 887, first movement exposition	89
4.2	Lacan's Graph of Desire	92
8.1	Speed and accuracy of harmonic recognition by musicians and non-musicians	154
9.1	Fernand Khnopff, *Listening to Schumann* (1883)	177

Music examples

1.1 Richard Wagner, *Parsifal*: Act II. (In reference to Kundry, Wagner writes: "Sie stößt hier einen gräßlichen Schrei aus". English: "She lets out here a grotesque scream")   31
1.2 Alban Berg, *Wozzeck*, Act III, scene ii, Marie's death (some parts not shown)   31
1.3 Alban Berg, *Lulu*, Act III, scene ii, Lulu's death (some parts not shown)   32
1.4 Franz Schubert, 'Der Doppelgänger', a representation of repetitive patterns in the setting of the first two stanzas of Heine's poem   35
1.5 Franz Schubert, 'Ihr Bild' from *Schwanengesang*   42
3.1 Richard Wagner, *Tristan & Isolde*, Prelude, bars 1–29   78
4.1 Franz Schubert, String Quartet in G major, D. 887, first movement, opening   87
4.2 Franz Schubert, String Quartet in G major, D. 887, first movement, closing bars   90
9.1 Robert Schumann, 'Chopin' from *Carnaval*, Op. 9   174

Acknowledgements

This collection brings together a number of established scholars and emerging voices. The impetus for developing this project arose initially at the RMA–SMA Music and Psychoanalysis Study Day held at the Department of Music at the University of Liverpool in 2013, an event at which a number of the chapter contributors presented. Others then joined the project, generously contributing their expertise and energy in the spirit of scholarly collaboration.

I would like to thank Heidi Bishop, Senior Editor, and Annie Vaughan, Editorial Assistant of Music Books at Routledge, for their guidance in bringing the collection towards completion, and Laura Macy for her encouragement during the early stages of this project. I am also grateful to the anonymous reviewers of the original project proposal and the manuscript. The final collection is doubtlessly stronger for their recommendations.

There are others to whom I am grateful for assistance in a myriad of forms. Some deserve particular mention. Kenneth M. Smith has been thoughtful and open in informally offering advice to an editor of a collection developing what is their first book project. I am would also like to thank Annika Forkert and Christopher Tarrant, who both kindly agreed to provide suggestions on an early version of the editor's introduction.

Finally, my thanks goes to all the authors whose chapters constitute the collection. They have participated fully in its emergence—providing feedback on each other's chapters at a draft stage, and engaging thoughtfully and generously in the process of the collection's making.

Samuel Wilson
Guildhall School of Music and Drama
London Contemporary Dance School

Contributors

David Bard-Schwarz has degrees in English (University of Virginia), Comparative Literature (Indiana University), German (Universität Hamburg), Interactive Telecommunications (New York University), and Music Theory (the University of Texas at Austin). He is Associate Professor of Music at the College of Music, the University of North Texas. He is married to violinist and Adjunct Professor of Violin (Texas Woman's University) Dr Ania Bard-Schwarz.

Alexander Carpenter is a musicologist and music critic. His research interests include the music of Arnold Schoenberg, popular music, and the relationship between music and psychoanalysis. He teaches music history and theory at the Augustana campus of the University of Alberta, where he is an Associate Professor and Chair of the Department of Fine Arts and Humanities.

Rachel Darnley-Smith is a music therapist and teaches at the University of Roehampton. She has written on a range of topics related to music therapy, including psychoanalysis, aesthetics, improvisation, and intersubjectivity in music making in late life. She is co-author, with Helen M. Patey, of *Music Therapy* (Sage Publications, 2003), and 'The Role of Ontology in Music Therapy Theory and Practice' in *The Music in Music Therapy* (ed. Jos De Backer and Julie Sutto, Jessica Kingsley Publishers, 2014). She is joint editor, with Sandra Evans and Jane Garner, of the forthcoming *Psychodynamic Perspectives and the Care of People With Dementia* (Routledge).

Stephen Downes is Professor of Music at Royal Holloway, University of London. He is the author of six monographs, including *Music and Decadence in European Modernism* (2010) and *After Mahler* (2013). He is also editor of *Aesthetics of Music: Musicological Approaches* (2014) and *The Szymanowski Companion* (2014). He is a past winner of the Wilk Prize for Research in Polish Music (University of Southern California) and was awarded the Karol Szymanowski Memorial Medal.

Kenneth M. Smith is a Senior Lecturer in music at the University of Liverpool. He completed his PhD at Durham University in 2009 and subsequently held teaching fellowships at Durham and Keele. While his research is analytical in focus, other areas of interest include: nineteenth- and twentieth-century music and philosophy, semiotics, psychoanalysis, and aesthetic theory. His monograph, *Skryabin, Philosophy and the Music of*

Desire (2013), is an interdisciplinary study of Skryabin's harmonic system and its roots in Russian culture and philosophy. Kenneth works broadly with neo-Riemannian theory and his current book project is entitled *Desire in Chromatic Harmony: A Psychodynamic Exploration of Fin de Siècle Tonality*. Kenneth also publishes on popular music and is co-editing *Expanded Approaches to Analyzing Popular Music* (Routledge).

Christopher Tarrant is a Teaching Fellow in Musicology at the University of Bristol, having taught previously at the Universities of Newcastle and Oxford, and Royal Holloway, University of London where he wrote his PhD thesis on Schubert's instrumental works. His research interests include intersections between critical theory and music analysis, analysis of music from the late eighteenth to the early twentieth centuries, and music from the Nordic region, especially Carl Nielsen.

Alexi Vellianitis is a research student at the University of Oxford, and stipendiary lecturer in Music at St Catherine's College. His doctoral thesis looks at the uses of urban music and street culture in twenty-first century British modernist music.

Samuel Wilson (editor) is Tutor in Music Philosophy and Aesthetics at Guildhall School of Music and Drama and Lecturer in Contextual Studies at London Contemporary Dance School. He completed his PhD in 2013 at Royal Holloway, University of London. His research explores music and subjectivity in the intellectual and material contexts of recent modernity. He has published on contemporary music and aesthetics, drawing on a range of theoretical perspectives—from psychoanalysis and Critical Theory to phenomenology and posthumanism.

Jun Zubillaga-Pow obtained his PhD in Historical Musicology and MA in Critical Methodologies from King's College London. He is a cultural historian and musicologist specialising in Germanic and Singapore cultures of the twentieth century. Jun is the co-editor of *Singapore Soundscape: Musical Renaissance of a Global City* (National Library Board, 2014), and *Queer Singapore: Illiberal Citizenship and Mediated Cultures* (Hong Kong University Press, 2012), and is currently co-editing two separate volumes on Schoenberg studies and Islamicate sexualities.

Introduction

Samuel Wilson

There is a growing interest in what psychoanalytic theory could mean for music and, conversely, what music might show us about psychoanalysis. Musicologists, music historians, analysts, and others continue to draw on psychoanalysis as a theoretical wellspring, in order to say something productively of music.[1] Indeed, even in much musicological thinking where explicit references are not made to psychoanalytic figures—such as Freud, Lacan, or Jung—these figures' ideas can be observed to have permeated these discussions; psychoanalytic thinking, it could be said, informs musicology and the intellectual cultures in which it is undertaken, both consciously and unconsciously.

The 'psychoanalysis' of this collection's title refers to something that is multifaceted and complex, an overlapping set of tendencies, interests, perspectives, and methodological inclinations here orientated around music's relation to the mind, meaning, and interpretation (among other things). In connection with the other two terms—music and musicology—it also evokes theoretical discourses that are related though distinct from the clinical practice of psychoanalysis and psychotherapy. Indeed, a theme that is present in many of the chapters that follow is the evocation of ideas themselves produced through an ongoing dialogue between artistic and cultural practices and those derived from psychoanalysis (principally indebted here to the ideas of Freud and Lacan). This enables the collection's contributors to engage rich traditions of psychoanalytically informed theories about music, the arts, and the cultures in which these unfold—as one might encounter, in very different ways, in the writings of commentators such as Theodor W. Adorno, Roland Barthes, and Slavoj Žižek.

This introduction outlines some trends, issues, and opportunities in connections between music, psychoanalysis, and musicology past and present. It aims, first, to provide the reader a critical survey of some significant and sometimes problematic themes that have emerged in psychoanalytic discourses on music. These themes have included music's debated associations with early childhood, the body and—more obviously problematically— its relation to "primitive" aspects of the mind and society, as well as music's enabling of a symbolic mastery of aspects of the world and the self. This opening discussion also serves to furnish the musically and musicologically oriented reader with psychoanalytic studies of music and examples that they may wish to follow up independently, including a number of historic accounts that form part of later theory's genealogy. Second, it is suggested that, through considering these studies, it may be demonstrated that in bringing together music and psychoanalysis one enacts a complex intermingling of different concepts and values. I hope to illustrate that ideas about music and psychoanalysis can be sketched in relation to one another—an idea echoed in many of the chapters that follow.

Music and sound in psychoanalysis

Musical sound and early childhood

One of music's challenges to interpretation is ontological: sound is its primary medium. What Lacan said of the voice in particular—that, just as it is uttered, it is lost—can in some sense be said of music more generally. For Lacan, the voice was associated with the *objet petit a*, the always receding, imagined object of desire that always eludes our final grasp.[2] Sound is a transient phenomenon, generally without a clear material referent—this can be said even more emphatically of *musical sound* in particular, in so far as music seems to rely on sound while simultaneously exceeding any reduction to it; even if one identifies its sound, the concept of music still seems to evade capture. 'Music is what we may call an objectless art', said the psychoanalyst Richard Sterba. He argued that, unlike non-musical arts, in which 'conscious and unconscious instinctual wishes are expressed and represented in the form of an image of the outside world', emotions in music are not represented 'in the form of images of the outside world'.[3] To make sense of a painting or sculpture one can always return to a concrete referent that is evidently connected to the world beyond it. These connections are seemingly resisted in music that has often been—at least within the domain of the Western art music tradition—regarded as inhabiting its own autonomous sphere. This difference is most pronounced in a contrast between figurative art and so-called "absolute" music, where the latter 'work of art is not a copy of reality'.[4] Indeed, in line with Lacan's *objet petit a*, this resistance to interpretation—that it escapes our grasp—might be one reason why we are drawn so compelling to music.

Music's apparently objectless quality, among other reasons to be discussed below, leads it to be often associated with early childhood.[5] This is because this era of development is itself often imagined and characterized as a time before the development of firm categories of subject and object (such as me and not-me); indeed, these are categories that also seem to blur as the music (not-me) washes over me; it is seemingly both within me and outside. Music, as mentioned above, does not provide the listener a solid and concretely delineated object but is often said to instead encompass the subject and thus complicate the self-other distinction.[6] This early infantile period is also often associated with a time prior to an individual's entry into a "symbolic" universe—predominantly language—that enables us to structure our experience of the world and ascribe it discernible meanings. (Some implications of this idea are discussed below.) This association with early childhood means that music, or at least aspects of it, are characterized as "regressive". Reviewing the relevant literature 'makes it obvious that the gratification which music provides is based on a deep regression to the earliest stages of extra-uterine mental development', opined Sterba.[7] Music's regressive characteristics are not necessarily negative, however. Ernst Kris, writing in 1952, was highly influential on later psychoanalytic discussions of art in his suggestion that one may view 'artistic activity as regression in the service of the ego'.[8] This is a form of regression in which the higher mental functions are withdrawn, and earlier forms come to dominate. This enables relaxation and relieving of the former from the stresses and strains of their constant use.[9]

Indeed, some have attributed music the capacity to recall or sublimate affects associated with specific aspects or developmental stages of early childhood. Isador H. Coriat was direct about this connection. He wrote that "the infantile interest in sound accompanying flatus may be transferred later in life to the subject of music and thus there is an anal erotic association of which music is the sublimation".[10] This idea developed the notion, presented as early as 1921 by Sigmund Pfeifer, that music enables for the listener a form of libidinal release or satisfaction, originally achieved through the 'ejection of pent-up primary narcissistic and autoerotic libido with a dematerialized substitute substance'[11]—air—via part of the body that is 'an erotogenic zone charged with libido',[12] such as the mouth or anus. Music was thus understood as 'a recapitulation of libidinal expression'.[13] While this specific reasoning, regarding erotogenic zones like the mouth and anus, is unlikely to be accepted universally, there was, particularly in psychoanalytic theorizations of music from the first half of the twentieth century, a general agreement that music enables forms of libidinal release that recall early childhood and the early developmental history of the subject.

Early infantile life is also often characterized as a relatively undifferentiated continuum, associated with the body, though a body not necessarily limited to its differentiation with the world beyond the threshold of the skin. Sound easily transverses those bodily limits that differentiate subjects from the surrounding world; it challenges boundaries of selfhood that are both physical (the skin) and psychical (the ego).[14] This is readily evident in loud and bass-heavy music that is experienced both as impacting *on* the body and simultaneously felt *within* it. Indeed, some suggest that this apparently pre-verbal, pre-symbolic realm is pre-echoed even before birth. Still within the womb, 'sounds from the outside world and the mother's body penetrate into the uterus, reverberating through the amniotic fluid and pulsing around the fetus's body as an audiophonic skin'.[15]

Mastery and the "oceanic feeling"

The psychoanalyst Heinz Kohut, like many others, pointed to music's provision of the experience of what Freud called an "oceanic feeling", of limitlessness.[16] The concept of mastery is often related to early childhood experiences and the oceanic feeling—and thus music is likewise associated with these same experiences. As David Bard-Schwarz summarizes, in oceanic fantasies, 'the boundary separating the body from the external world seems dissolved or crossed in some way'.[17] In this sense, music enables the subject's enjoyment of the imagined dissolution of its own limits. At the same time as entertaining the subject's suspension, music can also provide a fantasy for a subject reaching beyond its own limits. As with Freud's "oceanic feeling", music seems to recall what Lacan likewise characterizes as the 'undifferentiated and miasmic state' in which the young infant finds itself. This state, for Lacan, is prior to kinship structures and language, which emerge later.[18] Music—or at least aspects of it—are thereby imagined to exist prior to the symbolic conditions and grammar through which the self is recognized or articulated. Through an imagined dissolution of the boundary between self and other, the world becomes a pliable aspect of the self; music clothes the world under 'an extension of the psychic organization that brings the cosmos under the domination of the self'.[19] Similarly, it has been suggested by others that music recalls the gratifying motility that was experienced in very early childhood—a bodily experience that "constitutes a primitive narcissistic pleasure" and "affords a model for the domination of the objects in the external world". In this moment, the "acting person and the object that is influenced become one".[20] Musical movement here becomes a fantastical extension of bodily movement. But, as Bard-Schwarz reminds us, to be enjoyed as 'an object of play (unless one speaks of self-destructive fantasies)' this dissolution must be experienced from a 'fantasy position of mastery'.[21]

'Closing one's ears is a more complex task than closing one's eyes', wrote Martin L. Nass.[22] This is one reason why music has been said many times to illicit fantasies of mastery or enable the practice and development of healthy defense mechanisms; the experience of sound is unavoidable and, as such, its transmutation into music and musical practices permits fantasies of its control.[23] Yet it is not only sound in general that is mastered through music. Musicking enables mastery of other elements of life that are enlivened through acts of music-making. Through closely allying music and the body, this mastery has often been said to be that of, firstly, one's own body; Carroll C. Pratt suggested that 'auditory patterns [...] find correspondence with organic and visceral patterns in the body'.[24] Sterba expressed something similar, and heard music as a mastery of movement, one that recalls the ideal mastery of movement experienced in the early stages of infancy, from which autoerotic pleasure was gained. Music, he wrote, 'brings about not only regression to early infantile kinaesthetic pleasure, but also the intense pleasure of experiencing the dissolution of barriers between the self and the outside world'.[25]

Music is a quintessentially temporal art and its relation to mastery of the body has also been considered in this respect. Sybille Yate's 1935 essay is an early attempt to develop this idea. Time, Yates suggests, is a structuring and patterning device common both to the young infant's experiences and to the adult's musical world. Like many others, Yates saw music in general as related to the infant's mastery of this world—and this evocation continues to exert an influence on the adult's experience of music. 'Time is marked for the infant by the repetition of things which gradually become known', such as being fed, washed, and dressed.[26] Through such experiences, a rhythmicity is ingrained in the infant that persists into later life. Indeed, these rhythms are granted particular affordances: rhythms of feeding and excretion afford promises of satisfaction and release. Music was thus taken as an act of mastery that sublimates rhythms and their affordances in a more general sense. Bodily rhythms learned during infancy are echoed and mastered through music as a temporal art.[27] Others have suggested additional interpretations of music's temporal dimension, and its relation to early childhood; where, for example, music evokes those gentle rocking rhythms that are 'used in calming the distressed infant'.[28]

It has been said often that music enables the mastery of one's (internalized) relation to the mother figure. This is manifest in music's temporality, through features such as rhythm and the ordering of its events. In these terms, Eero Rechardt has suggested that the structure of music can echo the structure of aspects of upbringing. The 'Mother's leaving and returning' is transmuted in children's play—the *fort-da* game being the prototypical example[29]—and is likewise found in the musical "play" of adults too, as, for instance, in the tonal and thematic journeys that constitutes the classical sonata: 'Important elements in experiencing music contain play with give and take, disappearing the reappearing, getting lost and safely finding the way back home'.[30] Furthermore, Gilbert J. Rose, citing Yates's proposition about music's mastering of time, suggests that nuances in timing and pitch—such as swing and *tempo rubato*, and vibrato—constitute a playing with our relation to this imagined other. These nuances are manifestations of mastery through play. Rose suggests that

> the attraction of the "slight out of syncness" and "out of tuneness" might itself reflect that the original developmental union we hypothesize between infant and caretaker was less perfect than the one we are inclined to idealize in safe retrospect.[31]

In this view, treatments of time in music enable a management and imagined mastery of the mother-child relation. As Rose also points out, music can highlight temporal aspects of experience in general, aspects that would otherwise go unnoticed; music affords 'a representation of the emotional quality of subjective, lived time made audible—an auditory apparition of felt-time. Instead of vaguely sensing time as we do through our own physical life processes, we hear its passage'.[32] One could add that marking out time can also act as a form of mastery in itself: time, recognized and acknowledged in its unfolding, in music becomes rendered a "substance" to be shaped through aestheticized play. One moves from 'sensing time' to *making sense* of it through giving it shape musically.[33]

Performing psychoanalysis and music

Musics

It should be clear by now that, while a number of themes keep resurfacing, psychoanalysis and psychoanalytic theory are not singular phenomena; they are practiced through a myriad of forms, schools, and discursive practices. However, in this introductory discussion, I have been referring to "music" as if what were meant by this is self-evident—as if this were unproblematically singular in nature. In recent decades, however, musicology has sought to recognize and problematize this unitary "music" as diverse and plural. This potentially puts it at odds with some kinds of psychoanalytic approaches, those that have tended to take a particular kind of music as their object of study—unsurprisingly, Western art music of the common practice period— and assumed the universality of this particular. General conclusions about this universalized—capital "M"—Music have often relied on naturalized assumptions about the music referred to, or have functioned to supply broad comparisons of the psychological significance of different musical styles (for example, "classical" as compared with "jazz").

The problem of the assumed universalizing of a particular kind of music— and of its meaning—is readily apparent in some "vulgar" Freudian studies of symbolism. Angelo Montani's 1945 article, entitled simply 'Psychoanalysis of Music', is exemplary in this regard, an article in which the author suggests that the affective differences of major and minor modes are founded on the symbolic associations of their different third scale degrees.[34] The power of meaning through association is stretched over a number of steps. Montani notes first that, 'In the study of symbolism of the numbers we learn that the number [3] is associated with the "phallus" (i.e., ancient Hebrew graphy), the number 3 is the phallic number, the number of power'. At the same time, the names for minor and major suggest hardness and softness in various languages—and for this 'they do manifest quite clearly a sexual association'. Major and minor are in Italian "Modo Duro" and "Modo Molle" and in French "Mode Dur" and "Mode Moll", the author notes. Both derive from the Latin forms "durus" (hard) and "mollis" (soft). Major would thus effect a strong, hard possession of "the phallus" (in musical terms, the third scale degree); which itself stands symbolically for a position of power. The listener, when listening to this mode, thus also possesses and takes pleasure in this position of power. By contrast, the soft weakness and femininity of the minor mode, according to the author, recalls the *castration complex*, bringing with it repressed negative affectivity.[35] In this account, a tonal framework is assumed as normative—and indeed from this system features are isolated and decontextualized—such that they might be interpreted on the terms of an assumed, normative structure of subjectivity (and this is not even to mention the problematic gendering of this subject).[36]

Contrasting with this universalization of the particular, some recent commentators draw attention to the particularity of their focus. For instance, instead of promoting psychoanalysis as key to explaining music in general, some have argued in terms of specificity, for example, that '*classical* psychoanalysis and *classical* music are kindred spirits, perhaps more convergent than divergent',[37] and have as such identified points of correspondence between two particular forms of thought—one theoretical, the other musical. Others have pointed to the psychoanalytic questions begged by specific historical, aesthetic, or stylistic moments in art and music—as, for example, with modernist and postmodernist music. In his classic *The Psycho-Analysis of Artistic Vision and Hearing* (1953), Anton Ehrenzweig suggested that early twentieth-century art, in comparison with traditional, 'inhibited' art, 'proved useful for an investigation of unconscious form processes because—for a yet not fully explained reason—it more clearly revealed the workings of the artist's unconscious', thereby providing a more direct expression of these workings.[38] Modernist art and music both challenged representation and the assumed relationship between the artist and their materials. In visual art, in accordance with this perspective, one could hold up surrealism or primitivism as examples visibly arising from the unconscious and its processes; in music, expressionism or forms of improvisatory practice that encompass free-association and the (apparent) immediacy of play provide further possible examples.

Others have been wary of the view that the individual unconscious of the artist comes into view through modernist art in a more direct sense than in traditional art. By contrast, they claim that modernism problematizes the possibilities of representation and expression as such—the claims of traditional canonized cultural and aesthetic forms to be expressive and natural. Instead of modernist art constituting an immediately apparent sublimation of expression, as in Ehrenzweig's view, modernism became viewed as a critical practice that '"desublimates" cultural forms' so as to make their historical and social contingency apparent.[39] By shifting the focus from artist to the culture in which they were embedded, the "problems" and contradictions worked-through or expressed in modernist art were taken to foreground something societal over, or in addition to, something individual.[40] Postmodern music has similarly become understood as constitutive of, and indicative of a response to, a specific set of changing cultural conditions—and psychoanalytic theory might tell us about both these musics and their cultures, as well as something of the relation between the two.[41]

Music and the developing mind

A presumed "Music" enabled this object to be imagined as standing universally. This was often articulated by differentiating language from music: where language is rational, music is emotional; language principally engages the mind, music bears its trace first on the body; language is definite, music indefinite. Theodor Reik's comments were representative of this widely held view:

> Music is the universal language of human emotion, the expression of the inexpressible. [...]
> Human speech denotes the material reality, music is the language of psychic reality. [...]
> Music expresses what all men feel much more than what they think. Its language is an Esperanto of emotions rather than of ideas. [...][42]

Similarly, Carroll C. Pratt aligned music, and the emotions it stirs, closely with the body. He argued that emotions have 'their locus within the bodily structure'[43] and furthermore that music imitated these emotional structures: 'The ears of those who love music are filled with the form but not with the material of emotions.' As such, *'Music sounds the way emotions feel.'*[44] The implicit utopianism of such perspectives sometimes became explicit; Pinchas Noy suggested that the non-representational nature of "musical language", in contrast with the definiteness of language proper, meant that music could 'serve a [*sic*] language understandable to everyone'.[45]

This universalism draws from a narrative origin imagined since at least Rousseau: the idea that music and language developed from a system of ur-expression that unified both.[46] Ehrenzweig made this assumption explicit:

> It is not unreasonable to speculate that speech and music have descended from a common origin in a primitive language [....] Later this primeval language would have split into different branches: music would have retained the articulation mainly by pitch (scale) and duration (rhythm), while language chose articulation mainly by tone colour (vowels and consonants).[47]

The use of the word 'primitive' is important here: in past psychoanalytic literature, it has been used to refer both to the early infantile life of individuals and to the societies ("primitive peoples") as a whole; indeed, it does not merely indicate something chronological—it is a highly charged term that implies a teleological development from the primitive to the advanced, and thereby bestows or denies certain roles and values on that it proclaims.

Developmental psychological narratives or presuppositions have profoundly impacted psychoanalytic and psychological interpretations of music: of music as such, of aspects of it, and indeed, of its repertoires

Introduction 9

and canons. These narratives have been related both to individual and to societal developments.[48] Indeed, the two aspects have been correlated in what are now widely acknowledged as ideologically problematic accounts. Bruno Nettl's early article on 'Infant Musical Development and Primitive Music' provides one representative example (and one quite different in perspective from his later ethnomusicological work). The author argued that the musical play of infants echoes the musical forms used by "primitive" peoples; the implication is that the psychology of the child, akin to the psychology of the primitive, results in similar musical patterning. As Nettl put it, '[t]he simple form of repeating a single musical phrase with variations' is an early development in infants' music-making and can be found widely across cultures. 'It is the only form in some simple cultures', however.[49] Nettl concluded, tentatively, by effectively positing a weak form of recapitulation theory, in which ontogenetic musical development (the move from children's music to adults' music) correlates with the phylogenetic development of musical culture (that from primitives' music to "advanced" music): 'there is some correlation between the order of the appearance of musical traits in infants and the frequency of those traits in the musical cultures of the world'.[50] By extension, it is as if primitive culture and music embodies an earlier, childlike stage of the developmental process, having not yet achieved "adulthood".

Music's apparently "primitive" aspects were highlighted by a large number of past psychoanalytic writers. Richard Sterba pointed to the plenitude provided by musical experiences, one both social and sexual—something attesting to the close connection between libidinal expression and music. For Sterba, these primitive characteristics of music, which are present in all music in some form, were foregrounded most clearly in the music of the primitives themselves:

> The ecstasy at festivals of primitives is achieved by dance and music. The boundlessness and irrationality of the primitives at such occasions is brought about by the ecstasy of tones. At the same time the music of primitives is predominantly a common social process; there are only participants, no listeners. In primitive dances music and sexuality are practically identical.[51]

In this account, the primitive enjoys in music a celebration of liberated immediacy. In a manner reminiscent of early infantile life, this sonically (musically) and somatically (through dance) provides autoerotic gratification of both individual bodies and multiple bodies, socially "in harmony" with one another.[52]

It is easy to criticize constructions of "the primitive" such as this as obviously outdated, racist, and—one hopes—now superseded. However, there are at least two reasons, besides their inherent theoretical and historical interest, that I rehearse these accounts here. First, while one no longer finds references to "primitive culture" and "the primitives" in more recent scholarship, there is still, occasionally explicitly but more often implicitly, a role for the primitive aspects of the self—and this is in some sense informed by these earlier discourses. An implicit use can be observed where one finds appeals to "advanced", "highly developed", or "higher" aspects of music and the mind—and where these latter aspects connote implicit value. Here, while terms like "primitive" are left unsaid, their relational others remain. Indeed, in the manner of a Derridean supplement, terms such as "advanced" evoke these absent—"unconscious"—entities in order to take meaning through relation to them. This framework enables a presumed universality of aspects of music and the mind—a presumed hierarchy through which we again encounter the bestowing (or not) of value on particular musics, musical features, or ways of making or listening to music.

By way of an example representative of some theoretical tendencies encountered more broadly: in his essay on 'How Music Conveys Emotions', Pinchas Noy suggested that "High" music (which he closely associated with art music), in contrast with '[c]ommon or "pop" music', is more challenging as a listening experience; it requires more activity on the part of the listener, and is thus, in the end, all the more satisfying. He claims that if one were to

> arrange the various styles of music along a continuum from the "lowest" to the "highest" music, the difference is that while at the lower pole, music, by caressing, hypnotizing, or stimulating him directly, entices the listener into a passive and regressive attitude; at the higher pole it always attempts to challenge him into some kind of active involvement. The listener has to always do something and invest some mental efforts in order to get his satisfaction.[53]

Valuably, Noy pronounced the listener to be an active component in the musical experience. This contrasts with many psychoanalytic accounts of music that dominated the early twentieth century, which tended to consider the listener only secondarily as a passive receipt of musical meaning. However, it is interesting to note that Noy associated this activeness with a specific repertoire; it is only a particular kind of music that invites (a particular kind of) activeness, that leads to (a particular kind of) satisfaction. Indeed, it is notable that the "High" music that invites these modalities of activeness and satisfaction is also associated with a high degree of cultural capital, which seems to suggest that the performance of "activity" is not merely cognitive, on the part of the individual, but manifests sociocultural overtones.[54] Noy's concept of 'mental efforts' evokes a particular kind of listening, echoing perhaps the effort required in *structural listening*, that modality of listening, famously diagnosed by Rose Rosengard Subotnik, which 'concentrates attention primarily on the formal relationships established over the course of a single composition'.[55] Structural listening celebrates a form of active engagement of the music by the listener, through which they attempt to formally understand the musical object. This is a far-reaching idea which has its roots in Viennese classicism and romanticism but that is, in Subotnik's view, pronounced in the writings of Adorno and Schoenberg. As with structural listening, the listener encountered in Noy's account is not only 'active' but, through this activity, reinscribes a framework of aesthetic judgement that attributes value to music on these terms. This is not to say that this is not a meaningful mode of listening, just that it is necessary to recognize that it is historically and experientially contingent on one *of many* traditions and practices of music-making.

Thinking through the cultural implications of discourses surrounding music, as I have attempted briefly above, is indebted in large part to feminist and deconstructionist theories that call our attention to the ideological work implicit in dualisms, such as advanced and regressive, higher and lower, mind and body. From these theoretical orientations—themselves in part owing to psychoanalytic thought—it may be pointed out that one term in these dualisms tends to be favored over the other, and that these correspond to some degree (i.e., "advanced" with "higher" with "mind", "regressive" with "lower" with "body"). Indeed, on these terms, the widely encountered associations of musical features with the early infantile, the bodily, the pre-symbolic or the pre-linguistic, have been explored critically by a number of scholars. For example, Elizabeth Tolbert situates the music-language dualism within a dominantly logocentric cultural condition, in which a meaningful language is valued above and contrasted with an emotional and affective music. As she puts it, in this case music becomes

> the subordinate term in oppositions such as culture/nature, human/animal, mind/body, or reason/emotion [....] Logocentric concepts of music [...] uphold the hegemony of language, at least in part, by maintaining the hegemony of musics that disavow their emotional and sensual qualities.

She notes also that some of these perspectives bring to their discussion of music the same structure of domination; they seek to privilege that which is deemed cultural and rational in the music over its seemingly emotional or sensual qualities.[56]

It is notable, perhaps in part for this reason, that some commentators remain a "step back" from committing to ascribe pre-linguistic, sensuous qualities to music or musical sound itself; Bard-Schwarz, for instance, talks of music's ability to evoke '*fantasies* of a pre-linguistic sound world'—here music does not embody this world directly.[57] Furthermore, others have reflected on how music's association with specific forms of sensuality and femininity has been produced under particular historical and material conditions. For instance, Ian Biddle has considered how, in nineteenth-century opera, musical practices constituted ideas of femininity and its relation to the masculine; here femininity was invested as a site of (bodily, sexual) physicality and as a mode of 'affective consumption *par excellence*'.[58] Biddle suggests this was a symptom of what he calls 'opera's unconscious', something unspoken yet highly gendered:

> Opera's unconscious, then, is what men do not tell us: their access to opera as a technology, their dominance of the financial mechanisms by which opera operates, their consistent and overwhelming control, that is, of the operatic means of production, ensures that opera is materially guaranteed to act on women as its primary object and cause.[59]

Reflecting on familial rather than the material-economic conditions of production, Alexander Stein has argued that associating early infantile audial experiences with the mother exclusively puts us at danger of overgeneralizing the connection between sound and femininity; one could perhaps more productively talk of the 'polyregistral parental sound environment'. Indeed, through recognizing the gendered quality of the mother's and father's voices, one also recognizes the early infant's acoustic origins as contributing to sonic associations of gender.[60]

With these ideas in mind, one could caution a self-reflexive attitude, through which one is sensitive to the ideological and aesthetic performances one implicitly undertakes when performing psychoanalytic theorizations of music; these have implications for assumptions regarding things as diverse as the aesthetics of musical value, the status of the listener, and conceptions of gender.

Music, psychoanalysis, and musicology in relation

This self-reflexive inclination brings us to a second reason for having considered accounts that foreground issues of "the primitive", of value, of the politics of theory and of musical listening. These critical issues make clear that the meanings found in music and psychoanalysis have been—and perhaps still are—articulated in relation to one another: the animalistic energies of the Id have been imagined through the "liberated" moment of musical improvisation; the unconceptualizable pre-symbolic realm has been paradoxically traced conceptually through "oceanic" musical textures and elements of music's sounding.[61] One could say that music is invested theoretically, as well as emotionally. Furthermore, as noted above, these discourses contribute to the production of cultural and aesthetic meanings in addition to those that are "purely musical", or even "purely psychoanalytical". Simply put, these discussions manifest ideas about *both* musical and psychoanalytic cultures and values. Musicology thereby contributes to a sense of culturally manifested psychoanalytic theory.

This goes for particular features of music and for repertories as a whole. With hindsight, this is again clear if one investigates some historical accounts about music and psychoanalysis. One finds, for example, that *specific aspects* of music have been credited with profound connections to music's associations with early childhood and/or primitive experiences, as mentioned above. Rhythm has often been cited repeatedly in this respect. Heinz Kohut, for instance, considered those 'primitive rhythmic experiences', that belonged

> to that part of psychic life which Freud subsumed under the concept of infantile sexuality. The rocking of disturbed children and of schizophrenics and the ecstatic rites of primitive tribes may serve as examples.

He went on to note that '[r]hythm, of course, also plays an important role in mature sexuality, the only experience of the adult ego that equals the quality and relative intensity of infantile psychic life'.[62] Rhythm, in this account and many like it, is associated with immediacy, and music's somatic, bodily, (auto)erotic aspects. Indeed, even where rhythm is put forward as a mediating structure—rather than as immediately expressive—its status as a primary or primitive ordering principle is made explicit: for Eero Rechardt, 'Rhythm brings order to chaos. It is the beginning of orderliness in its most primitive form';[63] rhythm was for Sterba 'the taming of the original instinctual outbreak'.[64]

Through associating particular aspects of music with particular features of subjectivity—say, with the rawness of the Id—one performs a discourse that reinscribes or problematizes a larger set of meanings and ideological assumptions. By way of example: associating rhythm with the primitive body and autoerotic gratification has acted to enable the denigration, in the guise of an objective scientific discourse, of what were perceived as rhythmic musics. Isador H. Coriat reflected a widely held view when he wrote that 'the most potent element in jazz is a primitive rhythm'.[65] In discussions such as these, one aspect of music, rhythm, was attributed with a specific psychological significance; this effects generalized conclusions about not only this aspect of the music, but of entire musical repertoires deemed to celebrate this aspect. An early attempt to problematize these assumptions about jazz and the unconscious is provided by Norman M. Margolis's 1954 article, 'A Theory on the Psychology of Jazz'. Margolis casts this tendency in the light of different musics' places within society. He argued that

> the general Puritan, Anglo-Saxon tradition [...] dictated a rigid cultural conscience which required the repression of the objectionable impulses with which jazz had become associated and symbolized. But further, jazz in itself was a protest against this oppressive culture, and its acceptance implied a threat to the cultural conscience – a "return of the repressed".[66]

As such, he did not ascribe jazz with the characteristic of being absolutely and naturally more free to express the impulses of the unconscious; by contrast, he saw the ascription of this quality as contingent on jazz's alterity with respect to the dominant art music tradition; it was by contrast with this "serious" music—that which is imagined to be inhibited—that 'jazz came to symbolize the repressed Id drives'.[67] Indeed, he took this critique one step further: Jazz was not purely a protest music defined by its otherness to classicism's hegemony but it also encompassed aspects of this tradition, such as some rules of traditional European harmony, in order to protect itself from the raw Id. Jazz was thus characterized as manifesting an Id-Superego conflict.[68] To extend this idea, one could say that this conflict be best understood as one that derives not merely from the minds of individual people but also from the social situations in which they find themselves. Hence, a specific aspect of music (rhythm)—and the style that comes to be understood to embody it (jazz)—should not be understood to stand for aspects of the mind in themselves; these aspects and musics come to *symbolize* characteristics of the mind as part of a larger, relational discourse, a discourse that connects and produces the meanings of terms that are musical, cultural, and psychoanalytic—jazz and "serious music", freedom and constraint, Id and Super-Ego—with respect to one another.

What one finds in considering these accounts is that aesthetic judgements and cultural values are incorporated into psychoanalytic discussions of aspects of music, as well as of "Music" per se (again, capital "M"). These are implicit within a number of discussions regarding different musical genres and styles. The apparent structuredness of music is often regarded highly and correlated with "advanceness"; seemingly inarticulate and incoherent music is found lacking. Ehrenzweig, for instance, contrasted "highly developed" music with primitive music—music that, as he put it, 'would appear as being "all mortar and no bricks"'.[69] This metaphor suggests a music—and mind—not guaranteeing the well-formed and solid elements of adulthood, but one that bears the mental pliability of early childhood. The building metaphor is apt, it also conjures the misinformed image of the proverbial "mud huts" of the "primitives", which could likewise be imagined to be "all mortar and no bricks". The tone is often cited as the elemental brick that enables a developed structuring, a structure that, elevated developmentally through tones' coherent harmonic combination, enables a focused form of listening. By contrast, in primitive musics, these solid bricks are lost in the place of an 'endless glissando and vibrato passages with but a few resting points on articulate tone steps here and there on which our attention could settle'.[70] Notably, Sterba also used this metaphor of musical "bricks". He explicitly associated the building blocks of music with tone. However, for him, tone was the mark of an expression that preceded (yet that might ultimately rupture from) the socially determined structuring forces of music, such as harmony:

> The basic brick of music [...] is tone [....] It is the break-through of the instinct against inhibitions [....] The sequence of tone steps leads to melody [....] Harmony, another essential feature of music is predominantly a social product.[71]

Sterba's narrative of musical development thus led from the tone—which breaks through an original inhibition, silence—to the incorporation of this tone, via melody, within a multitude of tones (harmony). This paralleled a psychoanalytic narrative moving from the individual's drive to a social context that demands this tone's (this drive's) compromise with and coexistence amongst others. Yet, as may be inferred from Sterba's account, the tone's instinctual basis might still threaten to come into conflict with the inhibitions demanded by its later social context.[72]

Through relating psychoanalysis and music, psychoanalysts and musicologists have each been able to say something more not only of the music, but also of the theories brought to bear upon it. As Stein has argued, discussions about music, its philosophy, and its aesthetics, have 'always grappled with the manner in which music reflects, symbolizes, and communicates aspects of inner life'.[73] Indeed, there might be a value in recognizing implicit and explicit connections between music and psychoanalysis now, at this historical and cultural moment. A dialogue between music and psychoanalysis enables us to better reflect on the mind in the complexity of its artistic and cultural manifestations.[74]

While thematic and theoretical threads are interweaved throughout the nine chapters in the collection, the chapters are framed in two parts. The first part, 'Psychoanalysis, Musical Analysis, and Method' focuses primarily on interpretive and methodological concerns: psychoanalytic theoretical, music analytical, and historical and cultural themes of investigation. The chapters that make up the second part, 'Situating Music and Psychoanalysis', take their impetus from a range of contexts in which psychoanalytically indebted thought has and continues to be critically productive—whether this be the question of who or what is interpreted psychoanalytically in investigations of music, connections between psychoanalytic interpretations and music's aesthetics and wider artistic cultures, or music's situations of composition, performance, and listening.

The voice speaks up to begin the first part of the collection, in a chapter from David Bard-Schwarz. Exploring a range of psychoanalytic perspectives on the voice, Bard-Schwarz traces a number of critical connections between theories and theorists. Furthermore, he puts these theories into analytical practice through approaching voices as musically scored, as theoretical objects, and in the materiality of their sounding. In the second chapter, Alexander Carpenter develops this sense of productive links between ideas and figures from psychoanalytic and musical spheres. In the case of his focus, Freud and Schoenberg, these lines are traced as parallels rather than direct paths of connection. In oscillating between these two figures—their lives, legacies, and relations to those before and after them—Carpenter illustrates how attention to one enables us to more clearly see something in the other, and something of the culture in which both were embedded.

The third and fourth chapters put the psycho-analytic and the music-analytic into conversation. Both reflect on music analysis's object of investigation—music—as well as on music analysis itself, as a methodological practice to be examined critically. Kenneth M. Smith invigorates neo-Riemannian theory through the concept of desire, conceived of in psychoanalytic terms. Drawing on Lacan's view of metaphor and metonymy, Smith refracts his discussion through the lens of Wagner's *Tristan and Isolde*, and thereby demonstrates how psychoanalytic perspectives enable new interpretive insights into late romantic harmony and tonal functions. In contrast with this approach, Christopher Tarrant focuses principally on form. Through considering the role of fantasy in interpretation and music analytic practice, Tarrant explores sonata form and its role in the analysis of Schubert's music—its efficacy in past analytic readings and with respect to new observations. Furthermore, reference to the work of Žižek enables him to deliberate on music and music analysis's ideological content. The fifth chapter, by Alexi Vellianitis, which closes the first half of the collection, foregrounds issues of ideology and critique, and frames this through a discussion popular music (specifically, the music of Taylor Swift) understood in the context of contemporary capitalism. Žižek's work features here, too. Responding to Žižek's writing on violence, Vellianitis considers the possibilities and problematics of resistance to capitalist forces within music produced under its conditions.

The four chapters that constitute the second part of the collection reassess the musical contexts in which psychoanalytic observations are situated. Samuel Wilson begins by considering the plural identities—at first sight: composers, performers, and listeners—that are interpreted psychoanalytically in discussions about music. The reader is provided a chapter that interlaces a variety of psychoanalytic and psychoanalytically indebted sources, in a manner that critically explores paths and directions through, and potential pitfalls in, this perspectival landscape. While a number of contributors take Freud and Lacan's thought as points of inspiration, by contrast, in her chapter, Rachel Darnley-Smith progresses a Jungian concept: the 'Transcendent Function'. Darnley-Smith situates its relevance to music studies through the context of music therapy. She focuses in particular on improvisation as a means through which synthesis between conscious and unconscious elements are explored musically.

Moving from Darnley-Smith's discussion of music-making, Jun Zubillaga-Pow interprets situations of its reception. He reads and draws together a number of discursive and disciplinary threads—empirical, psychological, philosophical, and psychoanalytic—and knots them together around three central themes: listening, pleasure, and resistance. Zubillaga-Pow considers how listening relates both to the inner world of the self and the sonic world beyond. The final chapter, by Stephen Downes, puts the twin themes of masochism and sentimentality at its core. Through these, he traces creative and critical resonances between Schumann, Chopin, and Roland Barthes. Indeed, masochism and sentimentality are understood as themes both aesthetic and psychoanalytic in nature; one observes this where for instance they shape the felt nature of the body and its mediation by musical performance and musical sound.

To bring together these terms into interrelation—*music, psychoanalysis*, and *musicology*—is not to assemble isolated ideas from different corners of theory and practice. Each has a history of relating to its others. Just as our image of music is shaped by musicology, a now widely accepted idea, music and psychoanalysis each transform in relation to the other. Indeed, through bettering our understanding of the two, we come to more fully appreciate ourselves as complex, emotional, remembering, desiring beings.

Notes

1 See, for example, Ian Biddle, 'Listening, Consciousness, and the Charm of the Universal: What It Feels Like for a Lacanian', in *Music and Consciousness: Philosophical, Psychological, and Cultural Perspectives*, ed. David Clarke and Eric Clarke (Oxford: Oxford University Press, 2011), 65–77; Alexander Carpenter, '"This Beastly Science…": On the Reception of Psychoanalysis by the Composers of the Second Viennese School, 1908–1923', *International Forum of Psychoanalysis* 24, no. 4 (2015): 243–54; Stephen Downes, *The Muse as Eros: Music, Erotic Fantasy, and Male Creativity in the Romantic and Modern Imagination* (Aldershot and Burlington, VT: Ashgate, 2006); J.P.E. Harper-Scott, *The Quilting Points of Musical Modernism: Revolution, Reaction, and William Walton* (Cambridge and New York: Cambridge University Press, 2012); Freya Jarman-Ivens, *Queer Voices: Technologies, Vocalities, and the Musical Flaw* (New York: Palgrave Macmillan, 2011); Michael L. Klein, *Music and the Crises of the Modern Subject* (Bloomington: Indiana University Press, 2015); Lawrence Kramer, *After the Lovedeath: Sexual Violence and the Making of Culture* (Berkley and Los Angeles: University of California Press, 1997); David Schwarz, *Listening Awry: Music and Alterity in German Culture* (Minneapolis and London: University of Minnesota Press, 2006); Kenneth Smith, *Skryabin, Philosophy and the Music of Desire* (Farnham and Burlington, VT: Ashgate, 2013), among many others.
2 This idea is explored in detail in Bard-Schwarz's chapter. Also see David Bard-Schwarz, *An Introduction to Electronic Art through the Teachings of Jacques Lacan: Strangest Thing* (London and New York: Routledge, 2014), 79–80.
3 Richard Sterba, 'Toward the Problem of Musical Process', *Psychoanalytic Review* 33 (1946): 37.
4 Richard Sterba, 'Psychoanalysis and Music', *American Imago* 22 (1965): 97.
5 Pinchas Noy, 'The Psychodynamics of Music—Part 4', *Journal of Music Therapy* 4, no. 3 (1967): 83.
6 Cf. Martin Nass, 'Some Considerations of a Psychoanalytic Interpretation of Music' [1971], in *Psychoanalytic Explorations in Music*, ed. Stuart Feder, Richard L. Karmel, and George H. Pollock (Madison, CT: International Universities Press, 1990), 47. Nass is sceptical of assuming a breakdown of self and world in musical experiences.
7 Sterba, 'Psychoanalysis and Music', 111.
8 On this point, see Peter Brooks, 'The Idea of a Psychoanalytic Literary Criticism', in *Discourse in Psychoanalysis and Literature*, ed. Shlomith Rimmon-Kenan (London: Methuen, 1987), 5.

18 *Samuel Wilson*

9 See Heinz Kohut, 'Observations on the Psychological Functions of Music' [1957], in *Psychoanalytic Explorations in Music*, ed. Stuart Feder, Richard L. Karmel, and George H. Pollock (Madison, CT: International Universities Press, 1990), 37.
10 Coriat cited in Pinchas Noy, 'The Psychodynamics of Music—Part 2', *Journal of Music Therapy* 4, no. 1 (1967), 8. See Isador H. Coriat, 'Some Aspects of a Psychoanalytic Interpretation of Music', *The Psychoanalytic Review* 32 (1945): 408–18.
11 Sterba, 'Psychoanalysis and Music', 99, describing the view of Pfeifer.
12 Sigmund Pfeifer, 'Problems of the Psychology of Music in the Light of Psycho-Analysis. Part 1. Psychophysiology of Musical Sound', *International Journal of Psychoanalysis* 3, no. 1 (1922): 128. Paper originally presented on 22 October 1921.
13 Coriat, 'Some Aspects of a Psychoanalytic Interpretation of Music', 408, summarizing the view of Pfeifer.
14 David Bard-Schwarz develops this idea in relation to Didier Anzieu's notion of the "skin-ego" in his *An Introduction to Electronic Art through the Teachings of Jacques Lacan*.
15 Alexander Stein, 'Psychoanalysis and Music', in *Textbook of Psychoanalysis*, ed. Glen O. Gabbard, Bonnie E. Litowitz, and Paul Williams (Washington, DC and London: American Psychiatric Association, 2012), 559.
16 Kohut, 'Observations on the Psychological Functions of Music', 30.
17 David Bard-Schwarz, *Listening Subjects: Music, Culture, Psychoanalysis* (Durham, NC and London: Duke University Press, 1997), 7.
18 Maud Ellmann, 'Introduction', in *Psychoanalytic Literary Criticism*, ed. Maud Ellman (London: Longman, 1994), 16.
19 Sterba, 'Psychoanalysis and Music', 111.
20 Heinrich Racker cited in Sterba, 'Psychoanalysis and Music', 104. Here Racker is summarising an earlier [1939] paper by Sterba (a summary of which the author approves).
21 Bard-Schwarz, *An Introduction to Electronic Art through the Teachings of Jacques Lacan*, 52.
22 Nass, 'Some Considerations of a Psychoanalytic Interpretation of Music', 39. Lacan also pointed to the idea that one cannot close one's ears. On this point, see Bard-Schwarz, *An Introduction to Electronic Art through the Teachings of Jacques Lacan*, 53–54.
23 Pinchas Noy argued that musical aptitude is a practicing of our defence to the unavoidability of sound. Noy, 'The Psychodynamics of Music—Part 2', 18–19.
24 Pratt cited in *Ibid.*, 24.
25 Sterba, 'Toward the Problem of Musical Process', 42.
26 Sybille Yates, 'Some Aspects of Time Difficulties and Their Relation to Music', *International Journal of Psychoanalysis* 16, no. 3 (1935): 342.
27 *Ibid.*, 354.
28 Stein, 'Psychoanalysis and Music', 562.
29 In the "fort-da" game, Freud observed a young child repeatedly throwing a toy out of sight and pulling it back on a piece of string. Freud famously interpreted this as the child's attempt to symbolize the mother leaving and returning. Through play, the child becomes master of the toy's—and, symbolically, the mother's—disappearance and return. Thus, the child addresses its anxiety over the absence of the mother.
30 Eero Rechardt, 'Experiencing Music', *The Psychoanalytic Study of the Child* 42 (1987): 518.
31 Gilbert J. Rose, *Between Couch and Piano: Psychoanalysis, Music, Art and Neuroscience* (Hove and New York: Brunner-Routledge, 2004), 162

32 *Ibid.*, 97. At this moment, Rose supplements her psychoanalytic discussion with the aesthetics of Susanne Langer.
33 Mastery is not always successful, however. A classic example is provided in Heinz Kohut and Sigmund Levarie's paper, 'On the Enjoyment of Listening to Music', *Psychoanalytic Quarterly* 19 (1950): 64–87. For discussion and context see Allen M. Siegel, *Heinz Kohut and the Psychology of the Self* (London: Routledge, 1996), 38.
34 Angelo Montani, 'Psychoanalysis of Music', *The Psychoanalytic Review* 32 (1945): 225–27.
35 Montani, 'Psychoanalysis of Music', 226–27.
36 Others have more recently been explicit about the plural nature and historical specificity of subjectivities. See Lawrence Kramer's short foreword to a special issue of *19th-Century Music* on 'Chopin's Subjects'. 'Chopin's Subjects: A Prelude', 35, no. 3 (2012): (unpaginated).
37 Glen O. Gabbard's foreword to Julie Jaffee Nagel, *Melodies of the Mind: Connections between Psychoanalysis and Music* (London: Routledge, 2013), xi, emphasis in the original.
38 Anton Ehrenzweig, *The Psycho-Analysis of Artistic Vision and Hearing: An Introduction to a Theory of Unconscious Perception* (London: Routledge and Kegan Paul Ltd, 1953), xi.
39 Hal Foster, Rosalind Krauss, Yve-Alain Bois, and Benjamin H.D. Buchloch, *Art Since 1900: Modernism, Antimodernism, Postmodernism* (London: Thames and Hudson, 2004), 20.
40 Combining ideas from Freud, Marx, and others, this perspective is pronounced in Theodor W. Adorno's writing on musical modernism. The relation between individual psychology and society as he saw it was made explicit in his 'Sociology and Psychology' [1955], *New Left Review* 1, no. 46 (1967): 67–97. Elsewhere, Fredric Jameson has considered the libidinal qualities particular to any concept of modernity itself; 'the trope of modernity bears a libidinal charge; that is, it is the operator of a unique kind of intellectual excitement not normally associated with other forms of conceptuality'. *A Singular Modernity: Essay on the Ontology of the Present* (New York and London: Verso, 2002), 34.
41 See Rose, *Between Couch and Piano*, 158–59.
42 Theodor Reik, *Haunting Melody: Psychoanalytic Experience in Life and Music* (New York: Da Capo Press, 1983/1953), 8, 8, 15. Reik's clinical observations in *The Haunting Melody* are far more specific and, I would suggest, valuable than his comments about music in general.
43 Carroll C. Pratt, 'Music as the Language of Emotion' [Lecture delivered 21 December 1950] (Washington: The Library of Congress/The Louis Charles Elson Memorial Fund, 1952), 6.
44 Pratt, 'Music as the Language of Emotion', 26, emphasis in original.
45 Noy, 'The Psychodynamics of Music—Part 2', 7.
46 I would suggest that this construction evokes a primeval "mother" tongue, through which it manifests an implicit desire to return—a return to a mother imagined prior to a fragmented yet totalising Symbolic, culture.
47 Anton Ehrenzweig cited in Nagel, *Melodies of the Mind*, 19.
48 See Alexander Stein, 'The Sound of Memory: Music an Acoustic Origins', *American Imago* 64, no. 1 (2007): 64–66 for a discussion of an individual's development and its relation to sound and music, beginning with the earliest sounds of the intrauterine environment.
49 Bruno Nettl, 'Infant Musical Development and Primitive Music', *Southwestern Journal of Anthropology* 12 (1956): 89. Nettl's later work is more nuanced and self-reflexive in its treatment of "simple" music and its place within culture. For instance, in his *The Study of Ethnomusicology*, he states emphatically that

20 *Samuel Wilson*

"simplicity" in terms of musical parameters must be understood in the context of this music's role within the complexity of culture. See his *The Study of Ethnomusicology: Thirty One Issues and Concepts* (new edition, Champaign: University of Illinois Press, 2005), 269–70.
50 Nettl, 'Infant Musical Development and Primitive Music', 91. Nettl suggests that this correlation differs depending on the musical parameter in question (scale, form, rhythm, etc.) – each develops at different rates.
51 Sterba, 'Psychoanalysis and Music', 101.
52 Following this logic, one would be consistent in speculating that European art music performance practice is voyeuristic—audience members listen to the performance rather than partaking themselves.
53 Pinchas Noy, 'How Music Conveys Emotions', in *Psychoanalytic Explorations in Music: Second Series*, ed. Stuart Feder, Richard L. Karmel, and George H. Pollock (Madison, CT: International Universities Press), 143.
54 Noy is of course not the only writer to consider some forms music—popular music—as inviting a passive, "regressive" form of listening. Adorno famously did so, too. This was, for Adorno, indicative of the powers of mass culture to regress its denizens into unthinking beings; he read this regression as a symptom of a problematic historical and material situation. See his 'On the Fetish-Character in Music and the Regression of Listening' [1938], in *Essays on Music*, ed. Richard Leppert, trans. Susan H. Gillespie, 288–317 (Berkeley and Los Angeles: University of California Press, 2002).
55 Rose Rosengard Subotnik, 'Toward a Deconstruction of Structural Listening: A Critique of Schoenberg, Adorno, and Stravinsky', in *Deconstructive Variations: Music and Reason in Western Society*, 148–76 (Minneapolis and London: University of Minnesota Press, 1995), 148. Indeed, in his chapter in this collection, Alexi Vellianitis suggests that one might radically repurpose structural listening for non-classical repertoires.
56 Tolbert, Elizabeth, 'Untying the Music/Language Knot', in *Music, Sensation, and Sensuality*, ed. Linda Phyllis Austern (London: Routledge, 2002), 77–78.
57 See Bard-Schwarz, *Listening Subjects*, 19, my emphasis.
58 Ian Biddle, 'Opera's Unconscious, or What Men Don't Say', in *Masculinity in Opera: Gender, History, and the New Musicology*, ed. Philip Purvis (New York and London: Routledge, 2013), 206.
59 *Ibid.*, 212–13.
60 Stein, 'The Sound of Memory', 65–66.
61 See, for example, Bard-Schwarz, *Listening Subjects*, 12: 'In *Nixon in China*, the oceanic, undifferentiated texture of the opening[...]'.
62 Kohut, 'Observations on the Psychological Functions of Music', 23.
63 Rechardt, 'Experiencing Music', 514.
64 Sterba, 'Psychoanalysis and Music', 101.
65 Coriat, 'Some Aspects of a Psychoanalytic Interpretation of Music', 416.
66 Norman M. Margolis, 'A Theory on the Psychology of Jazz', *American Imago* 11 (1954): 273.
67 *Ibid.*, 272.
68 *Ibid.*, 275.
69 Ehrenzweig *The Psycho-Analysis of Artistic Vision and Hearing*, 84.
70 *Ibid.*
71 Sterba, 'Psychoanalysis and Music', 101–102.
72 It should also be noted that, while those like Ehrenzweig held onto the primitive/advanced hierarchy, the possibility of a limited degree of cultural relativism was sometimes also alluded to, at least in some respects. As Ehrenzweig put it, sacrifices are made for the West's achievement of a highly developed 'harmonic

articulation'—complexities of rhythm are forgone, for instance. He cites Indian music's supremacy in this regard, even suggesting, reflexively, that the West's rhythms may appear "primitive" by comparison to those of this other tradition. See Ehrenzweig, *The Psycho-Analysis of Artistic Vision and Hearing*, 163. Ehrenzweig suggested that different musics evinced aspects that were differently primitive or advanced—although this is not to imply that *all* music achieves advancedness in at least one respect; some music is still primitive through and through.

73 Stein, 'Psychoanalysis and Music', 552.
74 Nagel argues that a dialogue between music and psychoanalysis enables us to value and understand things in a manner that differs from the framework provided by currently dominant forms of thought—the values provided by instrumental rationality and the answers proffered by an uncritical and reductive scientism. See the final chapter in Nagel, *Melodies of the Mind*, 'Beyond the Concert Hall and Consulting Room', 109–19.

Part I
Psychoanalysis, musical analysis, and method

1 Speaking of the voice in psychoanalysis and music

David Bard-Schwarz

In this essay, I shall explore studies of the voice in psychoanalysis and music. I will look at essays and books that theorize the voice, and I will explore some limited analytical applications. These writings have been widely influential in shaping contemporary critical discourses. The essay is organized through a roughly chronological series of mostly twentieth-century writings with examples of music from across classical periods, and styles. The main purpose of the essay is to give readers who are familiar with current critical theory (psychoanalysis, theories of the voice) a resource comprising both a survey of theories of the voice as well as illustrations of how these theories can be applied primarily to musical-theoretical but also musical-historical criticism. A secondary purpose of the essay is to give readers who may be exploring theories of the voice and psychoanalysis for the first time a resource for exploring writings on the voice as a context with which to understand the various uses and misuses of the voice in traditional as well as contemporary classical musics.

While exploring the voice in the readings, I will locate each approach within its disciplinary and critical context, suggesting to the reader various paths of inquiry that can lead into a deeper understanding of the writings at hand, the musical examples cited, and their cultural contexts. Three red threads of discursive continuity run throughout this survey of theories of the voice: (1) the voice as a vehicle for the communication of meaning, (2) the voice as vehicle for the communication and/or expression of an aesthetic nature or emotion, and/or (3) the voice as object (of some sort) in and of itself. I shall also explore vocal signification and the body.[1]

Roland Barthes, 'The Grain of the Voice'

Roland Barthes' essay 'The Grain of the Voice' relies on an opposition of *phenosong* and *genosong*.[2] Barthes acknowledges (though without direct citation) that he has borrowed the terms from Julia Kristeva. I shall explore Barthes' essay by first looking at Kristeva's use of the terms *phenotext* and *genotext* in some detail and then proceed with Barthes' rereading of Kristeva and his application of his rereading to specific musical practices. Kristeva discusses the genotext as follows:

> What we shall call a genotext will include semiotic processes but also the advent of the symbolic. The former includes drives, their disposition and their division of the body, plus the ecological and social system surrounding the body, such as objects and pre-Oedipal relations with parents. The latter encompasses the emergence of object and subject, and the constitution of nuclei of meaning involving categories: semantic and categorial fields. Designating the genotext in a text requires pointing out the transfers of drive energy that can be detected in phonematic devices (such as the accumulation and repetition of phonemes or rhyme) and melodic devices (such as intonation or rhythm), in the way semantic and categorial fields are set out in syntactic and logical features, or in the economy of mimesis (fantasy, the deferment of denotation, narrative, etc.). The genotext is thus the only transfer of drive energies that organizes a space in which the subject is not yet a split unity that will become blurred, giving rise to the symbolic.[3]

Kristeva is thinking of the genotext as an attribute of, or entity contained within, the phenotext. She sees the genotext in close relation or proximity to the body, to subjectivity anterior to the split that constitutes the divided subject since Freud. Further, she views the genotext as articulation of threshold precisely at that fissure that will give way to psychic split. For her, the genotext is 'a process, which tends to articulate structures that are ephemeral (unstable, threatened by drive charges, "quanta", rather than "marks") and non-signifying (devices that do not have a double articulation)'.[4]

For Kristeva,

> [w]e shall use the term phenotext to denote language that serves to communicate, which linguistics describes in terms of "competence" and "performance". The phenotext is constantly split up and divided, and is irreducible to the semiotic process that works through the genotext. The phenotext is a structure (which can be generated, in generative grammar's sense); it obeys rules of communication and presupposes a subject of enunciation and an addressee.[5]

For her, the split of the subject into primary and secondary processes and the subject's full acquisition of language enable phenotextual articulation. The phenotext is constitutionally structured according to mutually exclusive binary oppositions of basic materials that undergo rules of transformation to become manifest texts—articulations to be shared among subjects in social space. For Kristeva,

> [t]he signifying process therefore includes both the genotext and the phenotext; indeed it could not do otherwise. For it is in language that all signifying operations are realized (even when linguistic material is

not used), and it is on the basis of language that a theoretical approach may attempt to perceive that operation.[6]

For Kristeva, the phenotext contains the genotext, and the boundary between them blurs and thickens as attributes of the latter become subordinate to the former.

When Barthes adopts Kristeva's terms to music, he substitutes "song" for "text" and transforms Kristeva's binary (in which a fluid boundary separates genotext and phenotext) into a more distinct binary opposition. Barthes is interested not so much in making a general, theoretical statement or category, as in explicating a personal source of pleasure. For him,

> The pheno-song [...] covers all the phenomena, all the features which belong to the structure of the language being sung, the rules of the genre, the coded form of the melisma, the composer's idiolect, the style of the interpretation: in short, everything in the performance which is in the service of communication, representation, expression, everything which is customary to talk about, which forms the tissue of cultural values [...] which takes its bearing directly on the ideological alibis of a period [....][7]

Barthes does not directly address the plethora of issues that arise when one discusses articulation, meaning, and expression in music. He jumps simply to a discussion of song. He discusses phenosong in terms of the language element inherent in song as well as conventional elements of music other than the linguistic.

For Barthes, the quintessential vocalist of the phenosong is Dietrich Fisher-Dieskau, in whose singing Barthes 'only [...] hear[s] the lungs, never the tongue, the glottis, the teeth, the mucous membranes, the nose'.[8] Barthes prefers musical performances in which the stain of the body not only remains but resonates openly. Rather than discuss such performances as geno-song, his language veers to the notion of "grain": 'The "grain" is the body in the voice as it sings, the hand as it writes, the limb as it performs'.[9] For Barthes, the quintessential vocalist of the geno-song is Charles Panzera. It can be difficult to follow claims such as Barthes' in analysis; writers may find recently developed software helpful for visualizing acoustic data that goes beyond pitch-specific notations of conventional notation. Screenshots of minute excerpts will illustrate how such software may be used. In Figure 1.1, I reproduce a sonogram of a recording of Dietrich Fisher-Dieskau performing "Im wunderschönen Monat Mai" from Robert Schumann's *Dichterliebe*; the passage shows Fisher-Dieskau's articulation of the words "als alle" from the beginning of the work whose first line is "Im wunderschönen Monat Mai als alle Knospen sprangen".[10]

In Sonic Visualizer, frequencies measured in Hz are in white font against black background arranged vertically on the left; sung language is generally

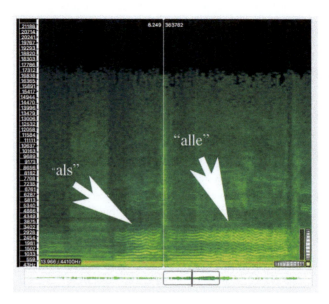

Figure 1.1 Robert Schumann, "Im wunderschönen Monat Mai" from Robert Schumann's *Dichterliebe*. Dietrich-Fischer Dieskau and Gerald Moore.

visual in the low 1000s, as here. One reads the image left to right, reflecting conventional representations of the passage of time. Dynamic level (how loud the signal is) is measured in colors on the spectrogram; from loud to soft, the colors move from red (rather loud) to orange, to yellow, to green (silent). You can see aspects of Fischer-Dieskau's performance of the words "als alle" through his even and controlled vibrato. Notice the neat "stacks" of waves; these waves show the control of Fischer-Dieskau's vocal production throughout the core of the notes he is singing; and looking horizontally, notice the clean "cutoff" after "alle". See Figure 1.2 for a sonogram of a performance of the precisely same excerpt from the same song:[11]

At the end of Panzera's articulation of "alle", there's a sudden "hole" in the vocal production; notice the dug out portion of the yellow wedge as the point of the diagram's arrow. This "hole" corresponds in the recording to a guttural articulation. I think Barthes would view these two screen-shots of sonograms from recordings as visualizations of his opposition of the phenosong (Fischer-Dieskau) and genosong (Panzera). Sonogram comparisons of the entire song show a plethora of other examples of this nature. Visualizations (as all musical examples) can cause one to continue to probe analytic claims. For example, one might notice that Panzera's articulations of the words "als" and "alle" are cleaner than Fischer-Dieskau's—cleaner in the sense that their beginnings and endings show more clearly marked thresholds. Such matters can be used to show differences in pheno-/geno-performances of any musician, playing any instrument.[12]

The voice in psychoanalysis and music 29

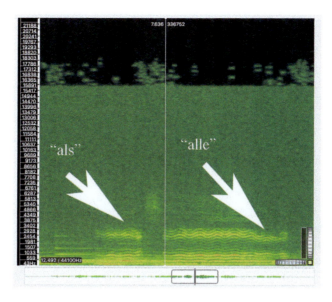

Figure 1.2 Robert Schumann, "Im wunderschönen Monat Mai" from Robert Schumann's *Dichterliebe*. Charles Panzera and Alfret Cortot.

Barthes' reading of Kristeva results in a simpler binary opposition, one in which singing in the realm of the phenosong subordinates the body to the clarity of perfection of execution and an evacuation of signification, articulation, and expression that might distract from codes exchanged in social space; singing (or playing an instrument) in the realm of the genosong lets the body as the source of signification sound in all its visceral and irreducible immediacy.

Michel Poizat, *The Angel's Cry*

The subtitle of Poizat's book quotes directly Sigmund Freud's *Beyond the Pleasure Principle*.[13] In this essay, Freud builds upon his theory of the pleasure principle as the principle that governs reduction of psychic tension. The work dates from 1920, and Freud would have been exposed to soldiers returning from the front of World War I with "shell shock"—a diagnostic forerunner of post-traumatic stress disorder. Freud was puzzled at the psychic function of traumatic nightmares that he had trouble understanding as functions of the pleasure principle. In theorizing "beyond" the pleasure principle, Freud posited the death drive, or drive to an inorganic state that brought traumatized veterans back again and again to painful memories that could not be incorporated into psychic life governed by the pleasure principle—tensions among the ego, id, and super-ego that could be managed through repression and return of the repressed in dreams, slips of the tongue, and jokes.

30 David Bard-Schwarz

Poizat's theoretical interest in the voice lies in performances in opera in which listeners experience an ecstasy quite beyond pleasure. Poizat explores the binary opposition of pleasure and *jouissance* from both historical and (implicitly) psychoanalytic points of view:

> this tension [between seeking gratification beyond a limit and mastering that limit in order to control gratification] would define, at its most stable or regular extreme, what the eighteenth century called pleasure; and at the other extreme, the point of greatest tension, closest to transgression, what can be defined only as the asymptotic term in a quest for the impossible, for pure and complete gratification, or, quite simply for *jouissance*.[14]

One dimension of *jouissance* of the voice in opera occurs, for Poizat, when the voice brings the listener from the world of language to the world of music (implicitly) "beyond". Poizat points out how the libretto often falls out of the hands of the avid opera fan—a literal correlate of the voice leaving the signifier behind: 'one can [...] speak of the falling away of the entire signifying order. Literally. Every opera lover knows at first hand the experience of the libretto falling out of his hands'.[15] Further, when the voice of opera brings the listener from the signifying chain of language into a *jouissance* of music, what it lays bare is a cry: 'when language disappears and is gradually superseded by the cry, an emotion arises which can be expressed only by the eruption of the sob that signals absolute loss'. For Poizat, "the Blue Note" (Poizat's turn of phrase) denotes that moment in music in which the voice in performance triggers a cry of *jouissance* in a listener.

Poizat examines the cry in opera from the point of view of an ambivalent charge between transgressing and maintaining a limit between the signifying chain of language and the less obviously signifying chain of music.[16] The cry as *jouissance* is 'an effect of the destruction or dissolution of language by music'.[17] Poizat discusses a number of cries/screams in opera, from Kundry's awakening in *Parsifal*, to Marie's death in *Wozzeck*, and Lulu's in *Lulu*.[18]

Of course, these cries are produced in all three of these operas on stage at the discretion of the singer, stage designer, director, and conductor. Kundry's awakening is accompanied by a fortissimo F half-diminished seventh chord (the same chord as the downbeat of the Tristan progression) moving to a G minor chord over an f in the bass as shown in Example 1.1.

The affect of agony is rendered by the absence of musical notation of the scream, the dissonant F half-diminished seventh chord whose resolution to G minor clashes with the held f in the bass, and the descending, semitonal voice-leading of all voices.

Both of Berg's operas include screams from their central female characters. In *Wozzeck*, Berg composes Marie's death at Wozzeck's hands in the context of the Act III scene involving variation on one note: $b\natural$ (see Example 1.2). Berg has Marie sing on the scene's note of obsession, $b\natural$, and

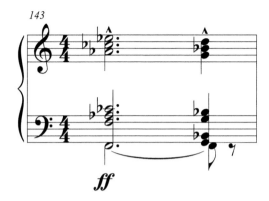

Example 1.1 Richard Wagner, *Parsifal*: Act II. (In reference to Kundry, Wagner writes: "Sie stößt hier einen gräßlichen Schrei aus". English: "She lets out here a grotesque scream").

Example 1.2 Alban Berg, *Wozzeck*, Act III, scene ii, Marie's death (some parts not shown).

it is with a harsh, very low $b\natural$ that Marie dies; note the marking on that low $b\natural$ in the basses—pizzicato with the basses' 'strings hitting the wood of the fingerboards' (my translation). This note is doubled by the harp and bass tuba (not shown). The $b\natural$ gathers more and more energy after Marie's death as it saturates the entire orchestral pitch space by the end of the scene. For Berg, the $b\natural$ and the expressive obsession that it embodies, goes well beyond any one-to-one correspondence between the note and a character or even an action; it pervades the environment like the terror of a nightmare. Berg composes Lulu's final words of negation to an iteration of the "Erdgeist fourths" that saturate the opera (see Example 1.3);[19] the orchestral articulation of her death (shown in the strings; the winds, percussion, harp, and piano double these pitches) condenses the entire pitch structure of the opera—presenting as aggregate three transpositions of the Erdgeist fourths (#1 = $c\natural–f\natural–f\sharp–b\natural$; #2 = $e\natural–a\natural–b\flat–e\flat$; #3 = $g\sharp–c\sharp–d\natural–g\natural$). In a subtle instance of semantic encoding, Berg has a crochet rest delay Lulu's cry of death.[20]

32 David Bard-Schwarz

Example 1.3 Alban Berg, *Lulu*, Act III, scene ii, Lulu's death (some parts not shown).

Poizat's approach to the cry can be applied to a wide variety of musical voices (human, instrumental, analog, or digital) at thresholds of a breach (of dynamics, texture, frequency, duration, etc.).[21]

Mladen Dolar, *A Voice and Nothing More*

Dolar begins his study of the voice by stressing that he is interested in a third term beyond the traditional binary of voice as carrier of meaning on the one hand, and embodiment of aesthetic pleasure on the other:

> I will try to argue that apart from […] the voice as the vehicle of meaning [and] the voice as the source of aesthetic admiration—there is a third level: an object voice which does not go up in smoke in the conveyance of meaning, and does not solidify in an object of fetish reverence, but an object which functions as a blind spot in the call and as a disturbance of aesthetic appreciation.[22]

Dolar begins to describe the object voice with a historical account of a speaking machine and chess automaton; the speaking machine was one of several similar devices produced in the late eighteenth century by Wolfgang von Kempelen. It had bellows that blew air through an aperture whose tension and opening were controlled by valves. The chess automaton was a device made by Kempelen and later taken over by Johann Nepomuk Mälzel; a dwarf hid inside a box and moved the limbs and controlled the movements and features of a chess-playing puppet. For Dolar, it is significant that at public showings of these two devices, the speaking machine laid bare its mechanical and non-anthropomorphic nature, while the chess-playing automaton seemed strangely human and anthropomorphic.

For Dolar, the order of appearance of the speaking machine followed by chess-playing automaton evokes two levels of "teleology"; first, the speaking machine made the chess-playing automaton more believable. Second, the speaking machine prefigured and made possible the more sophisticated chess-playing automaton. This suggests a mechanical and purely instrumental agency anterior to logocentric thought. Dolar reads this as a structure of infinite regress:

> the dwarf within the puppet himself turns out to be another puppet, the mechanical puppet within the anthropomorphic one, and the secret of the thinking machine is itself thoughtless, just a mechanism emitting voice, but thereby producing the most human of effects, an effect of "interiority".[23]

Dolar goes on to point out that the speaking voice was barely comprehensible as speech; what generated awe at its utterances heard in public was what Dolar calls the 'object voice'. The object voice is an acoustic embodiment of what Lacan called the *objet petit a*.

In Lacanian theory, the objet petit a has no abiding, internal consistency; it is more of a threshold phenomenon, something that we know to exist because it must (must like dark matter in outer space that scientists "know" exists but that no one can observe). It is far less what we anecdotally think of as an "object" as a place in which something of a certain kind can take its place, for a moment, in lieu of something else. It can be helpful to imagine the psychic apparatus as a circular drive of life force; but anything propelled along a path will simply run out and stop or burn out at some point (think of a short circuit of current, or a ball spun around a roulette table; it will eventually fall into a slot); or think of computer code. If you don't write a "repeat the loop" instruction the code will run once and simply stop. So, in electric circuits you build in capacitors, resistors, and transistors to slow down the current, to keep it moving so it neither stops nor burns out. And the psychic apparatus also has a block that keeps energy both moving and shaped, or slowed down. See Figure 1.3 for my sketch.

The sketch represents psychic energy moving counterclockwise along its circular path that necessarily and impossibly reaches and swerves around an inscrutable impediment; in the space of that constitutive gap that paradoxically propels and blocks energy, the objet petit a opens/lays bare a space or place of alterity. For Lacan, feces, the mother's breast, and (her) voice are quintessential embodiments of the objet petit a.

In applying this concept of voice as objet petit a to musical compositions, I suggest that one strategy is to hear a highly repetitive drive—a motion that continually circulates. This circulation should be more than

34 *David Bard-Schwarz*

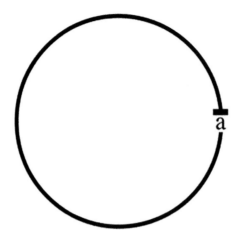

Figure 1.3 Representation of the Lacanian psychic apparatus.

a simple iteration of a short pattern (like a short circuit) and less than the repeat of a large section of a work that might tend to sound like doing something complete, one more time (the same or differently). I'm thinking of something like the four-bar phrases in Schubert's 'Der Doppelgänger'. In that work, a glance at the score will reveal that there are eight-bar phrases (divided into 2 four-bar phrases each) for Schubert's setting of the first two stanzas of the poem (during which the narrowing vision of the landscape of a town at night narrows from moon, to village, to street, to a man); the setting of the third stanza sets the narrator's realization that he is looking at himself. Yet I wish to discuss what happens to a repetitive structure for the musical setting of the first two stanzas (bars 5–8 + 9–12; 15–18 + 19–22; 25–28 + 29–32; and 34–37 + 38–41). There are diatonic mediant to dominant harmonies in B minor at the ends of each of these eight-bar phrases: III to V4/3 in bars 11 and 12, 21 and 22; Schubert sets up a pattern according to which the diatonic mediant (heavily voiced in close position of full triads in both right and left hands as opposed to the more vacant sonorities earlier) prepares the interrupted dominants of bars 12 and 22.

To represent the strain of the impending realization in the text that the narrator is not observing another person but is looking at a horrifying externalization of himself, the music begins to tear apart, as the diatonic mediant of bar 31 leads not to a dominant but to an augmented sixth chord (French—only one pitch is changed from the dominant; instead of $c\sharp$, Schubert darkens the sonority to a $c\natural$); the process of rupture continues as the diatonic mediant of bar 40 leads to a stronger augmented sixth chord (German—the $c\natural$ of the French chord is maintained and $f\sharp$ turns to $g\natural$). This process is summarized in Example 1.4.

The voice in psychoanalysis and music 35

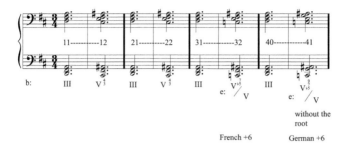

Example 1.4 Franz Schubert, 'Der Doppelgänger', a representation of repetitive patterns in the setting of the first two stanzas of Heine's poem.

The emergence of the augmented sixth chords in the space of the dominant sevenths (bars 12, 22, 32, and 41) suggests to me a Lacanian objet petit a—that thing that emerges in the necessary and impossible gap of the psychic apparatus. At the same time, it suggests to me an embodiment of Dolar's object voice—a voice that neither bears meaning nor is a source of aesthetic fascination. Schubert's object voice in 'Der Doppelgänger' is one whose alterity grows directly out of the repetition itself, as if the dominant 4-3 chords, through repetition, mutate and become something else, something other.

Dolar's notion of the object voice enables him to listen back to Saussure's semiotics from a new perspective.[24] While Saussure had defined the sign as a binary opposition between the signifier ("t-r-e-e" for example) and signified (the concept of a tree in the mind of a listener), Dolar is concerned with the signifier alone (after Lacan, Derrida, and others who view the signified as a concept always deferred, never reached unless an ideologically driven imperative marks a spot along the signifier's slide of infinite regress as "final"). As Saussure does, Dolar describes the essentially differential nature of the signifier: '[i]t is a strange entity that possesses no identity of its own, for it is merely a bundle, a crossing of differences in relation to other signifiers, and *nothing else*'.[25]

For Dolar, the linguistic aspect of the voice is 'what does not contribute to making sense. It is the material element recalcitrant to meaning, and if we speak in order to say something, then the voice is precisely that which cannot be said'.[26] For him, the voice is enunciated by a glitch: 'we stumble on the voice which is seemingly recalcitrant to the signifier: the accent, the intonation, and the timbre'.[27] In order to see an example of the kinds of things Dolar is hearing, let me examine a screenshot of a clip from Jacques Lacan speaking to an audience in 1972; Figure 1.4 is a visual representation of Lacan saying the words "le sujet" (the subject).[28]

The voice as Dolar describes it includes everything other than the words "le sujet" represented in the spectrogram above. One can see in the

Figure 1.4 Screenshot of Jacques Lacan speaking the words "le sujet" from *Lacan parle* (1972).

spectrogram what one can hear in the audio clip—Lacan's high voice; his intonation when speaking the vowel "e" in "sujet" is strongest at approximately 559 Hz. (A-440 is the pitch at which orchestras tune.) As is audible in the audio clip and very visible here, his voice tapers off at the end of the word "sujet". We can see that this tapering off consists of at least two elements: dynamics (loudness) and frequency (pitch). The frequencies of which Lacan's utterance of "e" in "sujet" consists taper; they look like terraces on a hill. The dynamics taper as well; the louder yellow lines yield to more quiet green lines to the right of the figure. And it is clearly a function of these stumbling blocks that allows us to recognize the voices of those we know. These stumbling blocks, then, *are* the voices that we recognize as voices.

This location of the voice as that stumbling block that carries but evades meaning opens the theoretical space for hearing non-articulate sounds produced by the body, and by its organs, as a (paradoxically) quintessential voice: 'the non-articulate itself becomes a mode of the articulate; the presymbolic acquires its value only through opposition to the symbolic, and is thus itself laden with signification precisely by virtue of being non-signifying'.[29] Consider a screenshot of the initial seconds of Cathy Berberian performing Luciano Berio's *Sequenza III*.[30]

Figure 1.5 shows Dolar's sense of non-articulate voice with the "tense muttering" followed by an intake of breath; the former is notated in the music;

The voice in psychoanalysis and music 37

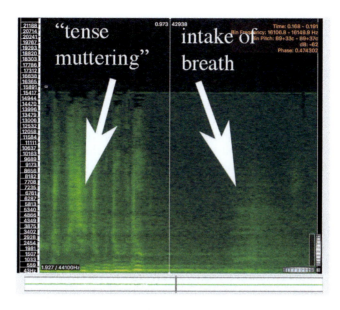

Figure 1.5 Screenshot of Cathy Berberian performing "tense muttering" at the beginning of Luciano Berio's *Sequenza III*.

the latter is an artifact of performance *not* notated in the work but a part of it, as the body of the performer bleeds into the fabric of the work. Most of the acoustic signature of the "tense muttering" is evenly distributed among the frequencies—an image of noise.[31] Yet if you look towards the bottom of the columns of "tense mutterings" towards the middle of the example, you can see traces of frequencies, trace amounts of pitched frequencies—the music inherent in all speech.[32] The purer object voice in Dolar's sense is the intake of breath; it feathers from and back into silence and its acoustic signature is evenly spread among the frequencies—a ghost of sound.

Dolar writes of two kinds of pre- and post-linguistic utterances; the scream is an example of the former, and we have examined it in some detail as the operatic cry in Poizat's writing, and the infantile reflexive expression and inaugural call for attention in the developing child in Anzieu's work.[33] Dolar considers singing an example of post-linguistic utterance, as well as laughter:

> Laughter is different from the other phenomena considered above [the cry, the scream, singing] because it seems to exceed language in both directions at the same time, as both presymbolic and beyond symbolic; it is not merely a precultural voice seized by the structure, but at the same time a highly cultural product which looks like a regression to animality.[34]

Writers have long discussed the shofar as a voice with a particular power, and for Dolar, it is an example of the object voice par excellence:

> [...] we have to recognize, in the sound of the shofar, the voice of the Father, the cry of the dying primal father of the primitive horde, the leftovers which come both to haunt and to seal the foundation of his law. By hearing this voice, the community of believers establishes its covenant, its alliance with God; they assert their submission and obedience to the law. The law itself, in its pure form, before commanding anything specific, is epitomized by the voice, the voice that commands total compliance, although it is senseless in itself.[35]

The sound of the shofar as the sound of God is related to the acousmatic voice—a voice for which one can hear but not see its source. It has been theorized as sound, speech, music produced by a person usually associated with a super-ego—an agency of alterity writ large—of the big Other.[36] It is most common in film, since we need to both see and hear. A well-known example of an acousmatic voice in classic Hollywood cinema is the voice of the Wizard of Oz that terrifies Dorothy and her companions. De-acousmatization occurs when the source of the voice is revealed; and this often shows the agent behind the voice as quite weak and small, as in the moment in *The Wizard of Oz* in which Toto (Dorothy's dog) pulls back the curtain to reveal the Wizard as a simple old man. Dolar points out a particularly uncanny form of the acousmatic:

> [v]entriloquism pertains to voice as such, to its inherently acousmatic character: the voice comes from inside the body, the belly, the stomach—from something incompatible with and irreducible to the activity of the mouth. The fact that we see the aperture does not demystify the voice; on the contrary, it enhances the enigma.[37]

Dolar absorbs two concepts from Giorgio Agamben that relate to the voice—*zoe* and *bios*: '*Zoe* is naked life, bare life, life reduced to animality; *bios* is life in the community, in the polis, political life'.[38] One might be tempted to think of bare life as the Lacanian Real, and it might in some discursive contexts be appropriate to see the former contained with the latter. Yet I read Agamben from the historical point of view (removing my Lacanian lens for a moment entirely) as a form of state-less disembodiment characteristic of post-9/11 geo-politics.[39]

For Dolar, the voice has three registers of its absence, silence: '[t]here are many kinds of silence, and perhaps we can group them for our purposes following Lacan's three registers: the Symbolic, the Imaginary, and the Real'.[40] Dolar suggests that the silence that follows the presence and absence of the Symbolic is a kind of symbolic silence. One needs to make an important distinction here: in symbolic structures, presence and absence move in infinite regress to an impossible vanishing point. Symbolic presence and absence is like the grey that is produced by alternations between black and white. Dolar (after Saussure) hears the silence of the full stop at the end of a sentence as symbolic silence—a silence that marks the symbolic work at its core (like the silence after a signifier which makes it possible to encode the meaning of the signifier).[41] The silence after any phrase of tonal music illustrates this form of symbolic silence in music, as the period at the ends of sentences does for language.

For Dolar, imaginary silence

> can overwhelm and enthrall the observer, a vision of supreme harmony, the oceanic feeling that Freud talks about in Civilization and its Discontents, cosmic peace. There are no voices to be heard, and for that very reason the silence speaks in an unalloyed presence, for voices would spoil the equilibrium, the alternation would bring imbalance. Silence functions as saturated with the highest sense, the mirror which reflects the inner and outer in a perfect match.[42]

Imaginary and symbolic silence are very different from one another; they both contain different dimensions of presence and absence, plenitude and lack. An infinite regress of black and white oscillation produces greys for the symbolic, and unyielding black and white binaries flip back and forth in the Imaginary). If silences after sounds enable their symbolic articulation, then Imaginary silences may interrupt, with an immediate plenitude, the flow of signification. The fermata has precisely this function. Complete absence of sound evokes the Real (as in the scene of *2001: A Space Odyssey* in which there is no "room" sound but utter silence as Dave is trapped by Hal outside the spacecraft).[43]

Conclusion: body, voice, acoustic gaze

I turn in conclusion from a discussion underwritten by the body to the acoustic mirror, and the acoustic gaze. In doing so, I understand the body as multivalent edges of flesh at the Imaginary, Symbolic, and Real. The body is the literal and figurative support we achieve in the mirror stage for the incorporation of our fragmented body parts into a coherent ego. According to Lacan, we achieve this (mis)recognition through the specularity of the (visual) mirror stage—through the organs of our eyes (as much flesh and blood as any other organ of our bodies). According to Anzieu, the (mis) recognition of the Lacanian mirror stage is supported by another organ of the body—the voice. In the acoustic mirror phase, we assemble fragmented body parts into a body ego, separate from the (m)other.[44] For me, the voice splits into (a) the voice of my body that I hear as it speaks to the (m)other, and (b) the voice of the (m)other that I (and others) hear. This split produces an acoustic alterity that opens the space for the voice not only of the other but the Other (writ large) as well. And the internalized knowledge of the voice of the Other is the acoustic gaze.

The voice can embody the gaze if it seems at some point that a voice impossibly but irrevocably listens to us rather than us listening to it. Lacan and others discuss the gaze in visual terms:

> I see that the other sees me, and that any intervening third party sees me being seen. There is never a simple duplicity of terms. It is not only that I see the other. I see him seeing me, which implicates the third term, namely, that he knows that I see him.[45]

An acoustic gaze would have to reproduce a ternary structure like the one Lacan is describing. It would have to involve the perception that a piece of music is somehow listening to the listener and that someone or something else is listening to both. For me, Schubert's 'Ihr Bild' produces such a structure. See Figure 1.6 for the poem.[46]

In the first two lines of the first stanza, the narrator begins a description of a dark dream he (presumably male as a surrogate of the poet?) had of staring at a picture or painting of a woman. In the second two lines of the first stanza, the beloved visage secretly comes to life. By the second stanza, we realize Heine is narrowing in (as in an iris-in technique in cinema) from "Bildnis" to "Antlitz" to "Lippen" to "Lächeln" to "Augenpaar".[47] In the first two lines of the second stanza, a wondrous smile pulls gently at her

>Ich stand in dunkeln Träumen
>Und starrte ihr Bildnis an,
>Und das geliebte Antlitz
>Heimlich zu leben begann.
>
>Um ihre Lippen zog sich
>Ein Lächeln wunderbar,
>Und wie von Wehmutstränen
>Erglänzte ihr Augenpaar.
>
>Auch meine Tränen flossen
>Mir von den Wangen herab -
>Und ach, ich kann es nicht glauben,
>Daß ich dich verloren hab!

Figure 1.6 Heinrich Heine, 'Ich stand in dunkeln Träuman' from *Die Heimkehr, Buch der Lieder.*

lips; in the second two lines of the second stanza, the narrator describes her eyes glistening as if from tears of pain. The "as if" is curious, implying that her eyes could be glistening from some other cause—such as what? In the first two lines of the third stanza, the imagery shifts to the narrator himself while remaining in the past; tears are falling as well from his cheeks. In the final two lines of the poem, the narrator falls into the present tense as he addresses the image, expressing disbelief that he has lost her.

The imagery of the poem is pervaded by the gaze; the narrator looks at the painting/picture/image and it's as if the act of his looking causes the image to come nightmarishly alive. There's an underlying subtext in the poem as well of a misrecognized mirror image. The images move along a trajectory of attributes of the other to attributes of the self, crossing the threshold from the former to the latter between the second and third stanzas. The other is the self trapped in a mirror. It's as if the "Auch" at the beginning of the third stanza covers the transformed identity of other (first two stanzas) to self (third stanza). Lacan has said that the gaze involves a triad of agencies—an object seeing an observer and another person seeing the object seeing the observer. In my reading of the poem, the painting/picture sees the narrator, and we the reader see the painting/picture seeing the narrator.

In setting six of the Heine poems from *Die Heimkehr* to music, Schubert was attracted to poems of psychic split and liked poems that had an unnamed, general quality. He liked poems that described general conditions of consciousness, not specific experiences or specific, named places. Schubert composes Lieder, particularly the Heine settings of *Schwanengesang*, so that the vocal line renders the text (either with traditional text-painting or more subtle inflections) and the piano at times accompanies, reflects, enhances the music of the voice that it supports, or (as a side-kick) the piano comments on the vocal line (either to the vocalist and/or to us as listeners). Schubert oscillates throughout 'Ihr Bild' between B♭ minor and the parallel B♭ major (see Example 1.5). The music begins hauntingly empty (bars 1–2),[48] filling in the empty octave B♭ with B♭ minor (bars 3–8), and then turning to B♭ major (bars 9–12) culminating in a perfect authentic cadence. B♭ major ironically sets the illusion that the portrait has come to life and the narrator has access once again (or for the first time) to his beloved. Schubert associates two musical details to the coming to life of the image of the narrator's beloved—the pitch-class $g♭$ associated with the gaze (see the downbeat of bar 5 with the tritone descent from c and the double-dotted rhythm) and the false happiness of B♭ major with which the setting of the first stanza concludes in bar 12. Yet it is not only the "happy" B♭ major that suggests an ironic illusion of happiness; the musical texture of the B♭ major from bars 8–12 is close position four-part harmony of chorales—signifiers of belonging in social space in Schubert's music.[49]

As the illusion of the picture coming to life deepens and Heine describes the lips and smile of the image, and tears welling up in her/its eyes "as if" from tears of pain, the gazing pitch-class $g♭$ becomes a key—G♭ major (for

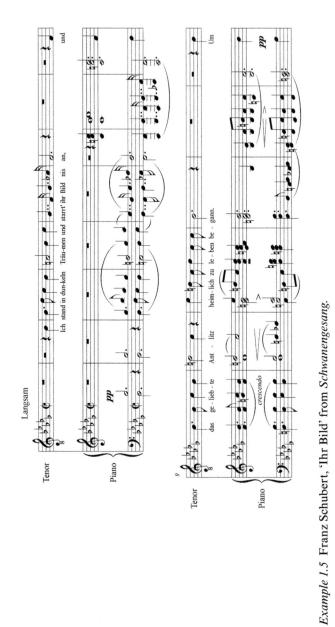

Example 1.5 Franz Schubert, 'Ihr Bild' from *Schwanengesang*.

Example 1.5 (Continued)

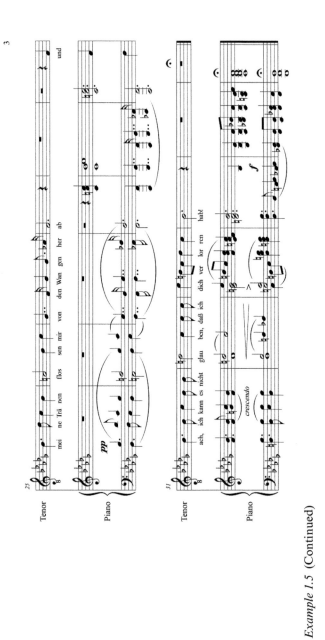

Example 1.5 (Continued)

the setting of the second stanza, bars 14–23). The piano accompaniment curtsies delicately in G♭ after the imperfect authentic cadence on the downbeat of bar 18, and again on the downbeat of bar 22. Schubert writes the one and only vocal ornament on a setting of the organ of specularity ("Augen") in bar 21—a delicate turn.

Schubert turns the music from illusion to reality with the freezing cold turn from G♭ major back to a near-exact repetition of the music to which he had set the first stanza of Heine's poem. The upbeat to bar 23, through bar 23, and the upbeat to bar 24, through bar 24, horrifyingly revisit the initial empty B♭ of the opening of the work as well as the courtesy of illusion that had echoed the false happiness of G♭ major. The chord on the downbeat of bar 23 is an Italian augmented sixth chord that moves directly to the tonic without the grace of a dominant harmony to soften the blow. The voice-leading is cruel; not only does $g♭$ resolve down to the $f♮$ of tonic B♭ minor, but, with a snarl, the $e♮$ doubles the gesture in contrary motion. Schubert gives us B♭ on the downbeat of bar 25, neither B♭ minor nor major, as if the shock of reality has evacuated the symbolic third of both sonorities.[50]

The narrator realizes his loss with the setting of the third stanza that almost repeats exactly the music of the setting of the first stanza. As with all near repetitions, the slight differences tell all; bars 12–14 are bars 34–36, except an additional voice is added and the hopefulness of the piano's comment on B♭ major in bars 12–14 turns to the dark of B♭ minor in bars 34–36.

To revisit Lacan's three positions of specularity inherent in the gaze: an object that looks at a subject; the subject seeing that the object looks at him/her; a third person who sees the entire scene and both of its specular dimensions. Schubert renders a musical gaze in 'Ihr Bild' through all of the parameters discussed above in which the picture is seen to respond to the narrator; and all of these details fuse the specular agencies of object and subject, making cause and effect indistinguishable. The brutality of bars 23–24 represent not so much an agent of specularity as the realization of a fusion of cause and effect with regard to the seemingly coming-to-life of the narrator's beloved. Schubert composes Lacan's third agent that observes all as the final two bars—the surplus voice (crucially an inner voice that thickens what had been close-position four-part harmony).

Notes

1 The body is a crucial component of Mladen Dolar's object voice (to be discussed below). The body is also closely linked to a distinction that Brian Massumi and others have drawn between emotion and affect. For Massumi, emotion is a socially based linguistic code that we articulate to ourselves and/or others at a ½ second remove from the visceral impact of affect. The body is clearly the carrier of affect for Massumi and others. The voice is clearly a vehicle for the introjection of signals from without, and a projection of signals from within. Yet what kind of "clearly" do I mean by these statements? I mean that there is no way to imagine the affective dimension of the voice without the body. However, the

precise distinction between the socially constructed "body" and some more essential, personal "body" are very difficult if not impossible to draw. It is perhaps helpful to think of the "body" as that dimension of the flesh we inhabit with edges towards and among all three of Lacan's psychic registers: the Imaginary, the Symbolic, and the Real. See Ruth Leys, 'The Turn to Affect: A Critique', *Critical Inquiry* 37 (2011): 434–72 and Melissa Gregg and Gregory J. Seigworth (eds), *The Affect Theory Reader* (Durham, NC and London: Duke University Press, 2010). My thanks to Alexi Vellianitis for pointing out this nexus of connections.
2 See Roland Barthes, 'The Grain of the Voice', in *Image-Music-Text*, trans. Stephen Heath (New York: Hill and Wang, 1977).
3 Julia Kristeva, *Revolution in Poetic Language*, trans. Margaret Waller (New York: Columbia University Press, 1984), 86. Kristeva's notion of the "symbolic" refers to elements of language involved in communication of meaning in a social context; Saussure's notion of signifier and signified are embedded within Kristeva's "symbolic". It is close to, but not identical with, the Lacanian notion of the Symbolic. See the Imaginary, Symbolic, and Real in Lacan in Dylan Evans, *An Introductory Dictionary of Lacanian Psychoanalysis* (London and New York: Routledge, 2006). Kristeva's notion of the "semiotic" refers to what less clearly participates in communication; it includes tone of voice, idiosyncratic speech patterns, and gestures. See Sara Beardsworth, *Julia Kristeva* (Binghamton, NY: SUNY University Press, 2004). For an introduction to the divided subject in Freud and Lacan, see Kaja Silverman, 'The Subject: The Freudian Model', in *The Subject of Semiotics* (New York: Oxford University Press, 1983).
4 *Ibid.*, 86.
5 *Ibid.*, 87.
6 *Ibid.*, 87–8.
7 Barthes, 'The Grain of the Voice', 182.
8 *Ibid.*, 183.
9 *Ibid.*, 188.
10 Recording at www.youtube.com/watch?v=BO538njaOIA. Accessed April 9, 2016. I used Sonic Visualizer to create the spectrograms that follow.
11 Recording at www.youtube.com/watch?v=mjcgBrJr9QQ Accessed April 9, 2016.
12 In this discussion, the terms sonogram and spectrogram are used as synonyms; there are technical distinctions to be made between them, but such distinctions lie outside the purpose of this chapter.
13 Michel Poizat, *The Angel's Cry: Beyond the Pleasure Principle in Opera*, trans. Arthur Denner (Ithaca, NY and London: Cornell University Press, 1992). See Sigmund Freud, *Beyond the Pleasure Principle*, ed. and trans. James Strachey (New York: W.W. Norton, 1961).
14 Poizat, *The Angel's Cry*, 7. Poizat's prose has been heavily influenced by Lacanian psychoanalysis; there are three works of Lacan in his bibliography, and he cites specific passages from Lacan from time to time. Since there is a strain of Lacan throughout Poizat's book, a word about *jouissance* is in order. In French, the word has sexual connotations of orgasm—suggesting a strong degree of pleasure. In Lacan, however (and in many applications of Lacan to a wide variety of texts), *jouissance* is (also, or rather) a pleasure in displeasure, such as a compulsion to repeat something unpleasant over and over again. *Jouissance* (also, or rather) has connotations of the unimaginable, that beyond either the Imaginary or Symbolic—some "thing" edged with the Real (that pulp "thingness" that necessarily and yet impossibly underlies all Imaginary and Symbolic structures, representations).
15 *Ibid.*, 37.

16 Poizat explores the history of this opposition: 'In "the King's corner," beneath the masculine emblem of the king, gathered those who championed a French music thoroughly committed [...] to the primacy of language. In "the Queen's corner," beneath the loge and under the feminine emblem of the Queen, gathered the partisan's of Italian music, proponents of lyric flight' (58).
17 *Ibid.*, 74–5.
18 These cries all align with Chion's notion of the female cry in classic Hollywood cinema representing female subjectivity at a limit (of consciousness, language, life itself) implicitly at the coercive hand of male subjectivity. See Michel Chion, *La voix au cinema* (Paris: Cahiers du cinema, 1952), 69.
19 For an early account of the relationship among motives in *Lulu* and the basic series (including the derivation of the Erdgeist fourths and the row), see Willi Reich, 'Alban Berg's *Lulu*,' The *Musical Quarterly* 22 (1936), 383–401.
20 Semantic encoding is a technique in literature of representing a temporal disjunction between the impact of a sensation and its verbalization.
21 By human, I mean the obvious agency of a human being singing; by instrumental, I mean an instrument heard in a melodic context; by analogue I mean a synthesized voice using analogue technology; and by digital, I mean a voice constructed or represented digitally and then output in an analogue environment.
22 Mladen Dolar, *A Voice and Nothing More* (Cambridge, MA and London: MIT Press, 2006), 4.
23 *Ibid.*, 10.
24 Many have looked back to Saussure as a way to spring theory forward, as it were. See Jacques Derrida, *Of Grammatology*, trans. by Gayatri Chakravorty Spivak (Baltimore, MD: Johns Hopkins University Press, 2013).
25 Dolar, *A Voice and Nothing More*, 17 (emphasis in the original).
26 *Ibid.*, 15.
27 *Ibid.*, 20.
28 <https://www.youtube.com/watch?v=6aqGYYBwKbQ> Accessed April 14, 2016. There are similarities between Dolar's notion of the linguistic voice and Barthes' geno-song. Among the differences: Fischer-Diskau and Panzera are singing texts and making a host of conscious and unconscious decisions concerning articulation and vocal production; Lacan is lecturing, explaining psychoanalytic content to a group of students, responding to a challenge by a disgruntled student.
29 Dolar, *A Voice and Nothing More*, 24. Just a reminder: Dolar means "" in its Lacanian dimension; the symbolic is language, law, social space, the infinite gradations of "grey" that mediate the brutal "black" and "white" binary oppositions of the Imaginary. The Real is that pulp thingness just beyond the Symbolic and Imaginary.
30 <https://www.youtube.com/watch?v=1hxjCIANddU> Accessed April 14, 2016.
31 One approach to "noise" is a sound that is spread across the audible spectrum— an "all frequency" sound in which you can't distinguish one frequency from another. The white noise of static is a good example of pure noise from this perspective.
32 A composer (one among many) who writes music that represents this music within the voice is Steve Reich; listen to *Different Trains* for an example of instrumental music that listens to taped voices and unfolds instrumental music based on the intervals heard in the spoken tapes.
33 See Didier Anzieu, *The Skin Ego*, trans. Chris Turner (New Haven: Yale University Press, 1989).
34 Dolar, *A Voice and Nothing More*, 29.
35 *Ibid.*, 53.

36 Dolar traces the term back to Michel Chion and Pierre Schaeffer (see *Ibid.*, 61). Although most uses of acousmatic voices in film and music describe functions of utterances uttered by people, it is not impossible to imagine usages of musical instruments not produced by vocal cords as representing/embodying acousmatic voices. The word "other" is the English word for "autre" in French; in Lacan, the word is sometimes written upper case; sometimes it is written lower case. "Other" with an upper case "o" tends to represent the big Other of the Symbolic order; "other" with a lower case "o" tends to represent the Imaginary other of the Imaginary—the image, as it were, of the other in the mirror.
37 For additional takes on the acousmatic in opera, see Carolyn Abbate, *Unsung Voices: Opera and Musical Narrative in the Nineteenth Century* (Princeton, NJ: Princeton University Press, 1991). Abbate defines voice as 'an aural vision of music animated by multiple, decentered voices localized in several invisible bodies' (13).
38 Dolar, *A Voice and Nothing More*, 106.
39 See Giorgio Agamben, *State of Exception*, trans. Kevin Attell (Stanford, CA: Stanford University Press, 2005).
40 *Ibid.*, 152. Dolar cites Dinouart who classifies ten kinds of silence. See Abbé Dinouart (No place given: Jérôme Millon, 1771), cited in *A Voice and Nothing More*, 154–55.
41 *Ibid.*, 152–53.
42 *Ibid.*, 155.
43 "Room" sound is ambient sound that is always present in recordings and movies; it is noise just below the hearing threshold that gives to space a "realistic" ambience. Dolar discusses acousmatic silence as the silence of God, or the silence of an analyst in the transference (*A Voice and Nothing More*, 161).
44 Anzieu, *The Skin Ego*, Chapter 11. See also, Édith Lecourt, "The Musical Envelope" in *Psychic Envelopes*, ed. Didier Anzieu (London: Karnac Books, 1990).
45 Jacques Lacan, *The Seminar of Jacques Lacan: Book I: Freud's Papers on Technique 1953–1954*, ed. Jacques-Allain Miller, trans. John Forrester (New York and London: W.W. Norton and Company, 1991), 218.
46 As reproduced at <http://www.staff.uni-mainz.de/pommeren/Gedichte/BdL/Heimk-23.html> Accessed April 18, 2016.
47 For an online translation, see <http://www.lieder.net/lieder/get_text.html?TextId=17768> Accessed 17 October, 2016. David Lewin suggests that the object of desire in the poem may be dead—suggesting not simply in the fact that "she's gone" but the phrase "zu Leben begann" implies that she is no longer living. See David Lewin, *Studies in Music with Text* (New York and London: Oxford University Press, 2006), 135–47.
48 In one of Schenker's first publications, he evocatively suggests that the reiterated B-flats with which 'Ihr Bild' opens suggest the blinking eyes of the male narrator gazing in disbelief at the image of his beloved as it comes to life. See Heinrich Schenker, 'Ihr Bild' in *Tonwille*, Vol. 1 (Vienna: Universal, 1921).
49 Modal irony pervades *Winterreise* as well; in *Winterreise* minor modes represent not so much sadness and direct experience; major modes represent illusion, memories of happiness that the narrator no longer experiences. There is a similar ironic use of close position, four-part harmony in 'Das Wirtshaus' and 'Die Nebensonnen'. The binary identification/alienation also suggests the ambivalence inherent in mirror (mis)recognition. My thanks to Alexi Vellianitis for this idea.
50 I mean to refer to reality in the colloquial sense, as opposed to the Lacanian Real.

2 Parallels between Schoenberg and Freud

Alexander Carpenter

Over the past few decades, a good deal of ink has been spilled—some of it, admittedly, by me—in an effort to directly link Arnold Schoenberg and Sigmund Freud. Such a linkage would, among other things, go a long way towards confirming the putative psychoanalytic *Zeitgeist* of *fin-de-siècle* Vienna, the connectedness between psychoanalysis and the aesthetic environment of Vienna generally, and would likely provide a clearer picture of the psycho-poetics of Schoenberg's revolutionary atonal, Expressionist music of the early twentieth century. Alas, much of this ink has been spilled in vain: no direct links exist between these men or their own discrete disciplinary projects, though a significant amount of circumstantial evidence suggests that Schoenberg was certainly familiar with Freud and his theories, and, of course, Freud and Schoenberg shared a number of friends and acquaintances; Schoenberg's students, Anton Webern and Alban Berg, were likewise familiar with psychoanalysis, and both came into contact with Freud and some of his followers. Music and psychoanalysis, in the fecund cultural environment of early twentieth-century Vienna, are clearly imbricated in complicated and sometimes nebulous ways.[1]

While it would certainly be helpful if the links between Schoenberg and Freud were more substantial, what is truly remarkable about these two epochal figures is not their connectedness as such, but rather the striking similarities between their lives. My argument here is not that Freud and Schoenberg were personally influenced by each other in some way nor that their respective enterprises directly informed each other, but rather that the powerful affinities between their contributions to the cultural and intellectual history of the twentieth century—arguably, Freud and Schoenberg engineered Copernican revolutions with respect to music and psychology, forever changing the way in which the self is understood and expressed, and the role that art plays in this expression—can be understood as an outcome of two lives lived in parallel.

Some superficial similarities

We could begin with the important if obvious similarities between Schoenberg and Freud: both were of Eastern European extraction—Schoenberg's father was Hungarian and his mother was Czech; both of Freud's parents were from Galicia, in what is now the Ukrainian-Polish border region. Both men were lapsed Jews: Freud famously a "godless Jew", and Schoenberg a converted Jew (who reconverted later in life); both lived in Vienna's Jewish ninth district, the Alsergrund; both were ignored or outright rejected by Vienna's cultural and intellectual institutions—neither Schoenberg nor Freud ever held a formal, permanent post in a major institution in the city; and both had a well-known, lifelong love/hate relationship with Vienna—Freud insisted 'Vienna oppresses me' and claimed he was never truly comfortable in the city (though he lived there virtually his entire life), while Schoenberg, who left and returned to Vienna a number of times, was likewise ambivalent about the "city of song" and once fiercely asserted 'I don't want to have anything to do with Vienna. I don't want to contract any new depressions there'.[2]

These are superficial similarities that are part of a much bigger picture. Though it appears that they never met, Schoenberg and Freud lived strikingly parallel lives, and it was the nature and course of these lives—shaped as they were by the shared milieu of Vienna, and by the shared inheritance of the intellectual traditions of Austro-Germanic culture—that gave rise to their originality, to their respective creative, intellectual, and theoretical bodies of work, and to their enduring legacies. In the following essay, I will draw some detailed biographical comparisons between Schoenberg and Freud, specifically examining the development of their respective theoretical enterprises, their relationships with their disciples and their responses to apostasy, and their concerns over priority. Again, while it remains impossible to directly connect Schoenberg's revolutionary modern music with the revolutionary psychology of Freud, it is possible to examine their lives comparatively, in direct and evocative ways, towards a deeper understanding of the social and cultural forces that shaped their milieu and their work, and the *Zeitgeist* of *fin-de-siècle* Vienna.

1923: *annus mirabilis* and structural models

1923 was a remarkable year for both Schoenberg and Freud. During this year, each man revealed his "structural model": perhaps more famously, Freud developed the Id-Ego-Superego model that supplemented his earlier topographical model; for Schoenberg, it was the 12-tone technique. To be fair, Schoenberg's "model" was really a "method", but I would argue that the purpose was the same, namely, to provide a solid theoretical underpinning and coherence for practice. In both cases, the "structural model" developed over a number of years and was revealed in nascent form prior to 1923. Moreover, each model/method became a central aspect of the legacies of Schoenberg and Freud. What follows is a comparative account of the development and revelation of Schoenberg's 12-tone method and Freud's structural model, and an assessment of their respective significance.

The 12-tone method

Schoenberg had what I consider to have been a brief "psychoanalytic period" in his compositional development, beginning roughly with his stylistic shift to free atonality in 1909 and ending around 1912. Much of the music of this period—including symphonic, chamber and stage works—was composed according to a new aesthetic that privileged an instinctive approach to composition, a radical approach predicated on the revelation or expression of the unconscious through music and the abandonment of the technical strictures of the major/minor system, functional harmony, traditional form, and motivic/thematic development. A decade later, Schoenberg's desire to (re)impose 'conscious control' on his music and to seek out the 'laws or rules' that govern 'order, logic, comprehensibility and form' in atonal music would lead him to the creation of the 12-tone method.[3] This method arose out of a period of exploration and experimentation that began towards the end of the First World War. Beginning in 1920, Schoenberg began communicating new ideas to his students and colleagues about form and the use of a melodic motive or basic shape, comprised of a row of pitches in a fixed intervallic order, as the basis of composition. Schoenberg called this rudimentary, nascent form of 12-tone serialism "composing with tones," which he described as a "very vague term" that captures the essential notion of using "a basic set of twelve tones" not as a traditional motive, but rather as the generative stuff of a composition, from which both melodic and harmonic content is derived.[4]

Schoenberg began tentatively experimenting with this new approach in the years immediately following the First World War, but did not begin composing in earnest until after 1921. Bryan Simms has argued that Schoenberg's creativity was catalyzed at this time through his dawning awareness of the neo-classical style emerging from France: while Schoenberg was decidedly ambivalent about the regressive, even pandering nature of the music of popular composers like Igor Stravinsky, he nonetheless conceded that neo-classicism was an aesthetic paradigm that could not simply be dismissed, and began composing his own essays in the style in order to compete and remain relevant within the vanguard of the modernists.[5]

Schoenberg's earliest 12-tone works include the Prelude from his Op. 25 *Suite*, the Sonnet from his Op. 24 *Serenade*, and the Waltz from his Op. 23 piano pieces: the Prelude was completed in 1921, the Waltz and the Sonnet, in early 1923. All three pieces emerged out of a nebula of experimental approaches that included elementary serial procedures and composing using basic sets and hexachordal groupings, in conjunction with Baroque and Classical forms. Ultimately, the 12-tone method was galvanized in these works, and it defined and dominated Schoenberg's compositional approach for the remainder of his life.

The importance of the 12-tone method for Schoenberg was manifold, but primarily it was intended as a method through which structural unity in panchromatic music could be achieved. The 12-tone method prescribes that a composition be forged from a single, ordered row of pitches—and its permutations—derived from the chromatic scale, deployed in serial fashion. The row unifies both the horizontal and vertical axes of music—melody and harmony, the whole of musical space—*a priori*, creating what Malcolm MacDonald memorably calls a "molecular" relationship between the preconceived tone row and the elements of a musical work: 'The note-row is, so to speak, the DNA molecule of twelve-note music: the agent which stamps every bar, every theme, every note, every chord, as belonging to a single, unique work'.[6] As I will argue below, Schoenberg's method—its rules abstracted from the fundamental principles of logic, order and cohesion—for imposing control upon the processes of musical composition can be profitably compared to Freud's structural model of the mind, revealing a striking affinity of thought between Schoenberg and Freud despite their putative ignorance of each other.

Freud: from topography to structural model

Freud's 'topography' of mind is already hinted at in 1895 in his first major publication, *Studies on Hysteria*, in which the terms *das Unbewusste* (the unconscious) and *Bewusstseinsunfähig* (inadmissible to consciousness) first appear, suggesting two distinct regions of mind.[7] The topographical model was subsequently introduced in *The Interpretation of Dreams* in 1900 and developed over the next two decades. In *The Interpretation of Dreams*, Freud allows that the 'psychic apparatus' does not necessarily have to be conceived in spatial terms (though he concedes that it may turn out that the mental systems are in a stable special arrangement); rather, Freud describes the 'agencies or systems' of the mind in terms of a temporal sequence, through which excitation passes during a psychical process.[8]

Freud regarded the spatial analogy as rather crude: he says as much in the *Introductory Lectures on Psychoanalysis*, but he also allows that a spatial analogy is 'the most convenient' for the purpose of general understanding.[9] Freud likened the systems of mind to a series of adjoining rooms (not an iceberg, as is popularly thought). The topographical model proposes that the mind consists of three systems—the Unconscious, the Preconscious, and the Conscious—that are related to each other spatially (i.e. at differently levels of depth or remove) but are not connected to the anatomy of the brain.[10] The Unconscious is the largest of the three systems or regions and contains mental impulses that are inaccessible to consciousness; residing in the liminal space between the Conscious and the Unconscious is the Preconscious, which comprises mental impulse with the possibility of being recalled to consciousness. In Freud's analogy of adjoining rooms, a mental impulse from the large 'entrance hall' (the Unconscious) can pass into the 'drawing room' (the Preconscious) if the doorman—whose function is to censor/repress—standing between the two rooms permits it; however, passing into the Preconscious is not a guarantor of an impulse becoming conscious—whatever passes from the Unconscious into the realm of the Preconscious must be 'noticed' by the Conscious, which occupies the same room as the Preconscious, standing 'as a spectator at the end of the [drawing] room'.[11]

Freud never completely abandoned the topographical model, but introduced a new model, the so-called structural model, in his 1923 paper 'The Ego and the Id'. Freud had already touched upon the elements of the new model in 1920s *Beyond the Pleasure Principle*, but in the 'Ego and the Id', he presented a complete synthesis, or perhaps rather a sublimation of the topographical model into the structural model. In this synthesis, the Ego is the 'entity which starts out from the system *Pcpt.* [perception] and begins by being *Pcs.* [preconscious]'; the Id is the entity that 'behaves as though it were *Ucs.* [unconscious]'.[12] In this model, the Ego and the Id are intimately linked: they are merged, as though in a round sack—Freud draws this model with the Id at the bottom, merging with the Ego towards the top, and the whole thing contained by the membrane of the perception system. The function of the Ego—the seat of reason and common sense—in this model is to check the passions of the Id, a task Freud likens to a man riding a horse: the Ego, insists Freud, 'is in the habit of transforming the Id's will into action as if it were its own'.[13] The tripartite structure of the topographical model is mirrored in the structural model through the addition of a third entity, the Super Ego or Ego Ideal. The Super Ego takes the form of 'conscience, to exercise the moral censorship': it is the 'heir of the Oedipus complex', having been formed as part of the task of repressing that very complex, while retaining the injunctive-prohibitive character of the Father.[14]

Schoenberg, Freud, and structure

This is all very familiar to anyone with even a passing knowledge of Freudian theory, but what does it have to do with Schoenberg and the 12-tone method? Like Freud, Schoenberg first tentatively presented his re-theorized approach in 1920, and then formally in 1923. Like Freud, he retained much of what his new model/method purported to supplant: just as the structural model worked in tandem with the topographical model, the 12-tone method did not obviate the fundamental techniques and musical thought that preceded it, but rather offered a new way of ensuring unity and comprehensibility in panchromatic music and provided a scaffolding for building large-scale atonal works.

What is most striking is the timing of Freud's and Schoenberg's re-theorizing: the desire to provide a more rigorous theoretical underpinning for their respective projects coincides almost exactly—Schoenberg's music from the summer of 1920 touches on rudimentary serial procedures, while the elements of Freud's structural model were likewise intimated that same year in *Beyond the Pleasure Principle*; Schoenberg revealed his 12-tone method to his students in February of 1923; Freud revealed his structural model in the

'The Ego and the Id' just a few months later, in April of that year. Freud and Schoenberg align at this time, furthermore, with regard to seeking greater 'coherence'—a term that, along with 'logic' and 'unity', comes up frequently in Schoenberg's writings, with respect to both 12-tone music and composition generally; Freud, in introducing the structural model and stressing the centrality of the Ego to the psyche, asserts 'the idea that in each individual there is a coherent organization of mental processes'.[15] Both Schoenberg and Freud, I would argue, introduce their new paradigms in 1923 in a sort of dialectical move, towards a greater systematization that simultaneously maintains a kind of fundamentally irrational, even numinous quality.

Responding to critics of his 12-tone music in 1931, Schoenberg confronted the charge that his music was 'constructed'. In his defense, he offered a view of composition that mirrors Freud's structural model insofar as it posits distinct processes, conscious and unconscious, which are separate but unified in the wholeness of the musical work. These processes, moreover, as in Freud's model, are temporal as much as spatial, proceeding from step to step, and from interiority to exteriority. The activity of "building"—of working with the musico-logical details—is analogous to the Ego's interaction or arbitration with reality, controlling, as Freud writes, 'the approaches to motility [...] to the discharge of excitations in the external world'.[16] Schoenberg's description of the compositional process also exemplifies the dialectical move he shares with Freud, as described above. For Schoenberg, the process is driven by something irrational, even metaphysical: "vision" or inspiration. Vision is realized through the building of the composition (its construction); the result is a work of art, the vision that is at once the sum of its parts—the vision is broken down and then reassembled through the process of composing, of working on the details—and more than the sum of its parts. What joins vision and the musical work, binding everything together, is musical logic, which can itself be unconscious: for Schoenberg, logic is even a "symptom" of unconscious processes—as he insists, one can find the 'symptoms of musical logic' present in a piece, 'even in places where I have not consciously put them'.[17] 12-tone composition, then, is not simply a new method of composing that is more systematic, but it is a manifestation of a broader aesthetic *Weltanschauung* that echoes Freud's model of mental processes, in which impulse (inspiration) is mediated through an agency (the Ego, musical logic) that gives form to the impulse. Schoenberg's new method, and Freud's new model, emerged from a shared need to articulate the logic and coherence of their respective theoretical enterprises, a need that was concomitant and coterminous in the *annus mirabilis* of 1923.

A question of priority

Another point of comparison between Freud and Schoenberg has to do with the notion that both men were revolutionary-heroic figures whose work and vision comprised a kind of absolute originality: this is a historiographic commonplace and warrants unpacking. Throughout their careers, Freud and Schoenberg struggled with rivals and disciples as they sought to assert the primacy of their respective discoveries: in Freud's case, he disavowed the fundamental knowledge that he surely possessed of Schopenhauer and Nietzsche and accused his rivals of plagiarism; Schoenberg vigorously defended the originality and priority of his greatest creation, the 12-tone method, in particular against the competing claims of Josef Matthias Hauer, a fellow Austrian theorist-composer and one-time collaborator in the development of the 12-tone method.[18] Priority and originality were abiding—perhaps even central—concerns for Freud and Schoenberg, concerns that drove both men to carefully shape and guard their respective identities, reputations, and legacies.

Freud: 'obsessed' with priority

While Freud's published writings typically include comprehensive literature surveys that acknowledge his sources and predecessors, it is also the case that Freud was, as Martin and Inge Goldstein claim, 'obsess[ed] with issues of priority' and that this obsession 'entered into his relationships with his associates and his rivals'.[19] Madalon Springnether likewise describes Freud's 'obsession' with 'priority and originality', going so far as to argue that Freud's 'whole theoretical endeavour was tied to his labour of self-creation'.[20] Freud's biographer Ernest Jones famously, if unctuously, claimed that "Freud was never interested in questions of priority, which he found rather boring", but "he was fond of exploring the source of what appeared to be original ideas, particularly his own".[21] The opposite is true: there are many instances in Freud's writing in which he expresses personal concern about priority: he was, as Frank Sulloway notes, 'continually reassessing his relationship to his forerunners, rivals, disciples, and posterity in terms of such priority issues. Characteristically, he even dreamt about priority matters'.[22]

Freud's concerns about priority are exemplified in two specific cases. First, there is Freud's feud with the sexologist Albert Moll over the issue of infantile sexuality, a concept that is foundational to psychoanalysis. Freud and his followers asserted that Freud was the original discoverer of infantile sexuality: the first, according to Ernest Jones, "not only to assert that infants normally experience sexual sensations, but to give a complete description of their variety".[23] Freud himself claimed in his *Three Essays on the Theory Sexuality* (1905) that "so far as I know, not a single author has clearly recognized the regular existence of a sexual instinct in childhood".[24] Moll published his *Investigations into the Libido Sexualis* in 1897—a full eight years before the publication of Freud's *Three Essays*—which he essentially re-published as *The Sexual Life of the Child* in 1909, in the wake of Freud's *Three Essays* and a 1908 paper entitled 'On the Sexual Theories of Children'.[25] Freud accused Moll of plagiarism, and a lifelong blood feud between the two men ensued. Freud, notwithstanding his claims that he knew of no one else who had addressed infantile sexuality, read Moll's book in the late nineteenth century, as attested to in letters to Wilhelm Fließ in 1897: Freud's exposure to Moll's ideas likely led to Freud's abandonment of the seduction theory. This was, as Lutz Sautereig observes, 'a disturbing and embarrassing moment for Freud [...] At the same time, giving up the seduction theory was also a decisive step for Freud and his understanding of childhood sexuality'.[26]

Lorin Anderson has described Freud's complex attitude and behavior with respect to priority and precedence, noting that, on the one hand, Freud 'was inclined to forget where some of his ideas originated, to appropriate ideas without due acknowledgment, to indiscreetly disclose the ideas of others, put to him in confidence'; on the other hand, 'he would recognize these traits, pay random and extravagant tribute to predecessors, and worry about plagiarism'.[27] While Freud's theoretical writings include acknowledgments and summaries of the contributions of his predecessors and contemporaries, it is the case that he also obscured his debt—and psychoanalysis' debt—to two major philosophers of the late nineteenth century, namely Nietzsche and Schopenhauer. Freud insisted he only read Nietzsche and Schopenhauer much later in life, and in so doing discovered serendipitous confluences between their work and psychoanalysis, including, for example, references in Schopenhauer's *World as Will and Idea* to a nascent formulation of the concept of repression, and in Nietzsche, to the idea of dreams as a path to understanding the human psyche, the unconscious and drives. Freud's one-time friend and colleague, Alfred Adler, observed early in the twentieth century that "[i]n Nietzsche's work one finds on almost every page observations reminiscent of those we make in therapy".[28]

Freud's claims that he never read Nietzsche or Schopenhauer, as is now well documented, seem profoundly disingenuous: Günter Gödde has made the case that Freud would have encountered and read the works of both philosophers as early as his student years in the 1870s, when he was a long-standing member of the *Leseverien der deutschen Studenten Wiens* (Reading Group of the German Students in Vienna).[29] In 1925, Freud allowed that Nietzsche, along with Schopenhauer, is a philosopher whose "premonitions and insights often agree in the most amazing manner with the laborious results of psychoanalysis".[30] Here, Freud does not relinquish priority so much as suggest that he, Nietzsche, and Schopenhauer have arrived at the same truths, via different and independent routes—the clinical labors of psychoanalysis provide a subsequent and independent confirmation of the philosophers' intuition.[31] Freud's putative avoidance of Nietzsche and Schopenhauer was, in his view, not about priority; rather, he insisted, it was to preserve his own "open-mindedness", to protect the originality of his own thought.[32]

Schoenberg versus Hauer

Josef Matthias Hauer was one of the chief sources of Schoenberg's anxiety about priority. Hauer is known to history principally as the putative co-initiator of 12-tone music. An Austrian composer, theorist, and contemporary of Schoenberg, Hauer seems to have come to the idea of a compositional method based on the 12 pitches of the chromatic scale independent of Schoenberg, and perhaps even earlier. John Covach indicates that Hauer discovered the '12-tone law' in the summer of 1919, and one of his compositions from that year—*Nomos*, Op. 19—already includes collections of 12 pitch classes; by 1921, Hauer had clearly articulated the idea that all 12 notes should sound before any are repeated, and had been experimenting with 'tropes' or hexachord pairs.[33] Like Schoenberg, Hauer asserted the supremacy of atonality over tonality, and viewed 12-tone composition in metaphysical terms, asserting that the 12 tones contained a 'spiritual truth'.[34] Where Schoenberg and Hauer diverged was in their respective views on the relationship between the composer and the music. Schoenberg viewed serial composition essentially through the lens of late Romanticism, regarding the composer as an expressive agent—Schoenberg's rows are composed, organic entities, and the creation of the row is the beginning of the composition. Hauer's view of composition was more in line with later high modernists like Pierre Boulez and John Cage, insofar as Hauer sought to radically suppress the intentions or expressive will of the composer in favor of the truth of the purity of 12-tone structures—he went so far as to generate rows using chance procedures.[35] Hauer was also more theoretically rigorous with respect to 12-tone composition and published a number of books and articles on the subject.

In 1932, Schoenberg wrote some fragmentary notes, collected under the title "Priority". In these notes, Schoenberg asserted that he was the progenitor of 12-tone composition, insisting that he wrote the first 12-tone piece in 1921, a few months before Hauer. Schoenberg insisted, too, that he developed completely independently of Hauer, that his thought with respect to atonality and composing with tones pre-dates Hauer's (going back as far as 1908), that he had already written a 12-tone theme in 1914—well ahead of Hauer—for an unpublished symphony, and that Hauer's approach was fundamentally different anyway: Schoenberg sought to use the 12-tone method as a means to build compositional coherence, while Hauer was merely experimenting with "a new sound" and was not strictly concerned with composition.[36] Schoenberg vehemently insisted that Hauer "does not have the priority", and that Schoenberg was "indisputably alone" in his use of the 12-tone row as a "basic shape" from which the material of the composition is generated: put side by side, Hauer's and Schoenberg's first 12-tone pieces demonstrate, in Schoenberg's words, that "I have the (and if one my say so, the exclusive) priority".[37]

Like Freud, Schoenberg asserts his priority over his would-be competitors—including his own disciple Anton Webern, as discussed below—going so far as to employing legalistic arguments (assembling and interpreting evidence, establishing time lines, and even citing witnesses) all the while maintaining in the same breath that he does not care about priority: "It is a matter of complete indifference to me who has the priority [...] the question of priority is completely unimportant to me".[38] The striking similarities between Schoenberg and Freud, with respect to their concerns with priority, reveal that both are fiercely determined to protect the originality of their respective enterprises, arguably at the expense of what might have been fruitful collaborations with like-minded contemporaries, and even at the expense of the historical record itself.

Disciples and apostates

The early history of the psychoanalytic movement is defined by two major activities or energies: psychoanalytic theory's hardening orthodoxy, and the concomitant apostasy of a number of the movement's earliest acolytes. Freud, as is well known, demanded deference from his followers and strict adherence to his theoretical enterprise; Schoenberg, though certainly not as dogmatic, also surrounded himself with a circle of reverential devotees who protected him and were likewise expected to be loyal. Schoenberg and Freud are very much alike insofar as neither suffered dissent or apostasy gladly.

Freud's apostates: Jung and Adler

According to Edoardo Weiss, an Italian psychoanalyst and early Freudian, Freud—while knowing that the theories of psychoanalysis he was developing would evolve and be revised over time—was "very protective of the great field of his scientific investigation and theory he had christened psychoanalysis, and he resented any distortion or misinterpretations of his concepts".[39] Following a series of high-profile defections from the psychoanalytic movement between 1911 and 1913, Freud tightened his grip on the discipline and his followers, demanding personal loyalty and situating himself squarely at the center of the movement and as the *sine qua non* of psychoanalytic knowledge: in 1914, in the immediate wake of Jung's secession, Freud would declare that "I consider myself justified in maintaining that even today no one can know better than I do what psycho-analysis is".[40] Interestingly, while Freud was ostensibly non-musical, he would characterize the failures of the disloyal disciple-apostates (especially the Jungians) of the psychoanalytic movement in musical metaphors, stating 'The truth is that these people have picked out a few cultural overtones from the symphony of life and have once more failed to hear the mighty and primordial melody of the instincts'.[41]

Freud never forgave apostates, and especially Jung and the members of the Vienna Psychoanalytic Society who defected with Alfred Adler. Jung and Adler are of course the most famous Freudian apostates: Adler was one of the earliest members of Freud's circle in Vienna; Jung connected with Freud later, becoming the dauphin of the psychoanalytic movement. Adler and Jung dared to challenge the orthodoxy of psychoanalytic theory, and both moved away from Freud's exclusively sexual aetiology and developed their own theoretical corpora.

Early on, Freud not only viewed Jung as a Swiss Christian savior who could help psychoanalysis transcend its reputation as a "Jewish science" and overcome the anti-Semitic resistance it faced, but he also characterized Jung as an able helper, as Joshua to his (Freud's) Moses, suggesting that it would be Jung who would explore "the promised land of psychiatry".[42] Eventually, Jung deviated from Freudian theory on the issue of a strictly sexual—and therefore mechanistic-reductionist, in Jung's view—interpretation of the libido, and instead posited the notion of a more generalized fundamental life force as the main human drive, which entailed rejecting the Oedipus complex, and developing his own "analytic psychology". Freud promptly dismissed his former disciple as "brutal" and "sanctimonious",[43] and would ostracize him from his circle, never fully recovering from the betrayal. The Oedipal elements of their relationship are obvious: Freud not only characterized Jung's apostasy as pathological—Jung, as Freud wrote to Karl Abraham, was "crazy"—but he also believed that Jung harbored a death wish for him.[44]

Alfred Adler, though not the crown prince Jung had been, nonetheless played an important role in the early history of psychoanalysis. Adler was a strong supporter of Freud's from the earliest meetings of Freud's Wednesday Psychological Society, beginning in 1902. He was not a pupil of Freud as such, but rather a colleague and a key member of the inner circle of psychoanalysis until 1911. Adler broke with Freud for the same reasons Jung did: namely, Adler was not an orthodox adherent to Freudian theory, but rather had his own ideas and theories—believing, like Jung, that sex was not the whole story and, while allowing for the role of unconscious forces, also suggesting social pressures as a key component of the development of personality—that competed directly with Freud's. Adler would be the first major dissenter from Freud's psychoanalytic movement, founding his own school of psychotherapy, the Society for Individual Psychology, in 1912. Freud's response to Adler's disloyalty, as with Jung, was to diminish and pathologize: Freud lamented the "disgraceful defection" of a former friend and colleague now demonized as "little Adler [... a] malicious paranoiac."[45]

The parallels between Freud's circle and Schoenberg's will become clear. Each man had a cause and an enterprise to jealously safeguard: for Freud, it was the primacy of his own insights and discoveries, embodied in the scientific legacy of psychoanalysis; for Schoenberg, it was the expressive gains from the radical overthrow of the tonal system and the modern music it engendered. Both Freud and Schoenberg drew their followers in tightly, surrounding themselves with a protective ring of supporters and insisting upon an almost religious devotion and loyalty: each man was Moses—or even Christ—within his own circle.

Schoenberg's apostates: Eisler, Krenek, and Weill

Alex Ross argues that Schoenberg took 'personal' umbrage at 'Weimar's young composers [and their too-accessible work...] it was a question of betrayal'.[46] Schoenberg reserved particular vitriol for fellow composers who not only shirked their responsibilities to modern music—by turning towards such heresies as jazz and by actively courting public approval for their works—but who also criticized atonal music, if not Schoenberg directly. Austrian composer Ernst Krenek's rejection of Schoenberg was a combination of apostasy—Krenek turned away from atonality, to compose more fashionable *Zeitopern* that embraced popular idioms—and a personal if indirect attack against Schoenberg's 12-tone method. Krenek employed masturbation as a metaphor to describe the activities of a "self-gratif[ying] composer"—clearly Schoenberg and his school—"who sits in his studio and invents rules according to which he then writes his notes"; Schoenberg responded by lashing out at Krenek as a mere populist, accusing him and his ilk of writing music "only for whores" instead of serving the cause of and suffering for authentically modern music.[47]

Kurt Weill, a one-time would-be disciple of Schoenberg's, was also attacked by the composer as an apostate—albeit indirectly in Schoenberg's annotations of an article by the younger composer—for not only being a populist, but for calling on modern composers to give up their radical pursuits and to reorient their music towards a broader audience. Modern composers should strive to be more understandable, argued Weill; Schoenberg, in sharp contrast, echoed his remarks about Krenek, accusing Weill's generation of composers of dumbing down music for the general public, of writing idiotic music for idiots.

Schoenberg also turned directly on former acolytes and students, including Theodor Adorno and Hanns Eisler. In 1946, Adorno criticized Schoenberg's late 12-tone music in the book *Philosophy of Modern Music*, which juxtaposed Stravinsky and Schoenberg in a broader discussion of the socio-political implications of modern music. Schoenberg's response was to attribute unscrupulous motives to the philosopher—his "attack was an act of vengeance"—and to dismiss him to the rubbish heap of the out-of-favor who dared disparage any of Schoenberg's work: Adorno immediately became merely "another disloyal person [...] now I know that he has clearly never liked my music".[48]

Hanns Eisler, who studied with Schoenberg in the early 1920s and was one of the first of Schoenberg's students to adopt the 12-tone method, made the mistake of admitting that he did not like modern music, nor "the modern" generally. Schoenberg wrote to his brother-in-law, Alexander von Zemlinsky, seeking clarification of Eisler's deviant views and asking 'Did [Eisler] say he is turning away from this modern stuff? [...] that he doesn't understand twelve-note music? [...] that he simply doesn't consider it music at all?'[49] Eisler's views infuriated Schoenberg, who accused Eisler of 'treason' and of failing to adhere to the 'laws of loyalty' that Schoenberg had established for his circle; he further describes Eisler as a nihilist and cynic, who makes 'snap judgments' that are successful 'solely in café-haunting circles'.[50] Schoenberg rejected Eisler's claims of 'complete loyalty' towards Schoenberg 'personally' and to his 'cause', and asserted that Eisler was free to hold his own views: Schoenberg maintained that he would 'never resent' a person with views diverging from his own, but rather would feel sorry for him, as though he were disabled—like someone with 'one short leg, a clumsy hand, etc.'.[51] Here are still more congruences with Freud and his relationship to the acolytes of psychoanalysis: unconditional loyalty to the project of modern music—as defined by Schoenberg—is a requirement for the members of Schoenberg's circle, just as Freud required unswerving commitment to the orthodoxies of Freudian psychoanalytic theory: heretics, secessionists, and apostates are deficient, disabled, and disposable.

Schoenberg: Oedipal conflicts with Webern

While Schoenberg was known, on the one hand, to be a genial and warm person, with a decidedly magnetic personality and a quick wit, it is also true that he could be acerbic, angry, dour, and depressed. He was also known, as Allen Shawn points out, for his 'famous need for unswerving loyalty from his students'[52]; Christopher Hailey echoes this, suggesting that Schoenberg exerted a 'tyrannical influence upon his students' and imposed 'demands for absolute loyalty' upon them.[53]

Anton Webern was Schoenberg's most devoted student-disciple. While it is also the case that Schoenberg's other famous student, Alban Berg, served "the Master" with equal fervor as acolyte and dogsbody, it was Webern who manifested an unhealthy emotional and psychological dependence on Schoenberg. Webern resided 'at the borderline of complete psychological dependence' on Schoenberg, as Friedrich Wildgans argues; Allen Shawn describes Webern's feelings as 'sometimes cross[ing] over the line into religious adoration'; and in a similar vein, Julie Brown argues that Webern and Schoenberg's circle of devotees constituted a kind of messianic cult, with Schoenberg as a Christ figure—confirmed in Webern's words to Schoenberg: "I believe that the disciples of Jesus Christ could not have felt more deeply for their lord than we for you".[54]

The Freud-Jung relationship—in which Jung, in his own words, felt towards Freud "uncompromising devotion" and "unconditional veneration" that was "'religious'-enthusiastic" in its fervor[55]—certainly maps neatly onto the Schoenberg-Webern relationship in this regard. There was also a strong Oedipal aspect to the Webern-Schoenberg relationship, which is to say that there existed a kind of tense competition between master/father and disciple/son, having to do in this case specifically with the issues of priority and originality. Schoenberg—who insisted, with respect to the advent of the 12-tone method and his relationship with Hauer, on his "outstanding originality" and "completely independent achievements" not only in music but in painting, poetry, theory, and politics[56]—complained vociferously to the pianist Erwin Stein that Webern was, in Stein's words, "a predatory disciple" who aggressively emulated Schoenberg, following each new stylistic development and immediately taking it on, albeit in what Schoenberg would describe dismissively as an "exaggerate[d]" form.[57] Christopher Wintle has documented some of Schoenberg's vitriol towards Webern, observing that Schoenberg seemed to see Webern as a rival even when he was Schoenberg's student, accusing the younger composer of "follow[ing] all my developments. [Webern] always tries to surpass everything."[58] More acutely, Schoenberg was troubled by Webern's incursions into 12-tone composition, and was suspicious that Webern was clandestinely trying out Schoenberg's embryonic method during the First World War. When the 12-tone method was clearly emerging around 1921, Schoenberg tried to keep his "imitators", especially Webern, at a distance—"I am annoyed by them: I even do not know anymore what is mine and what is theirs"; and Schoenberg directly accused Webern of "infidelity", of seeking to displace Schoenberg as "the innovator".[59] In the early 1930s, Schoenberg reflected upon Webern's dangerous proximity a decade earlier, complaining that "Webern was breathing down my neck, and scarcely after I had written a piece he wrote a similar one; how he carried out ideas, plans, and intentions that I had expressed in order to get ahead of me!"[60] Like Freud, Schoenberg fostered close relationships with his followers, but he also feared their infringements upon his creativity and originality, and upon his reputation as a singular innovator. It is tempting to argue that the rigor with which Schoenberg and Freud insulated their work—from assaults from without and within—not only shaped but perhaps even ossified their thought, achieving the opposite intended effect, namely to preserve independence and "open-mindedness".

Conclusion

How did it come about that Freud and Schoenberg should lead such strikingly parallel lives? An argument that I am tempted to close with relates to each man's well-known identification with the figure of Moses. This identification hinged upon the fact that Moses was a revolutionary figure, an exile, and a law-giver: an individual destined to deliver a difficult message to a nation that was not necessarily ready to receive it, and to never reach the promised land.

Moses was a source of inspiration to both men—one of Schoenberg's greatest works is his unfinished oratorio *Moses und Aron*; Freud's final book was *Moses and Monotheism*—and served as a touchstone for the investigation of their respective religious and artistic/intellectual identities. Moses represents a point of convergence for Freud and Schoenberg, a point at which the parallel I have been drawing in this essay meet. Or, perhaps better, these parallel lines emerge from Moses: to draw upon metaphors from biology, the Freud-Schoenberg relationship is better understood not so much as cross-pollination—and this is the most common historiographical approach—but more as parallel evolution, in which very similar traits found in different individuals, from different locales, are attributable to a common ancestor.

Parallel lines never touch, and perhaps this is the best way to think of Freud and Schoenberg in early twentieth-century Vienna: as closely related, and indeed contextualizing each other and serving to define one another, with respect to time and place, but never quite converging.

Notes

1 See, for example, Lewis Wickes, 'Schoenberg, *Erwartung*, and the Reception of Psychoanalysis in Musical Circles in Vienna until 1910/1911', *Studies in Music* 23 (1989): 88–106; Robert Falck, 'Marie Pappenheim, Schoenberg, and the *Studien über Hysterie*', in *German Literature and Music: An Aesthetic Fusion, 1890–1989*, ed. Claus Reschke and Howard Pollack (Symposium on Literature and the Arts, Houston, 1989), 131–45 (Munich: Fink, 1992); Alexander Carpenter, 'Schoenberg's Vienna, Freud's Vienna: Re-examining the Connections between the Monodrama *Erwartung* and the Early History of Psychoanalysis', *The Musical Quarterly* 93, no. 1 (2010): 144–81; Alexander Carpenter, '"This Beastly Science...": On the Reception of Psychoanalysis by the Composers of the Second Viennese School, 1908–1923', *International Forum of Psychoanalysis* 24, no. 4 (2015): 243–54.
2 See Peter Gay, *Freud: A Life for Our Time* (New York: W. W. Norton, 2006), 9; Lorraine Gorrell, *Discordant Melody: Alexander Zemlinsky, His Songs, and the Second Viennese School* (Westport, CT: Greenwood Press, 2002).
3 Arnold Schoenberg, 'Composition with Twelve Tones (1)', in *Style and Idea: Selected Writings of Arnold Schoenberg*, ed. Leonard Stein (New York: St. Martin's Press, 1975), 218.
4 Schoenberg cited in Bryan R. Simms, *The Atonal Music of Arnold Schoenberg, 1908–1923* (Oxford: Oxford University Press, 2000), 181.
5 *Ibid.*, 188.
6 Malcolm MacDonald, *Schoenberg* (Oxford: Oxford University Press, 2008), 142.
7 Frank Sulloway, *Freud: Biologist of the Mind* (New York: Basic Books, 1979), 64.
8 *The Standard Edition of the Complete Psychological Works of Sigmund Freud*, ed. James Strachey, Vol. 5, *The Interpretation of Dreams* (London: Hogarth Press and the Institute of Psycho-Analysis, 1953), 536–37.
9 *The Standard Edition of the Complete Psychological Works of Sigmund Freud*, ed. James Strachey, Vol. 16, *Introductory Lectures on Psychoanalysis* (London: Hogarth Press and the Institute of Psycho-Analysis, 1963), 295.
10 J.N. Isbister, *Freud: An Introduction to His Life and Work* (Cambridge: Polity Press, 1988), 168.
11 Freud, Vol. 16, *Introductory Lectures on Psychoanalysis*, 295–96.
12 *The Standard Edition of the Complete Psychological Works of Sigmund Freud*, ed. James Strachey, Vol. 19, *The Ego and the Id and Other Works* (London: Hogarth Press and the Institute of Psycho-Analysis, 1961), 23.
13 *Ibid.*, 25.
14 *Ibid.*, 36–37.
15 *Ibid.*, 17.

16 *Ibid.*
17 Arnold Schoenberg, 'Constructed Music', in *Style and Idea: Selected Writings of Arnold Schoenberg*, ed. Leonard Stein (New York: St. Martin's Press, 1975), 107.
18 See John Covach, 'The Zwölftonspiel of Josef Matthias Hauer', *Journal of Music Theory* 36, no. 1 (1992): 149–84.
19 Martin Goldstein and Inge Goldstein, *The Experience of Science: An Interdisciplinary Approach* (New York: Plenum, 1984), 373.
20 Madalon Springnether, 'Reading Freud's Life', in *Freud 2000*, ed. Anthony Elliot (New York: Routledge, 1998), 146–47.
21 Jones cited in Sulloway, *Freud: Biologist of the Mind*, 467.
22 Sulloway, *Freud: Biologist of the Mind*, 467. Robert Merton's, *Sociological Ambivalence and Other Essays* (New York: Free Press, 1976) includes a survey of Freud's writings that documents over 150 instances where he expresses concerns about priority, *pace* Ernst Jones.
23 Jones cited in Sulloway, *Freud: Biologist of the Mind*, 469.
24 Freud cited in Sulloway, *Freud: Biologist of the Mind*, 469.
25 'Über Infantile Sexualtheorien' was published in *Sexual-Probleme* in December 1908. See Sigmund Freud, 'The Sexual Theories of Children', in *The Standard Edition of the Complete Psychological Works of Sigmund Freud*, ed. James Strachey, Vol. 9, *Jensen's 'Gradiva' and Other Works* (London: Hogarth Press and the Institute of Psycho-Analysis, 1959), 209–26. Freud also published 'Zur sexuellen Aufklärung der Kinder (Offener Brief an Dr. M. Fürst)' in 1907. See Freud, 'The Sexual Enlightenment of Children', in Vol. 9, *Jensen's 'Gradiva' and Other Works*, 131–39.
26 Lutz D.H. Sautereig, 'Loss of Innocence: Albert Moll, Sigmund Freud and the Invention of Childhood Sexuality Around 1900', *Medical History* 56, no. 2 (2012): 168.
27 Lorin Anderson, 'Freud, Nietzsche', *Salmagundi* 47/48 (1980): 6–7.
28 Adler cited in Anderson, 'Freud, Nietzsche', 28.
29 See Günter Gödde, 'Freud and Nineteenth-Century Philosophical Sources on the Unconscious', in *Thinking the Unconscious: Nineteenth-Century German Thought*, ed. Angus Nicholls and Martin Liebscher (Cambridge: Cambridge University Press, 2010), 266.
30 Freud cited in Anderson, "Freud, Nietzsche," 4.
31 *Ibid.*
32 *Ibid.*
33 John Covach, 'Hauer, Josef Matthias', *Oxford Music Online*. Oxford University Press, Online at http://www.oxfordmusiconline.com/subscriber/article/grove/music/12544. Accessed May 10, 2016.
34 *Ibid.*
35 *Ibid.*
36 Schoenberg cited in Joseph Auner, *A Schoenberg Reader: Documents of a Life* (New Haven, CT: Yale University Press, 2003), 236–38 *passim.*
37 *Ibid.*, 237–40 *passim.*
38 *Ibid.*, 238.
39 Weiss cited in Daria Colombo, 'Freud and His Circle', in *Textbook of Psychoanalysis*, 2nd edition, ed. Glen Gabbard, Bonnie Litowitz and Paul Williams (Washington, DC: American Psychiatric Publishing, 2012), 12.
40 Freud citied in Colombo, 'Freud and His Circle', 12.
41 *The Standard Edition of the Complete Psychological Works of Sigmund Freud*, ed. James Strachey, Vol. 14, *On the History of the Psycho-Analytic Movement, Papers on Metapsychology and Other Works* (London: Hogarth Press and the Institute of Psycho-Analysis, 1957), 62.

42 Freud cited in Robert Smith, *The Wounded Jung: Effects of Jung's Relationships on His Life and Work* (Evanston, IL: Northwestern University Press, 1997), 48.
43 *Ibid.*, 52.
44 Paul Roazen, *Freud and His Followers* (New York: DaCapo Press, 1975), 261; Gary Lachmann, *Jung the Mystic: The Esoteric Dimensions of Jung's Life and Teaching* (New York: Penguin, 2010), 85.
45 Freud cited in Roazen, *Freud and His Followers*, 207.
46 Alex Ross, *The Rest Is Noise* (New York: Picador, 2007), 217.
47 Krenek and Schoenberg cited in Alex Ross, *The Rest is Noise*, 217.
48 Schoenberg cited in Auner, *A Schoenberg Reader*, 335.
49 Letter to Alexander von Zemlinsky, March 3, 1926, in Arnold Schoenberg, *Letters*, ed. Erwin Stein, trans. Eithne Wilkins and Ernst Kaiser (Berkeley: University of California Press, 1987), 119.
50 Letter to Hanns Eisler, March 10, 1926, in *Ibid.*, 120.
51 Letter to Hanns Eisler, March 12, 1926, in *Ibid.*, 121.
52 Allen Shawn, *Arnold Schoenberg's Journey* (Cambridge, MA: Harvard University Press, 2002), 219.
53 Christopher Hailey, *Franz Schrecker 1878–1934: A Cultural Biography* (Cambridge: Cambridge University Press, 1993), 63.
54 See Friedrich Wildgans, *Anton Webern*, trans. E. T. Roberts and H. Searle (London: Calder & Boyars, 1966), 51; Shawn, *Arnold Schoenberg's Journey*, 180; Julie Brown, 'Understanding Schoenberg as Christ', in *The Oxford Handbook of the New Cultural History of Music*, ed. Jane Fulcher (Oxford: Oxford University Press, 2011), 120–21.
55 Jung cited in Peter Gay, *Freud*, 204.
56 Schoenberg cited in Auner, *A Schoenberg Reader*, 238.
57 Erwin Stein cited in Christopher Wintle, 'Webern's Lyric Character', in *Webern Studies*, ed. Kathryn Bailey (Cambridge: Cambridge University Press, 1996), 230.
58 Schoenberg cited in *Ibid.*, 230.
59 *Ibid.*
60 Schoenberg cited in Auner, *A Schoenberg Reader*, 236.

3 The psychodynamics of neo-Riemannian theory

Kenneth M. Smith

Energetic?

The seminars of Jacques Lacan unlocked new doors to our unconscious desires. The unconscious is now shown to work both in and through language, just as language works in and through the unconscious. Rewiring the Freudian circuits of desire from what philosopher Nick Land has called "libidinal materialism", Lacan approached what we might call *libidinal idealism*—a desire inscribed in an Imaginary-cum-Symbolic metaphysics.[1] Although philosophers of desire have since asked us to strip from our unconscious minds the linguistic processes that cool the searing libido into frozen oedipal coordinates, this is not easy to achieve.[2] Music, as Schoenberg's "language of the unconscious"[3] can figure in this, and I propose a benefit in theorizing a musical experience between these two poles.

Theorists often associate music's psycho-energetic potential with Ernst Kurth and his wonderfully descriptive insights into the psychological depth of Wagner's and Bruckner's Romantic harmony, frequently driven by the Schopenhauerian-Freudian topic of *desire*.[4] Yet this powerful driving force that works through our imaginations to generate *Affekt* is marginalized in more formalized music-theoretical systems. This is striking given their reliance on Hugo Riemann, fascinated as he was by the compelling powers of *Tonvorstellung*—"Imagination of Tone", as translated by Robert W. Wason and Elizabeth West Marvin[5]—that was to become a major theory that would trace the production of a metaphysical enjoyment from acoustic stimuli. As Ian Bent recently reminded us: 'Riemann outlines a new psychological theory of "selecting and ordering" on the part of the mind', which indicates an acute psychological interest.[6] A listener is psychologically alive[7] and actively engaged with sonic hopes and expectations that allow the Imaginary part of our musical encounters to guide us. And desire has the controlling share in the whole experience,[8] staging in the imagination the act of listening.[9]

The concept of desire can animate anew some rather lifeless aspects of music theory as practiced in North America. I use the classic neo-Riemannian *Tonnetz* as my playground, the familiar net of tones that was developed by Czech theorist Otakar Hostinský (1847–1910),[10] who claimed:

[...] we have only a three-fold mutual and immediate relationship that leads us to new tones, those of the fifth, the major and minor third. If, for example, we take the pitch *c*, then the direct relations: *g* and *f*, *e* and *a*♭, *e*♭ and *a* can be schematised as follows:

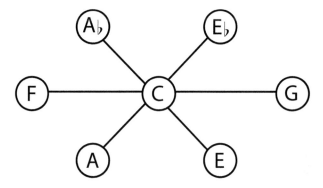

[*Figure 3.1* A central nub of *c* on Hostinský's Tonnetz.]

Naturally the grade of the relationship is strongest in the direction of the fifth and the weakest in the direction of the minor third.[11]

This final sentence has passed practitioners of *Tonnetz* analysis by. The kind of music that is successfully modeled by the famous **P** (Parallel), **L** (Leading-note exchange), and **R** (Relative) transformations is nowadays bound up with discourse on meandering triadic progressions, which explore "voice-leading parsimony" and for which a tonic is not normally invoked.[12] Nora Engebretsen calls this type of analysis 'tonic-blind';[13] chords simply transform into each other via common-tone frugality, the metaphor of pitch *space* becoming doubly apt as both the topological field of movement and the inter-planetary field of zero-gravity. Where can we locate the desire to move from one chord or pitch to another? Richer conceptions of the tonal energetics, such as Daniel Harrison's 'discharge' (of pitches $\hat{7}$–$\hat{8}$ and ♭$\hat{6}$–$\hat{5}$), are not captured by this particular *Tone-net*,[14] and yet Hostinský is clear that the chords do *not* simply drift from one into the other; the three axes have different strengths of tonal attraction and repulsion, and are thereby ideal conduits for the libidinal energy that Wagner and post-Wagnerians sought to channel. But what makes minor thirds the weakest carriers of libidinal energy, and major thirds and fifths the strongest, and how do they register in our Imaginary/Symbolic reconstruction of these tones and pitches?

One of the most fruitful branches of Riemannian theory is the *Funktionstheorie* that Riemann never successfully integrated into his *Tonvorstellung*, or his *Tonnetz* maps. From this perspective, Brian Hyer's dissertation on *Tristan and Isolde*[15] shrewdly located Lacanian semiotic drivers in Riemann's energetic theory of Symbolic tonal function: **T** (tonic), **S** (subdominant), and **D** (dominant). Hyer, who is largely responsible for Riemann's renaissance, claims that **D** is a signifier for **T**; with a (somewhat loose) Lacanian knot, Hyer ties signification to desire. I intend to cultivate this idea of signification in the Lacanian unconscious and evaluate the role that these three functions play in driving a Symbolic system that filters through the Imaginary kingdom, often through substitution of one chord for another representative of the same function. Apart from the PRL transformations that occupy the *Tonnetz*, David Lewin's DOM transformation (which moves the chord to its tonic as if it were a dominant) is energetic, only superficially produced by combinatory LR transformations.[16] It works along the x axis of the *Tonnetz* (← or →). However, to me, the DOM is more of a discharge than a "transformation", which explains the prominence that Hostinský bestows it on the *Tonnetz*. Desire is aroused most strongly when it is aligned with expectation and realization, and this is strongest when we travel the circle of fifths. The **S** route (DOM^{-1}) is noticeably weaker.[17] Hence, Riemann's predilection for the **TSDT** rather than the **TDST**; one drives into the circle of fifths, the other drifts backwards.[18] Like Riemann, I take it as read, then, that the root-based motion by fifths along the leading axis of the *Tonnetz* drives the change of tonal function most compellingly and is the principal path of libidinal harmonic energy.

Static?

Minor-third related chords are notoriously static, though they work their way diagonally ↗ and ↙ on the *Tonnetz*. Passages of minor-third progression, particularly of tense tetrachords, famously outline the meta-tension of the diminished-seventh, thereby standing at a crossroads between four pathways.[19] Each of these three octatonic zones has a problem. Each contains four highly tense dominant-seventh chords. For example, one collection might contain four dominant-sevenths: C^7, E♭^{7}, F♯^{7}, A^7 that, all things being equal, would each aim to resolve to F, A♭, B, D. However, these are contained in a different collection. Neither the major leading-note ($\hat{7}$) of each seventh-chord (*e*, *g*, *a*♯, *c*♯), nor the minor leading-notes (♭$\hat{6}$) are present *within* the home collection. Thus, *discharge* (Harrison's term for these two leading-note resolutions) is impossible within a single octatonic collection.[20] Ergo, diatonic discharge is only possible *between* octatonic zones; it passes through them. Whenever minor-third relations are brought into diatonic practice (particularly chromatically, i.e. C major → A major, rather than C major → A minor), diatonic energy is dammed/stored-up. The four blocked chords can be perceived as a single group:[21] a distinct collection of octatonic pitches that can only resolve into an alternative octatonic faction. Note also that, like the three diatonic tonal functions, there is a tripartite division of the chromatic universe into three octatonic zones. Is there a homology between them? The three cardinal functions are certainly dispersed evenly between the three octatonic regions. Because discharge is impossible within a single collection, we might speculate that minor-third-related chords can generally represent a single function.[22]

Magnetic?

Neo-Riemannian theory markedly privileges major-third relations that collect three chords and their modal equivalents into another single region or zone (north, south, east, west in Cohn's hexatonic universe). These work ↖ and ↘ on the *Tonnetz*. This hexatonic system is formed, however, from P and L transformations. This latter transformation, I claim, alters a function by discharging $\hat{7} \rightarrow \hat{8}$. Each chord in a major-third cycle (say C, E, A♭) has its leading-note registered in one of the other chords. So, for example, C major's leading note *b* appears in E major/minor and also as *c♭* in A♭m. The alternative leading note ($\hat{6}$ in the minor key: *a♭* in C minor) is also apparent, both in A♭ major/minor, and in E major (as *g♯*). Thus, when circulating in hexatonic space, it is difficult to avoid both of Harrison's categories for discharge at every change of chord. Thus, while octatonics save function, hexatonics spend it. In fact, moving downwards by a major third creates the clearest discharge (C→A♭) while moving upwards tends to backtrack (like DOM^{-1}). However, there is always interpretative wiggle-room for how we might hear functions in Riemann. As David Kopp claims,

> Thus a functional analysis of the progression C major—E minor—F major might be **T–Dp** [dominant preparation] –**S**, indicating significant harmonic change occurring between the first two chords. It could also be **T–Ŧ–S**, implying a less pronounced change. Riemann favors the latter analysis, in line with his statement that leading-tone change chords normally follow the archetypes from which they are derived.[23]

Ŧ is Riemann's symbol for the tonic heard as leading-note exchange (i.e. when E$_m$ follows C). Riemann's opposite interpretation, and the clearer to my mind given the presence of $\hat{7}$, is to hear E$_m$ as metaphorical G substitute (one of its minor-third relatives), thus, **T$_p$** in Riemann's nomenclature (P indicates Riemann's *relative*). Figure 3.2 attempts (and fails) to plot the opening of *Tristan* (see Example 3.1) on a plain *Tonnetz*. The net naturally collapses because it requires that we reduce the tetrachords to triads. A minor is musically indicated first by (what I take to be) the leading-note appoggiatura ♭$\hat{6}$–$\hat{5}$. The subsequent *Tristan* chord is reduced to a simple F major when the half-diminished chord becomes a French-sixth that resolves to E^7, retrospectively defined as being rooted on F.[24] As well as its inability to recognize tetrachords, the *Tonnetz* does not register kinesis particularly well unless it is by common-tone. The move from the grey triangle (indicating that A$_m$ is hypothetical) to the F is interesting

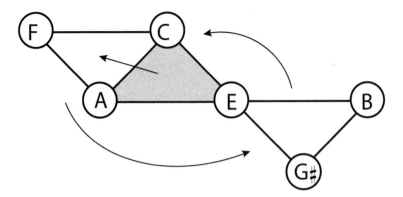

Figure 3.2 Problematic *Tonnetz* reduction of Tristan's opening progression.

for several reasons: (1) it shows the clear L transformation between the two that suggests we could hear F as 𝄪 (which is worth retaining in our memories, as this is a promissory note soon to be cashed-in); (2) the north-west move registers a $\hat{7}\to\hat{8}$ discharge in F, creating a tectonic shift that may incline us towards an **S** hearing; (3) it highlights the chords' common-tone proximity to each other, which only comes to light after reducing them to 'ideal' (triadic) forms. Visually, the semitone motion from F to E is disjointed on this spatial map of triadic objects, and thus the *Tonnetz* seems somewhat unfit for purpose when analyzing patterns functional tension.

Psychodynamic?

One solution to the problems defined above is Lendvai's *axis system*, in which octatonic cycles serve as agents of the three functions (see Figure 3.3). These cubes (as I draw them) may discretely rotate and nonetheless represent **T**, **S**, or **D**. The three paradigmatic representations of function in Lendvai's center of gravity are the major-third cycle. Passing temporally through the central reservation, triadic progressions are generated by revolving functional cogs. Candace Brower submits that, '[b]ecause hexatonic and octatonic collections constitute closed regions contained within a larger chromatic space, we may conceive of them as we do the diatonic collection—as containers or objects which may themselves be set in motion'.[25] I would further argue that these cogs are instead set in motion *by* the diatonic system. Thus, a version of the opening of *Tristan*—the $[A_m]\to F^{\varnothing 7}\to E^7\to[A_m]$—emerges if we recalibrate the outer cogs towards the new rotation shown in Figure 3.4.

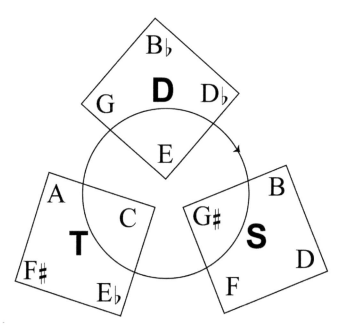

Figure 3.3 Conception of Lendvai's Axis System, based on hexatonically related C–E–G♯.

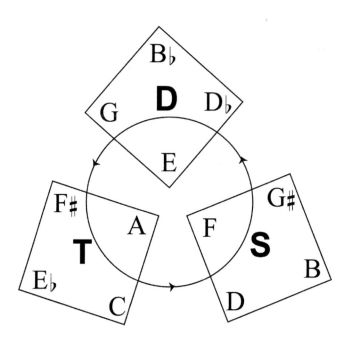

Figure 3.4 Rotation of Axes to show the opening Tristan progression.

C♯	F♯	B	E	A	D	G	C	F
A♯	D♯	G♯	C♯	F♯	B	E	A	D
G	C	F	B♭	E♭	A♭	D♭	G♭	C♭
E	A	D	G	C	F	B♭	E♭	A♭

Figure 3.5 Conception of Weber Space, with collapsed major & minor, and rotated 90°.

I linearly conceptualize this in Figure 3.5 so as to better account for temporality; this yields a different *Tonnetz*, one attributed to Gottfried Weber by Fred Lerdahl.[26] Along the *x*-axis we imagine the circle of fifths; up/down the *y*-axis we capture the minor-third functional group.[27] This visual aid expresses chord progressions from left to right, passing through time. These two axes form the bloc of metaphor and metonymy that Lacan grafted linguistically onto our unconscious minds, forming specific Imaginary-Symbolic relations that obscure the Real sonic objects we confront.[28] This Lacanian slant ushers us closer to Riemann whose *Tonvorstellung* attempted a philosophically monist account of the material encounter with sound that we find in Hermann von Helmholtz. Riemann's corrective *Tonvorstellung* is contextualized by Benjamin Steege: '[t]he mistake Helmholtz made is now easy to recognise; he sought to explain from the nature of sounding bodies concepts that can only be explained from the nature of the perceiving in mind'.[29] In exploring Riemann's *Klangvertretung*, Hyer claims,

> the tonic, dominant, and subdominant, that is, are *representational* constructs. Both the dominant and subdominant *represent* the tonic, though not, of course, in the same way: the dominant represents the tonic lying a perfect fifth below, while the subdominant represents the tonic lying a perfect fifth above.

Further,

> [a]s representations, the dominant and subdominant combine a *material form*, a chord, and a more extensive, immaterial content, an *idea*, for which it stands. A dominant is a mental image or schema—a *concept*—that involves, besides the actual chord, the relations it articulates with other harmonies in the *Tonart*.[30]

These dimensions of 'representation' clearly work on both musical and psychological levels. These musical relations can be articulated in the language of psychoanalysis as *metaphor*. For me, as for Lacan, representation must articulate itself metaphorically. Lacan's formula for metaphor is:

$$f\left(\frac{S'}{S}\right) S = S\,(+)\,s.$$

The signifying function is represented by "fS" which contains "S'/S" where signifiers are metaphorically exchanged.[31] The formula states that the substitution attempts to cross 'the bar' (between an object and its representation), though this positive (+) effect does not indicate full success. So, for example, C may be represented/substituted by A minor to achieve a certain discharge of G^7's $b{\rightarrow}c$ and $f{\rightarrow}e$, but the C major satisfaction still runs a deficit. We might regard both as representatives of the **T** function, particularly in a work like *Tristan*, whose first act famously celebrates a 'double-tonic complex' of C/A.[32] This **T** function, however, cannot be established without a **D** function, and vice-versa.

The formula for metonym is more clearly allied with desire:

$$f\,(S...S')\ S \cong s\,(-)\,s$$

Here the temporal succession of signifiers produces the signifying function (*fS*), forcing it to slide under the bar between signifier (S) and signified (s), keeping it nonetheless intact without attempting to cross it. This means that signification fails, but desire is produced. For Lacan, 'desire is a metonymy' in categorical terms, where it becomes a copula for new signifiers.[33] Harrison proposes, incorrectly to my mind, that the **T**, **S**, and **D** are 'sensuous-functional relationships', and that neo-Riemannian motion is, by contrast, 'energetic'.[34] I would subvert this by suggesting that the **T** propels to the **S** which propels to the **D** which propels to the **T**. This is a pressurized system, in which desire is almost as hydraulic as Freud's hot libidinal engine. However, the significance bestowed on these grammatical values are more Lacanian, for Lacan famously exchanged the libido's sweltering engine room for pure linguistic coordinates. For Lacan, desire is found in our Imaginary engagement with the Symbolic (the power of language, the Big Other); '*desire is the desire of the Other*'.[35] These musically morphological categories are always in motion, and their sliding under the signifier is the driving force; we are never sure that the **T** *is* the **T**, and thus our temporary identification with functions is always awaiting a *point de caption*—an Imaginary moment of fixity. This, too, always arouses our suspicion, which perpetuates desire. Harrison's assertion that neo-Riemannian patterns are energetic is troublesome because, while we do find substituted discharge motion through hexatonic space, the *Tonnetz* as it stands does not register this dynamism because it has no inherent sense of *direction*. In short, the metaphorical axis is chord substitution (minor third based, where no discharge can occur, but functional consolidation *can*), and the metonymical axis is about chord-chaining and combination, that produces desire (diatonic fifths and major thirds that discharge functions into new ones), as shown in Figure 3.6.

Funktionstheorie has always been caught between these two poles of metaphor and metonymy, because Riemann did not actually define or intend it to be about syntax (the metonymic axis). As Hyer reminds us, 'As tonal functions, the tonic, dominant, and subdominant are inert, if not immobile: neither the dominant nor the subdominant conveys a strong urge to push to the tonic'.[36] Yet it *has* to have a syntactical dimension, whether Riemann realized it or not.[37] Chord progressions need to be articulated metonymically. Yet even here, there is a gap, a lacuna. The **T** needs the **D** in order for itself to be understood as **T**, while the **D** needs the **T** for itself to be understood as **D**. We have a double-bind here; the functions create a chicken/egg situation for themselves, both arising by positing the other in the Imaginary realm until it becomes crystallized as Symbolic. A further Lacanian dimension is articulated around this central lack. Suzannah Clark praises Michael Siciliano for demonstrating that 'all but the final transformations in [Schubert's] *Trost* make their way consistently around the RPL cycle, and he argues that the cycle created by neo-Riemannian relations replaced the lack of a single tonic known to diatonic theory'.[38] Lendvai himself describes, 'the most peculiar feature of the system is that its *center* is being marked by a "Black Hole"'.[39] This zero point is the Freudian-Lacanian *lack* that motivates desire.

The theory described above privileges root motion, and collapses major and minor distinctions. The former may seem particularly curious when considering that the high level of ambiguity that characterizes Wagner's tense chords. Part of the tension inherent in a simple V_7 is that, for all of its clarity, it could always be used as a German-sixth. This aspect of the theory itself is Riemannian-cum-Lacanian. Riemann claims that the mind

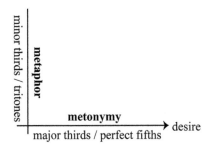

Figure 3.6 Metaphor & metonymy and substitution and combination chord relationships.

"moves directly toward rejection of more complicated structures, where other possible meanings suggest themselves that weigh less heavily on the powers of interpretation...".[40] We will consider this in a Lacanian light at the close of the chapter, but his proposition that we experience complex structures by mentally reducing them to simple ones is Imaginary in a pure Lacanian sense (it is Imaginary that we might hear the pitches *g-b-d-f* as V^7 rather than a German-sixth in a particular context). Yet the **T**, **S**, and **D** are Symbolic and metaphorical placeholders that we simplify our equations to.

Hysteric? Neurotic? Schizophrenic?

Nietzsche famously called Wagner an hysteric: Wagner's problems were 'all of them problems of hysterics—the convulsive nature of his affects, his overexcited sensibility, his taste that required ever stronger spices, his instability which he dressed up as principles'.[41] Žižek, however, analyzing these words from a Lacanian perspective, has more recently claimed that an hysteric is someone who cannot cope with the torn fabric of the Symbolic order—someone who glimpses a sense of the Real.

> Wagner does not yet venture this step into hysteria: the problem with him is not his hysteria, but rather that he is not hysterical enough. Although his dramas provide all possible variations of how love can go wrong, all this takes place against the fantasmatic background of the redemptive power of full sexual relationship.[42]

We might reasonably consider Isolde to be a proto-Freudian hysteric (untamed, suicidal, later suffering hallucinations of *Tristan*'s transfiguration). Yet is Wagner the hysterical one? Are we? Not according to Žižek. Before we can begin to psychoanalyze those who perforate it, the Symbolic packaging of the opera's harmony must be analyzed.

In fact, *Tristan* (especially distilled in the Prelude) almost religiously rotates **T→S→D→T** as a Symbolic harmonic paradigm (Zizek's "fantasmatic background"?). My interpretation adds to the continued *seriation* of analyses[43] of this *locus romanticus* of transitional harmony, though I believe it is the only one to demonstrate the clear functionality of **T→S→D** in terms of its root driving force, in which Real sounds are coerced into an Imaginary-Symbolic dialectic: Imaginary in the sense that we interpret chords in particular ways (yours may or may not coincide with mine), Symbolic in that this works dialectically with a practice of reducing to a syntactical function. The Imaginary and the Symbolic thus play tennis with each other, allowing 'the game' to be played out.

The inaugural appoggiatura of *f→e* sets the tone for the four hours to follow, and to my hearing, it masks an A_m chord, outlined above and shown on Example 3.1. The French-sixth that follows has a double-identity as VI

♭$^7_5$ on F or B that could lead to E^7 or B♭^{7}. This ambiguity can be celebrated on the metaphor-metonym grid, though the E^7 that does materialize retrospectively acts as a *point de capiton* that points us to A minor as **T**. This *call* is left unanswered (serving itself as a *point de capiton*, letting us know that desire will be frustrated in the opera, or that we will be at least set on the path of object-chasing in the Freudian libidinal tradition). The vacuum that follows voices the lack that we are being encouraged to mentally fill with our own Imaginary *objet petit a* Lacan's 'object-cause' of desire.[44] This continues in the subsequent phrase that outlines a *b→g♯* ascent, projecting its E^7 across the void. The **T** of A is articulated as a *lack* by being skipped over—*übersprungen* in Riemann's terms[45]—and its presence in the imagination is clear because the **TSDT** cycle reboots at **S** with a fresh French-sixth on either A♭/D, steering us to the G^7 **D** of C major. Because the opening is hitherto a loose variant transposed three semi-tones upwards, we can note that no functional *modulation* has taken place; a missing A minor is functionally identical to a missing C major, not because both have been mislaid, but because they cannot discharge into each other, cast in the same octatonic die.

Hear how the *a* is only heard as a chromatic passing note on the way to the **S** *Tristan* chord in bar 10. Wagner is working hard to shrink the **T**, not only as a chord, but as a pitch. This is not just achieved by entirely denying it, but also by rendering it as an evanescent entity. It arrives again, however, as the seventh of B^7 in bars 11–13. B^7 is prolonged as a newly clarified **S** function (though this is technically rendered 𝔻 for Riemann (**D** of the **D**) B^7 substitutes for the D$_m$ iv); what before was an equivocal French-sixth is now a more tangible, yearning II^7. The object of its yearning comes again after reaching out across a void in the sumptuous E^7 of bar 16. The famous deflection in bar 17 positions F where we would expect a clear A$_m$. Note, however, that the pitch *g♯* resolves to *a*, and *d* resolves down to *c*. Thus, although F would hold an **S** function in Lendvai's system; in Riemann's, we would likely hear it as **T̵**. The tension between these two hearings is the vital aspect for me; it is from the space between them that the subsequent D^7 appears as a natural egress; it comes as either an **S** continuation of F, or as a **T→S** discharge from A$_m$. For clarity, this is marked as *übersprungen* in Example 3.1, showing that the A$_m$ **T** object has once more been evaded. In the recovery of this failure, the musical subject becomes more ardent, increasing harmonic pace through a prototypical series of rotations. These are sometimes compacted. For example, the D^7 of bar 18 resolves to C$^6_4$ which is technically a **T** functioned substitute, but adopts **D** function if we consider the heavy emphasis on the fifth. Bar 19 attempts the same sequence, but presently unpacks the full G→G^7→C motion. This event continues C^7→C♯^{o7}. The diminished chord cannot adequately be denoted on the standard *Tonnetz*, nor in Weber space; one would need to appeal to the kind of geometries that Dmitri Tymoczko, Edward Gollin, and Richard Cohn offer, though again we would sacrifice the sense of teleological direction.[46]

Of course, we might wish to question whether desire is truly teleological. In Lacanian theory drives seek to constantly aim and miss its object, but to continue circulating it, the object being an Imaginary enactment in the Symbolic order of what life might be beneath it.[47] More recent psychoanalytical critique from Deleuze and Guattari, and his model of desire machines, re-contextualises this Lacanian drive as a more teleonomical desire, one which territorializes and reterritorializes cybernetically.[48] The act of orbiting an Imaginary gratification, while slowly recalibrating in response to feedback acquired from successes/failures, is seemingly what we confront in this sequential passage, for when we arrive at a full A major on bar 22, it is on a 'feminine cadence'. Even this is approached from its T tritone substitute E♭; we surely feel that A minor is waving us through. In subsequent phrases, a loosely dispersed chain of fifths C♯→F♯→B→E is interspersed with its functional substitutes that conspire to veil its path. But through bars 26–29 the way is cleared, and the progression is given a clear footing (Example 3.1).

The remainder of the prelude's rotations—its principal nodes and copulas—are tabulated in Figure 3.8. As I hear them, the progressions seem to start from **T** representatives: A, C and F♯. Sometimes the path is direct; sometimes it is windy; oftentimes, it employs two representatives of a function side-by-side, resulting in a static suspension without discharge. Such is the case with the initial A–F♯$_m$ in bar 44. This is hardly treading water, however. The semitone slump from A→G♯, while discharging (**T**→**S**), would be relaxing or deflating, where the piece is more generally working to ever-increase its charge. The mediating power of F♯ serves to make the discharge up to G♯ a breakthrough of strength and elation (like the IV→V motion that is the only permitted diatonic whole-tone action). Remember that octatonics trap energy rather than liberate it.

A longer passage that achieves a different aesthetic is the libido-damming C–E♭–A–E♭ at bar 61. This engages both of C's R transformations—upper and lower—further weakening the alluring potential of the **T** by dispersing it across an octatonic collection that resolves *en masse* to D/B, before alighting upon E in bar 62. In the ensuing bars, the A is selected from this octatonic reservoir to continue the line of fifths: A→D→E. Snippets of fifth-discharges flow outwards, always rerouted by substitution. In these few bars, we acknowledge Robert Bailey's "double-tonic complex" of C/A major/minor, but we see this as a salient part of a deeper system of activating static octatonics to release their energy through a metonymic circle of fifths, which is constantly being deflected by metaphorical substitution.

My analysis observes no real modulation. Can it really be true that Wagner's prelude does not modulate? I propose that modulation can easily take place, whenever we sense a new Imaginary **T** object grabbing our attention. This happens all of the time. However, at a deeper level, I propose that we are bound to the C, A, F♯, E♭ axis as a subterranean **T**, and that all other phenomena work around this, despite it being hollow at its core—Lendvai's "Black Hole". At bar 84, we pause as we began, on E^7.

Example 3.1 Richard Wagner, *Tristan & Isolde*, Prelude, bars 1–29.

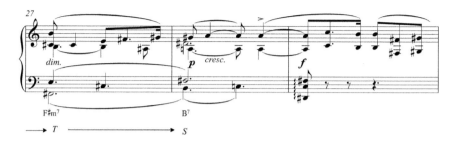

Example 3.1 (Continued).

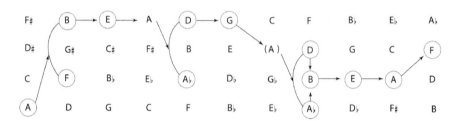

Figure 3.7 Richard Wagner, *Tristan & Isolde*, Prelude, bars 1–17.

Bar	Progression	Function
44	A–F#$_m$→G#→E/C#→	T→S→D
47	F#→B (C#)	T→S→D
51	A→C→F→D→G^7/C#/E	T→S→D
55	C^7→A→B(→E)→D/B //	T→S→D
59	C→A♭→D→B→E (b. 60$_5$)	T→S→D
61	C^7→E♭→A→E♭→D/B→E	T→S→D
63$_3$	A→D→E	T→S→D
65	A→D→E^7→G^7	T→S→D
72$_6$	C→F→B→C$^6_4$	T→S→D
75	C→A$_m$→D^7→G^7	T→S→D
77	C Ø^7→FØ^7→E^7 (b. 84)	T→S→D

Figure 3.8 Richard Wagner, *Tristan & Isolde*, Prelude, table of rotations, bars 44–77.

In closing: a *Gedankenexperiment*. The nearness of the rotation of tonal function to Lacan's model of the drive that moves around its Imaginary object begs an interesting question. The arch-critic of Lacan, Gilles Deleuze, contended that Lacan's reduction of complex mental phenomena to the triangle of "daddy, mommy, me" was a project that utterly missed the point of difference (by reducing everything to the *same* Oedipal triangle).[49] Deleuze could equally level the criticism at *Funktionstheorie* that reduces the wild, tensile energies of a *Tristan* chord to a generic nub on a root of F. However, Deleuze's critique was of the neurotic way of thinking (which was 'normal' for Lacan), urging us to open new pathways, and unlock novel ways of breaking the molds artificially enforced on us by the big Other. Deleuze does not deny that Oedipus exists, he maintains only that Oedipus is evil. It is perhaps nothing more than ironic that the **T, S, D** is a familial triangle. With a mock Deleuzian tongue in our cheek we might hear the **T** as the "mommy" that we always desire to return to; the "Father" as the **S** other figure that seems to occupy the Mother's attention, taking it away from ourselves, the many **D**s that are the most torn, the most directed, the most subjectified. Might we equally reduce things to the Freudian ego (**T**), the Id (**D**), and the Superego? Doubtless, we could re-order or re-shuffle our chess-pieces here and there, and one may take a radically different approach to a theory of the tonal functional grammar at stake, but the point is that the reductive powers of Oedipus (as Deleuze uses it to stand for a broad sense of reduction of differences to archetypes) flourishes in *Funktionstheorie*, and this puts us on the path of neurotic, rather than hysterical, desires.

Notes

1 Nick Land, *The Thirst for Annihilation: Georges Bataille and Virulent Nihilism (an Essay in Atheistic Religion)* (London: Routledge, 1992), 99.
2 See for example: Gilles Deleuze and Félix Guattari. *Anti-Oedipus* (London: Continuum, 2004); Jean-François Lyotard, *Libidinal Economy* (London: Continuum, 2004).
3 Schoenberg cited in Alexander Rehding, *Hugo Riemann and the Birth of Modern Musical Thought* (Cambridge: Cambridge University Press, 2008), 197.
4 See Ernst Kurth, *Romantische Harmonik und ihre Krise in Wagners 'Tristan'* (Bern and Leipzig, 1920) and *Musikpsychologie* (Berlin: Max Hesse, 1931).
5 Robert W. Wason, Elizabeth West Marvin, and Hugo Riemann, 'Riemann's "Ideen zu Einer 'Lehre von den Tonvorstellungen'": An Annotated Translation', *Journal of Music Theory* 36, no. 1 (1992): 69–79.
6 Ian Bent, 'The Problem of Harmonic Dualism: A Translation and Commentary', in *The Oxford Handbook of Neo-Riemannian Theories*, ed. Edward Gollin and Alexander Rehding (New York: Oxford University Press, 2011), 169.
7 This is apparently true of transformation theory, in which a listener performs mental actions on the sounds s/he hears.
8 Ludwig Holtmeier reminds us that even Rudolph Louis thought of musical reduction as a product of "drive guided" dynamic aspects of *Will*. Edward Gollin and Alexander Rehding, 'The Reception of Hugo Riemann's Music Theory', in *The Oxford Handbook of Neo-Riemannian Theories*, ed. Edward Gollin and Alexander Rehding (New York: Oxford University Press, 2011), 34.

9 One of Lacan's most famous additions to psychoanalytic theory is the triangulation of three areas of experience: the Real (base material), the Symbolic (the external world of signs of symbols that a subject must enter), and the Imaginary (the mental platform upon which the subject interacts with images and identifications). The concepts evolved over Lacan's career from the 1930s to 1980s.
10 According to Richard Cohn, the *Tonnetz* was discovered twice: once by Leonhard Euler (1773) and again by Oettingen (1866). See his 'Tonal Pitch Space and the (Neo-)Riemannian *Tonnetz*', in *The Oxford Handbook of Neo-Riemannian Theories*, ed. Edward Gollin and Alexander Rehding (New York: Oxford University Press, 2011), 322.
11 '[...] so haben wir blos eine dreifache wechselseitige und unmittelbare Verwandschaft, die uns zu neuen Tönen führt: die der Quinte, der grossen und der kleinen Terz. Wenn wir z. B. vom Tone *c* ausgehen, so sind die directen Verwandten: *g* und *f, e* und *as, es* und *a*, also schematisirt [...]Selbstverständlich ist der Verwandschaftsgrad in der Quintenrichtung am stärksten, in der Richtung der kleinen Terz am schwächsten'. Otakar Hostinskÿ, *Die Lehre von de musikalischen Klängen. Ein Beitrag zur aesthetischen Begründung der Harmonielehre* (Prag: Altenburg, 1879), 66–67.
12 Triads appear as triangles on the *Tonnetz*, bringing together their three pitches. Three distinct operations, transform one triad into another, maintaining common-tone relationships. Cohn outlines *Parallel* (i.e. C major→C minor), *Relative* (i.e. C major→A minor), and *Leittonwechsel* (C major→E minor). See his 'Introduction to Neo-Riemannian Theory: A Survey and a Historical Perspective', *Journal of Music Theory* 42, no. 2 (1998): 167–180.
13 Engebretsen, Nora. 'Neo-Riemannian Perspectives on the *Harmonieschritte*, with a Translation of Riemann's *Systematik der Harmonieschritte*', in *The Oxford Handbook of Neo-Riemannian Theories*, ed. Edward Gollin and Alexander Rehding (New York: Oxford University Press, 2011), 353.
14 Daniel Harrison, *Harmonic Function in Chromatic Music: A Renewed Dualist Theory and an Account of Its Precedents* (Chicago, IL: University of Chicago Press, 1994).
15 Brian Hyer, 'Tonal Intuitions in "Tristan und Isolde"' (PhD diss., Yale University, 1989).
16 Lewin, David, 'On Generalized Intervals and Transformations', *Journal of Music Theory* 24, no. 2 (1980): 243–251.
17 Whereas DOM is Lewin's symbolic shorthand for the 'dominant transformation' by which a chord would move from, say, C to F, DOM-1 is a DOM transformation in the opposite (subdominant) direction so C to G. The indicator '-1' implies a single class of transformation, working in two directions.
18 The issue is contentious. Suzannah Clark claims that the **D** '[c]an be gained by combining LR'. See her 'On the Imagination of Tone in Schubert's *Liedesend* (D473), *Trost* (D523), and *Gretchens Bitte* (D564)', in *The Oxford Handbook of Neo-Riemannian Theories*, ed. Edward Gollin and Alexander Rehding (New York: Oxford University Press, 2011), 300. Cohn only sees the need for PLR. David Kopp claims the need for **D** because the most common move should not behave as a compound. See Kopp, *Chromatic Transformations in Nineteenth-Century Music* (Cambridge: Cambridge University Press, 2002). I would agree with Kopp, as the principle would be against Hostinskÿ's authority of the **D** on the *Tonnetz*.
19 Engebretsen notes that these intervals are 'well used for modulations', demonstrating, for example, that C can move to G_m effectively via E♭. See 'Neo-Riemannian Perspectives on the *Harmonieschritte*', 370.
20 Harrison, *Harmonic function in Chromatic Music*, 90.

21 Note that the octatonic collection is formed from the successive arrangements of P and R transformations; if we played with only these two transformations, we would, over time, realise our limitation to a closed group.
22 This hearing is prohibited by Carl Dahlhaus, but promoted by Ernő Lendvai. Dahlhaus, 'Structure and Expression in the Music of Scriabin', in Schoenberg and the New Music, trans. Derrick Puffett and Alfred Clayton (Cambridge: Cambridge University Press, 1987), 206; Lendvai, *Béla Bartók: An Analysis of His Music* (London: Kahn & Averill, 1971), 3–4.
23 Kopp, *Chromatic Transformations in Nineteenth-Century Music*, 89.
24 Note that E^7 too suffers a loss of its seventh when plotted on the *Tonnetz*.
25 Candace Brower, 'Paradoxes of Pitch Space', *Music Analysis* 27, no. 1 (2008): 29.
26 Fred Lerdahl, *Tonal Pitch Space* (Oxford: Oxford University Press, 2001), 42.
27 Diagonally we have the hexatonics, but these push along the same axis because of their discharge potential.
28 The 1957 seminar was published as 'The Agency of the Letter in the Unconscious or Reason Since Freud'. See Jacques Lacan, *Écrits: A Selection*, trans. Alan Sheridan (London: Tavistock Publications, 2004), 193.
29 Benjamin Steege, '"The Nature of Harmony": A Translation and Commentary', in *The Oxford Handbook of Neo-Riemannian Theories*, ed. Edward Gollin and Alexander Rehding (New York: Oxford University Press, 2011), 83.
30 Brian Hyer, 'What Is a Function?', in *The Oxford Handbook of Neo-Riemannian Theories*, ed. Edward Gollin and Alexander Rehding (New York: Oxford University Press, 2011), 98.
31 See Lacan's essay 'The Agency of the Letter in the Unconscious or Reason Since Freud' in Jacques Lacan, in Lacan, Jacques. Écrits: a Selection, trans. Alan Sheridan (London: Tavistock Publications, 2004), 161–197.
32 Robert Bailey, *Richard Wagner, Prelude and Transfiguration from 'Tristan and Isolde'* (New York: W.W. Norton, 1985), 121.
33 Lacan, *Écrits*, 193.
34 Harrison, 'Three Short Essays on Neo-Riemannian Theory', in *The Oxford Handbook of Neo-Riemannian Theories*, 558.
35 Jacques Lacan, *Seminar XI: The Four Fundamental Concepts of Psychoanalysis*, trans. Jacques Alain Miller (London: Vintage, 1998), 38.
36 Hyer, 'What Is a Function?', 108.
37 For discussion, see Scott Burnham, 'Method and Motivation in Hugo Riemann's History of Harmonic Theory', *Music Theory Spectrum* 14, no. 1 (1992): 1–14.
38 Clark, 'On the Imagination of Tone in Schubert's *Liedesend* (D473), *Trost* (D523), and *Gretchens Bitte* (D564)', 301; see Michael Siciliano, 'Toggling Cycles, Hexatonic Systems, and Some Analysis of Early Atonal Music', *Music Theory Spectrum* 27, no. 2 (2005): 221–248.
39 Ernő Lendvai, *Symmetries of Music: An Introduction to the Semantics of Music*, ed. Miklós Szabo and Milós Mohay (Kecskemét: Kodály Institute, 1993), 66.
40 Riemann cited in Wason, Marvin, and Riemann, 'Riemann's "Ideen zu Einer 'Lehre von den Tonvorstellungen'"', 88.
41 Friedrich W. Nietzsche, *The Birth of Tragedy, and The Case of Wagner*, trans. Walter Kaufmann (New York: Vintage, 1967), 166.
42 Slavoj Žižek, '"There Is No Sexual Relationship": Wagner as a Lacanian', *New German Critique* 69 (1996): 11.
43 Jean-Jacques Nattiez, 'The Concepts of Plot and Seriation Process in Music Analysis', trans. Catherine Dale, *Music Analysis* 4, no. 1/2 (1985): 107–118. There are several pertinent analyses of the *Tristan* prelude, additional to those mentioned by Nattiez: Robert Bailey's study score is replete with psycho- and musico-analytical insight that accounts for a 'double tonic complex' (Bailey, 1985); Lawrence Kramer rehearses an interdisciplinary interpretation of *Tristan* and

the sexuality explicated through music analysis (Kramer, 1990: see Chapter 5 'Musical Form and Fin-De-Siècle Sexuality', 135–175); Daniel Harrison uses the prelude to elucidate what he calls 'Accumulative analysis' (Harrison, 1994, 153–157) in which distinct levels of functional meaning are set into dialogue; Hoffman's thesis explores the concept of enharmony in neo-Riemannian theory (Hoffman, 2011); from a different perspective, Lerdahl attempts to model the tension patterns of the prelude (Lerdahl, 2001, 183–186); most recently, Monahan follows in a different vein by isolating voice-leading energetics (Monahan, 2016).
44 For an explanatory discussion of the objet petit a, see David Bard-Schwarz's chapter in this collection, p. 33.
45 Hugo Riemann, *Systematische Modulationslehre als Grundlage der musikalischen Formenlehre* (Hamburg: J.F. Richter, 1887), 16.
46 See Dmitri Tymoczko, *A Geometry of Music: Harmony and Counterpoint in the Extended Common Practice* (New York and Oxford: Oxford University Press, 2011); Edward Gollin, 'Some Aspects of Three-Dimensional "Tonnetze"', *Journal of Music Theory* 42, no. 2 (1998): 195–206; Richard Cohn, *Audacious Euphony: Chromatic Harmony and the Triad's Second Nature* (New York: Oxford University Press, 2012).
47 Lacan, *Seminar XI*, 174–186.
48 Deleuze and Guattari, *Anti-Oedipus*.
49 *Ibid*.

4 Schubert, music theory, and Lacanian fantasy

Christopher Tarrant

Schubert analysis is obsessed with propping up its own symbolic order. In recent decades, analytical and theoretical writing on his music, and his sonata forms in particular, has coalesced into a new orthodoxy that responds to the old-style view of Schubert's music as structurally deficient. This can be seen in the multifarious analytical articles published since Webster's 'Schubert's Sonata Form and Brahms's First Maturity' in 1978, which seek in their various ways to promote Schubert's particular treatment of sonata form, and to defend it against charges of inadequacy, incoherence, and a perceived inability to match the aesthetic inheritance of Beethoven's sonata exemplars.[1] Clark's *Analyzing Schubert* is representative of this analytical tradition, one of whose central aims is, put in Lacanian terms, to encourage a perception of Schubert's music through the lens of its own symbolic order (as it has been identified by David Beach, Richard Cohn, Charles Fisk, Peter Pesic, and others) rather than erroneously employing analytical systems based on Beethoven's practice, which she constructs as foreign to Schubert's music. This tradition of Schubert scholarship can be seen as a general push towards framing Schubert's treatment of form as a logical process, contra the inherited postwar view, which, culminating with Brendel, portrayed Schubert as a compositional somnambulist.[2]

Musicologists since the late 1970s, whose scholarship has helped to build a much more congenial picture of Schubert as a composer of sonata form, have employed a variety of methods in their attempts analytically to defend Schubert from obloquy. Many of these center on his treatment of tonality as a vehicle for formal experimentation and expansion. This includes the employment of hexatonic theory, which favors structures and procedures such as major-minor equivalence, equal division of the octave, mediant relationships in general, and 'crossing the enharmonic seam'.[3] Where the pre-1978 treatment of Schubert's music seemed unable to remove itself from the perceived hole in the music's symbolic order, manifested in charges of formal disorganization, excessive length, poor thematic quality, unorthodox treatment of tonality, and so on and so forth, the more recent assessment of Schubert since Webster has been to construct a new 'official' reading of the repertoire. This new reading emphasizes the ways in which Schubert transcended the inherited Classical forms by 'inflecting' them, as Rosen argued. It is a reading that largely suggests that an analytical machinery drawn from Beethovenian exemplars ought to be variously modified, reorganized, or rejected in favor of one more appropriate to the structures apparent in Schubert's music. The result of this, it might be argued, has been to replace one hegemonic theoretical tradition and its Beethovenian-Schenkerian prejudices with another, now equally hegemonic tradition of Schubertian-Riemannian partisanship.

What this chapter aims to demonstrate is that this new official reading is reliant on a fantasmatic support, and that a traversal of this fantasy, through an analysis of the first movement of Schubert's G major String Quartet, D. 887, can offer a much more radical reading of Schubert's engagement with sonata form. In traversing this fantasmatic support, we create a necessary critical distance between music theory and the repertoire that it attempts to address. This involves the critical step of stripping the fantasy of its power— of revealing it as a fantasy *as such*—an idea that I will return to at the end of the chapter. Lacan is essential here not least because his complex conceptions of desire and fantasy, which, while highly theoretical and abstract in his own work, have since been developed into practical philosophical tools by Slavoj Žižek, provide the most developed nomenclature for teasing apart the object of study and the lens through which we observe it. This process results in a double rejection, both of the old-style evaluation of Schubert's supposedly incompetent handling of form, and of the more recently constructed official reading of Schubert as a 'non-Beethovenian'.[4]

There is considerable suspicion of a teleological view of Schubert and, by proxy, the application of a theory such as Hepokoski's and Darcy's *Elements of Sonata Theory* to his music.[5] In *Analyzing Schubert*, Clark makes the following criticism the opening gambit of her final chapter on Schubert's sonata forms, and the various analytical approaches that can be used. She writes:

> The norm according to Sonata Theory remains a one-sided masculinist view of 'human experience,' which, moreover, is characterized by the "perfect" human experience. While the authors promised to provide a fresh perspective on sonata form, they reassert the privileged teleological, masculine paradigm that has been the subject of sustained feminist critique. Why are we still being presented with an apparently old-style version of sonata form?[6]

Her objection is essentially a political one. Why should a teleological theory which favors stereotypical masculinist musical metaphors for human actions (goal-directed motion, motivic efficiency, logic, and so on) based on the "old-style" misogynist Beethovenian model continue to occupy a privileged position in music theory? It has to be said that when Hepokoski and Darcy remark that the sonata is "perfect", the scare quotes are theirs, not hers, and that, furthermore, the adjectives used to characterize this "perfection"—"elegance", "proportionality", and "completeness"—seem not to be gendered one way or another.[7] On issues of goal-directed motion, it would seem that Schubert is just as capable of achieving this as anyone else. The transitional drive to the medial caesura is an example of this, and in Schubert's music can in cases be more excessively emphatic and inevitable than many of Beethoven's.[8] Further to this, few scholars nowadays would argue that Schubert's handling of sonata form is inelegant or incomplete, and the old charges of excessive length and "sprawling" tendencies, particularly in his finales (which is where the problem is perceived to reside) are not upheld by Sonata Theory. To challenge the privileged status quo, however, requires intentional intervention. Both Clark's Neo-Riemannian model and Hepokoski's and Darcy's dialogic one work to structure the way we listen. Both function, as I will argue, as a fantasy screen, and both should be subjected to interrogation. Sonata Theory is not any different on that level to any other theory when it comes to explaining music and how we hear and engage with it. The only brief remark on the G major Quartet that is made in *Elements of Sonata Theory*, however, concerns the P^0 introductory idea.[9] Illuminating as this is, it does not provide an adequate foothold for an analysis of the movement as a whole.

Observations concerning the psyche have been a relative commonplace in Schubert scholarship, but are rarely thorough. The state of Schubert's mental health in biographical writings has been particularly explicit. Elizabeth Norman McKay's biography, for example, is littered with references to a mental condition—cyclothymia—of which Schubert is said to have been a sufferer.[10] Other more directly textual studies have come close to attributing symptoms of psychological disorder to analytical observations of Schubert's music. Along with Robert Winter's comparison of a section of Schubert's Piano Sonata in A, D. 959, to a nervous breakdown, Susan Wollenberg writes of 'Schubert's use of tonal and modal colouring' as being 'characterized by his perception of major and minor as two sides of a divided character'.[11] She goes on to write of the G major Quartet:

> The introductory bars present an intensely compressed version of the 'divided character' type [...] Famously, in D 887-i the duality expressed in the opening of the movement is distilled even further when it is recalled at the end, to the point where major and minor almost coalesce. It's as if the opening bars put a proposition which is explored in different ways in the course of the movement, including the role reversal at the start of the recapitulation. [...T]he choice of keys for Theme II responds to the major-minor ambivalence presented at the start.[12]

This, in Lacanian terms, represents the 'official' reading of the work—a reading that is the result of an informed appreciation of the text from an analyst who is properly installed in the symbolic order. The problem with such

Example 4.1 Franz Schubert, String Quartet in G major, D. 887, first movement, opening.

a reading—in fact, *any* reading—is that it is reliant on a fantasy space to render it meaningful. The impression Wollenberg gives is one of completeness and consistency, an impression that all loose ends have been neatly tied up. From a Lacanian perspective, however, a different conclusion can be reached for this movement and, indeed, the work as a whole, since the idea of 'major-minor ambivalence' is revisited throughout.

The clues to such a Lacanian reading can sometimes be found in the small details of the text that may otherwise be overlooked. The tonal language on the surface of the music, which shifts—often violently—between major and minor, is most plainly demonstrated in the P^0 gesture that opens the quartet (see Example 4.1). This is a typical gesture for Schubert: P^0 acts as an in-tempo introduction before the start of the exposition proper, but is countergenerically included within the expositional repeat, and is in some cases presented again at the start of the recapitulation.[13] In the G major Quartet, P^0 is presented more subtly at this point (bar 280): the major/minor opposition is reversed and rescored as a more contented gesture. This psychological reversal does suggest some kind of amelioration or synthesis in the intervening bars between the expositional medial caesura and the end of the development section. The P^0 gesture is visited one final time in the closing bars of the movement in its original stormy form, with major and minor versions of the tonic pulling against one another before finally settling on a chord of G major. The opposition of major and minor versions of the tonic is structurally crucial and produces a harmonic emblem that leaves an indelible mark on the rest of the work. It may even be worth entertaining the idea that the designation of G major as the key of the work is no more than arbitrary, since so much of the surface as well as the structure is governed by relationships with the tonic minor.

The handling of tonality within the quartet has been a perennial topic of debate. On the largest scale of the overarching formal and tonal plan of the first movement, G major and G minor are treated as equally valid tonal centres. This is expressed in the secondary zone by the principal key in which the essential expositional closure (EEC) is delivered, D major, enveloping a central B♭ section (bar 110). This secondary zone presents a problem for Schenkerian analysis, in the first place because Schenkerians have been unable to agree where the prolongation of D major begins, and in the second place because of the large amount of material that occurs after the initial cadence in the dominant at the end of $S^{1.1}$, which can be thought of as excessive (Figure 4.1).[14]

One solution is to understand D major as a normative secondary key for a sonata in G major, B♭ as normative for a sonata in G minor, that both are equally valid tonal goals, and that in generating this structure, Schubert constructs a double-tonic complex that governs the quartet. This would be along similar lines to the 'directional tonality' first proposed by Robert Bailey in his work on Wagner's harmonic practice, and later discussed by Kinderman and Krebs in *The Second Practice of Nineteenth-Century Tonality*; that is to say, a piece may begin in one key and end in another, usually separated by the interval of a third.[15] While this cannot be said of Schubert's Quartet in G major, it is still logical to talk of two distinct tonics operating within a broader nexus, since major and minor versions of the same tonic bring with them their own distinctive structural properties and generic associations.

We are also presented with a hexatonic relationship between two keys that are also normative S-theme keys for major and minor sonatas, respectively, one of which is diatonic and accessible to a Schenkerian approach (D major), and therefore potentially 'dialectical' in Dahlhaus's terms, and the other which is chromatic and resistant to Schenkerian theory— Dahlhaus's 'lyric-epic' (B♭ major).[16] The 'missing' key from the hexatonic orbit is found at the point of the III: HC medial caesura, whose F emphasis completes the cycle of major 3rds. In a sense, both readings, the dialectical and the lyric-epic, are valid, but only if the fantasy is in place: a Lacanian reading of this situation can show that a certain group of analysts, as argued below, have sought to tear down one fantasy only to erect another.

Turning to the closing bars of the first movement, it is plain that major and minor are being juxtaposed in a final 'summing up' gesture that is ordinarily found in large Type 3 first movements.[17] This is a return to the opening P^0 module that generates an effect of culmination (see Example 4.2). The bars at the end of the movement achieve this with particular flair, with antiphonal exchanges that coincide with the alternation of mode between the two pairs

Bar	Module	Key
1	P^0	I/i
15	P^{Theme}	I
24	P$^{Var\,1}$	I
33	P$^{Var\,2}$ → TR$^{(failed)}$	I
54	P$^{Var\,3}$ → TR	I
63	III: HC MC	V/III
65	S$^{1.1Theme}$	V
78	S$^{1.1\,Var\,1}$	V
90	S$^{1.2}$	V
109	I: HC PMC	V/I
110	S$^{1.1\,Var\,2}$	♭III
122	S$^{1.2}$	♭III
141	III: HC PMC	V/♭III
142	S$^{1.1\,Var\,3}$	V
154	EEC	V
154	C^1	V
164	C^2 → RT	V

Figure 4.1 Quartet in G major, D. 887, first movement exposition.

of instruments. However, any sense of the two modes beginning to 'coalesce' here is immediately undermined by the final two bars. Far from the unusual antiphonal scoring and the summative play between major and minor, we are presented with the most generic of final gestures: the simple presentation of the tonic major with a downward arpeggiation in the bass voice. The conceptual goal of achieving a synthesis between the opposing modes is dashed with this disarmingly simple gesture, which effectively undoes the problematic that has been generated over the course of the movement. The essence of the gesture, however generic its surface, is obligatory in the narrow symbolic order that the music is channeled through: that of the common-practice era sonata and its associated tonal obligations. In this case, such symbolic inconsistencies originate from the impossibility of reconciliation of major and minor tonalities. The Lacanian response to this is that symbolic inconsistencies are covered over with fantasies that act as a symbolic support and serve to restore the impression that the symbolic order is consistent and

Example 4.2 Franz Schubert, String Quartet in G major, D. 887, first movement, closing bars.

meaningful.[18] It is significant, then, that we remain analytically invested in the ending as a moment of closure, especially when this moment is not achieved unproblematically. This is addressed in Hepokoski's and Darcy's Sonata Theory by the controversial category of "deformation", perhaps the clearest example in music theory of a fantasy taking its own inconsistencies into account in advance.

Criticisms (in the prosaic sense) of Schubert's handling of form and tonality are rare, especially since the professionalization of Schubert analysis that has taken place since 1978. However, J.P.E. Harper-Scott has constructed a startling reappraisal of the situation that critiques the inherited story of the New Musicology of the early 1990s.[19] He remarks that:

> Modern musicologists are quite clear that while Beethoven's musical techniques formed the basis of theories like Schenker's, as well as our listening practices, those of Schubert, formerly considered aberrant or unrefined, actually present a critique of our assumptions about musical practice in the nineteenth century. But in a specific sense, it is Beethoven—and Haydn—who are the ideology critics and Schubert— far from being the willing embracer of the musically deviant, the gay composer who does not follow Beethoven's alpha-male models—who is the mystifier of the interpellative violence of tonality.[20]

Harper-Scott argues that Beethoven and Haydn, albeit in separate ways, present a critique of the hegemonic structuring of tonal music from Bach to Schoenberg. It is Beethoven who declares his challenges at the outset, which are to be violently and ritualistically conquered, thus bringing the 'interpellative violence' of the tonal system into clear view (i.e. Beethoven is not the source of the violence, as claimed by McClary, but tonality itself—the violence is systemic, rather than symbolic).[21] Haydn, on the other hand, exposes the arbitrariness of the structural ordering of tonality by exposing it as such—as something to be toyed with. This is clear from Harper-Scott's example of the finale of Haydn's C major Piano Sonata, Hob. XVI:50, in which the B♮ in bar 10 is not harmonized in the usual way, as the leading note in the context of a G major dominant harmony, but as a 'zany' B major harmony leading to a 'confused fermata'.[22] Unlike Beethoven, this challenge to the structural order is not violently conquered, but left unresolved. Beethoven, then, is the revolutionary who exposes the violence in the system, and Haydn is the satirist, pointing to its arbitrariness. Schubert, on the other hand, is the collaborator who, through hexatonic modulations, equal treatment of major and minor, opening fifth space *around* rather than *from* the tonic, and so on, aims to show that genuine freedom can be found in the tonal system.

In his comparison with Haydn, for instance, Harper-Scott tries to construct Schubert as the composer who indulges and enlarges the tyranny of the tonal symbolic order, and Haydn as the activist who 'toys' with its inherent arbitrariness. Schubert, however, can be found doing similar things—at the end the finale of his Piano Sonata in A major, D. 959, for example. In its final statement, the theme begins to disintegrate, as bar-long silences are introduced. The harmony also begins to unravel, with the German augmented sixth at bar 342 resolving directly to the tonic, rather than to its proper destination, the dominant. It would seem that Haydn and Schubert are experimenting with the same idea. However, notwithstanding this comparison, the impression given by Haydn is one of the awkwardness of the ideological structuring, enacting the role of the court jester who makes fun of the king: he creates an ideological space where normal social and, in this case, tonal norms are suspended, sometimes with comedic effect. The case in Schubert's music is quite the opposite. The events that would otherwise be considered odd or tonally deviant are brought into the fantasy, presented seriously and earnestly as genuine normality within the structural order.

Not only does Schubert perpetuate the hegemonic structuring of tonality (and sonata), but he actively gulls the listener into believing that he is doing the opposite. That is to say, in the G major Quartet, he overtly constructs the 'challenge' at the start that cuts to the core of the tonal system—that major and minor are in conflict—and then attempts to convince the listener not only that genuine freedom can be found in the tonal/sonata system through an experimental and progressive exploration of sonata space, but furthermore that by the end of the musical utterance he has neutralized the problem and successfully synthesized the opposing modes. Far from Beethoven's or Haydn's sonata practice, Schubert serves not to expose the arbitrary imposition of symbolic tonal and sonata goals, but to muddy the water (through expanding the tonal map, introducing foreign forms, such as variation into the sonata, and so on) and thereby to identify with the hegemonic symbolic order rather than to present a critique of it. We are led to believe that

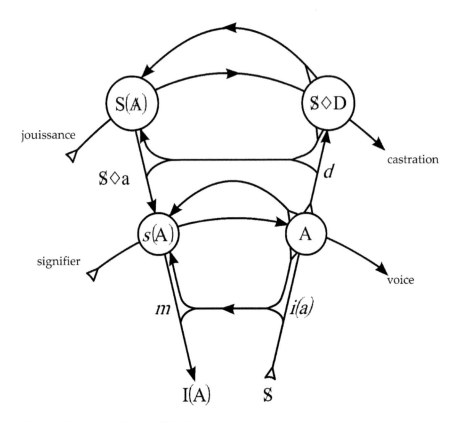

Figure 4.2 Lacan's Graph of Desire.

equality between major and minor is a case of Schubert breaking the rules by opening up a welcoming new ideological space. What Schubert does in his continued treatment of major and minor is to promise something in his music—something more 'open' or 'gay' or 'non-Beethovenian'—only to back down, folding this promise back into the structural ordering of sonata space. The important thing is not the meaning he promises through modal equality, but simply the form of the gesture itself.

This leads us to Lacan's graph of desire (Figure 4.2). In the case of the G major Quartet, the vector of the barred subject ($) can be followed from the bottom right of the graph to the bottom left, giving an account of the circuit of desire in the work. At the first intersection, the vector of the barred subject is penetrated by the signifying chain, and at this junction, Lacan locates the Big Other (A), the universe of contingent rules which governs the musical language. The vector leading vertically upwards from this point, which is the source of Lacan's fathomless '*Che vuoi?*', can be considered to be the genesis of 'musical meaning': not in the sense that the music does not 'make sense' to us, but rather that it holds messages that escape the observation of structures considered to be objectively 'in' the work, to use Hepokoski's and Darcy's phrase.[23] This can be considered an offshoot, or an excess that results from the process of 'quilting' the signifying chain (the process by which a fixed point of reference organizes a succession of otherwise meaningless signifiers) and escapes signification. Here we locate desire (d), the phenomenon of the splitting of what is said, and what is meant. This is the location of musical meaning, that is to say, the point at which Hepokoski's and Darcy's 'empirical realm' stops and where 'that of hermeneutics' begins.[24]

The point at which this offshoot of desire is perforated with the vector of *jouissance* is the location of the drive ($S \Diamond D$), the impossible junction between enjoyment and the signifier. In the standard model, this would be the location of the partial 'erogenous zones' that are arbitrarily shot through with enjoyment. For the present musical example, this could be a signifier of major and minor tonalities existing as one simultaneous entity, and hence 'impossible'. It would be possible to envisage such a situation, but only in a context that is so distant from Schubert's universe as to be utterly meaningless and incompatible with the present work. This might be found in analytical mechanisms such as Allen Forte's pitch-class set analysis, intended for atonal music, in which the major and minor triads are signified by the same pitch-class set (3–11), and therefore incompatible with any meaningful tonal analysis.

It may be the case that we need not even venture into the twentieth century to find an adequate homology for this. From Wagner onwards, major and minor were in many instances regarded as freely interchangeable, and the near collapse of the tonal system can be glimpsed earlier in works by Debussy and Liszt—his *Bagatelle Sans Tonalité*, S.216a, is perhaps the most convenient example of this. The observation that Schubert uses major and minor versions of the tonic so frequently that Wollenberg considers it to be a 'fingerprint' belies a more fundamental observation, however, that when Schubert does this, the two modes alternate—that is to say, one may be substituted for the other, with far-reaching consequences, but they are never fully synthesised and sounded as a unified musical signifier. For Schubert, interchangeability of mode is commonplace, but they each still come under the sign of either major or minor, which remain in marked opposition, rendering their true synthesis beyond the structural horizon of Schubert's universe.

The point of crisis is reached at the second intersection of the vector of *jouissance*. The sign of the barred other ($S\slashed{A}$) is analogous to the realization that such an utterance (a simultaneous expression of major and minor tonalities) is impossible within the ideological structuring of sonata form in the 1820s. There is no such sign within the Schubertian universe, and at this point the inconsistency in the symbolic order is exposed as a symbol of lack. The principal ($S\slashed{A}$) statement in the G major Quartet is the P^0 module in the first movement, in which major and minor are in close proximity, but can only be expressed partially and successively. We might say that the necessary components for the complete musical statement are present, but they can only be symbolized at a certain level of isolation from one-another, as a string of partial musical objects.

Moving down the left side, fantasy (S◊a), which appears opposite desire (d) on the graph, functions as an ideological support for the fractured symbolic order, accounting for gaps and inconsistencies. In the present instance, the fantasy is music theory as such, as it presents a picture of completeness in the work and accounts for any anomalies, taking its own failures and shortcomings into account in advance, adapting and morphing to accommodate whichever text is exposed to its gaze. Suzannah Clark has expressed a similar view, although not psychoanalytically, about Sonata Theory. She remarks that 'The Sonata Theory of Hepokoski and Darcy [...] has a geometry, an arc, that is treated as "sacred," though it is not explicitly labelled as such'.[25] Clark is right to point out that the sacred arc of Sonata Theory is a dubious concept, but she is wrong to dismiss the theory as a result. What is interesting here is not the observation that Sonata Theory is flawed, but the sacred aura that allows it to carry on functioning.

The result of the process of filling in the gaps and inconsistencies with fantasy is the signified of the Big Other (s(A)), which occurs at the second point of intersection of the signifying chain. This is where the various 'official' readings of the work can be located—readings that propose that desire has been satisfied, that all loose ends have been tied up, and that these can be demonstrated through observations of structures thought, to use Hepokoski's and Darcy's phrase, to be objectively 'in' the work. The Lacanian answer to such a proposition would be that desire is *never* fully satisfied—in such a case, we would stop listening to sonata form because we would no longer desire it—but that some modicum of satisfaction can be harnessed with the aid of a fantasy screen.

Following the vector down to its final point we reach the identification with an aspect of the big Other (I(A)), the reassurance that the forms found within the work are structured properly—that Schubert 'did it right'.[26] However, what a Lacanian psychoanalysis shows about this string quartet is that, with the help of theory, not only does Schubert 'do it right', but that his music actively contributes to the buttressing of an ideological frame of which he has hitherto been constructed as a principal critic.

Clark, in her introduction to *Analyzing Schubert*, makes the following remark:

> The impact that the choice of "lens" of music theory has on the perception of a musical work may be put in the following fantastical terms. Imagine owning a pair of spectacles that allows only a specific shape, say circles, to be perceived by the observer. He or she would enjoy the full moon, see clocks, round tables, and wheels. Then imagine replacing these spectacles with a pair that allows only right angles to be seen. Suddenly rectangular tables would come into view, as would the corners in

a room, picture frames, books, and so on. Now imagine walking into a room where everything is circular but our observer is wearing the wrong glasses. The circles are there, but the glasses do not reveal them. The result is chaos or blindness—all because of the choice of lenses.[27]

Her point is that the choice of analytical system is crucial. Her 'right angles' are a clear reference to Beethoven's music, with its strongly defined, architectural structures, and the lenses that enable the observer to view them are Schenkerian. Her 'circles' are obviously metaphorical of Schubert's more enigmatic mode of composition, and the lenses allowing one to view this are neo-Riemannian ones.

Clark's spectacles, were they positioned on Lacan's graph of desire, would be located at the big Other (A), the mechanism through which phenomena appear meaningful. However, in light of the analysis presented above, it pays to remove oneself one more step from the analytical entanglements that Clark is concerned with. Although the lens metaphor is a useful form of meta-analysis, let us consider for a moment that the spectacles, rather than blocking out certain shapes, actually fill in the gaps, allowing them to form a coherent whole rather than producing something merely partial or successive. Clark's spectacles enact the process of signification, perforating the music and reducing it to what is symbolizable. Whether you are looking at circles or squares in this scenario does not affect their function. The spectacles that I am suggesting are those that, far from filtering out information, 'fill in' what is missing, or lacking, in the field of view. This posits them as $S\lozenge a$ objects, without which the text would appear as a purely successive and therefore meaningless utterance—an unquilted, inarticulate, and chaotic stream of desire emerging in sound over time. Projected onto a fantasy screen, the coordinates of desire can be articulated, and its objects identified. These would include such 'objects' as medial caesurae and essential expositional closure that, without a fantasy screen, would evade us. One of the effects of this is that Sonata Theory, like any functioning fantasy, can grow and change and enlarge itself to be able to cope with whatever ruptures are revealed in the symbolic order. Clark constructs it as a conservatively Schenkerian theory that promotes a masculinist view of sonata form, whereas it is actually capable of growing and changing to accommodate the 'lyric-epic' chromatic structures identified by Dahlhaus at the same time as the 'masculinist' diatonic ones.

As much as psychoanalysis can reveal layers of meaning that were hitherto inaccessible, the reverse is equally demonstrable: that psychoanalysis can strip away the fantasies that render phenomena meaningful in the first place. To add yet another perspective to the metaphor of the neo-Riemannian 'spectacles' that Clark uses in *Analyzing Schubert*, 'Lacanian spectacles' behave more like the sunglasses in John Carpenter's *They Live* (1988).[28] In this film, our protagonist is down on his luck, homeless, unemployed, has no prospects, and in a world which seems normal to him: the America he is used to—full of media and advertising. By chance, he acquires a pair of sunglasses, which, when donned, reveal in plain text the 'real' messages that are being transmitted through 'reality' as it appears. These include billboard slogans such as 'OBEY AND CONFORM', 'MARRY AND REPRODUCE', 'CONSUME', 'DO NOT QUESTION AUTHORITY', and, on the bank notes, 'THIS IS YOUR GOD'. This, it is possible to say, is the effect that psychoanalysis can have on human behavior and, in particular, the cultural traces that humans generate in the form of artworks. Like Žižek's 'third pill'—a reference he makes to *The Matrix* (1999) in *The Pervert's Guide to Cinema*—the spectacles allow our protagonist to separate the 'real world' and its arbitrarily enforced authority from the symbolic fictions that such authority would not function without. In music theory, and in Sonata Theory in particular, these symbolic fictions are strong, and serve as a crucial support for the way we understand musical works to be meaningful. This is heightened in Hepokoski's and Darcy's Sonata Theory by the language they employ, which is full of whimsical images and metaphors that ventriloquize their musical exemplars. Sonata Theory, therefore, is not only a way of situating musical works in a theoretical frame, but also of actually structuring the way we listen. It highlights the ways that musical works can be informative to the broader experience of human subjectivity.

Our desires are not our own. They are other to us, and we have to be taught how to access them. Yet there is a problem. These desires, for money, power, sexual intercourse, or medial caesurae, can never be fully satisfied. Žižek makes this point when he writes:

> when we encounter in reality an object which has all the properties of the fantasized object of desire, we are nevertheless necessarily somewhat disappointed; we experience a certain "this is not it"; it becomes evident that the finally found real object is not the reference of desire even though it possesses all the required properties.[29]

So, whether the I: PAC ESC is properly established or not is not the point in hand, or, as Harper-Scott said, 'Mozart would have been out of a job centuries ago'.[30] The point is that Sonata Theory teaches the human subject how to locate desire in the musical text. It fixes the coordinates of their desire. To put it in Žižekian terms, sonatas do not give us what we desire: they tell us how to desire.

The way this affects Schubert analysis is twofold, and performs a kind of double motion. As with any analytical or meta-analytical study, it informs a deeper and more profound structural understanding of the text. This serves to contribute something to a mature tradition of Schubert analysis, a tradition that has constructed Schubert's music as a kind of meta-analytical prism—his music is a critical lens for 'analysing analysis', and has become a crucible of theoretical rigor. This is demonstrated in Cohn's *Audacious Euphony*: his very first musical example is an extract from Schubert's Piano

Sonata in B♭, D. 960, which he uses as a means of undermining the logic of conventional chordal analysis.[31] Yet the second part of the double motion creates what Žižek would call a 'radical ambiguity'. This unpicking of music analysis is itself undermined by the final traversal of the fantasy. We arrive at a situation at the end of the psychoanalytic process where the fantasy screen between the desiring subject and the real kernel is completely removed, resulting in a radically new relationship between subject and other, one in which language and fantasy are seen for what they are—symbolic constructions of a radical otherness.

This can result in what is sometimes referred to as a 'negative therapeutic reaction'.[32] The result of the process is both successful and unsuccessful. On the one hand, a deeper understanding of the way that music analysis functions has been achieved. This is particularly important when concerned with a composer such as Schubert, whose music has become a barometer of theoretical integrity. On the other hand, after having 'gone through' the fantasy, the structures are revealed to us in all their brutality and arbitrariness. The choice that remains is whether to beat a hasty retreat and allow the fantasies once again to swell, restoring the support for a meaningful normality, or to embrace the real kernel for what it is, in its arbitrariness, contingency, and in the absence of the support that brings consistency and meaning to our experience of music.

Notes

1 See David Beach, 'Schubert's Experiments with Sonata Form: Formal-Tonal Design versus Underlying Structure', *Music Theory Spectrum* 15, no. 1 (1993): 1–18; Richard Cohn, 'As Wonderful as Star Clusters: Instruments for Gazing at Tonality in Schubert', *19th-Century Music* 22, no. 3 (1999): 213–232; Charles Fisk, 'What Schubert's Last Sonata Might Hold', in *Music and Meaning*, ed. Jennifer Robinson (Ithaca, NY: Cornell University Press, 1997), 179–200; Peter Pesic, 'Schubert's Dream', *19th-Century Music* 23, no. 2 (1999): 136–144; James Webster, 'Schubert's Sonata Form and Brahms's First Maturity', *19th-Century Music* 2, no. 1 (1978/1979): 18–35.
2 See Alfred Brendel, 'Form and Psychology in Beethoven's Piano Sonatas', in *Musical Thoughts and Afterthoughts* (Princeton, NJ: Princeton University Press, 1976), 41–42.
3 For more on this, see Richard Cohn's, *Audacious Euphony: Chromatic Harmony and the Triad's Second Nature* (Oxford: Oxford University Press, 2012).
4 Suzannah Clark, *Analyzing Schubert* (Oxford: Oxford University Press, 2011), 161–174.
5 James Hepokoski and Warren Darcy, *Elements of Sonata Theory: Norms, Types, and Deformations in the Late-Eighteenth-Century Sonata* (Oxford: Oxford University Press, 2006).
6 Clark, *Analyzing Schubert*, 204.
7 Poundie Burstein provides an excellent problematization of these gender politics, detailing the various inherent contradictions in such constructions and how they relate to the G major Quartet. See his 'Lyricism, Structure, and Gender in Schubert's G Major String Quartet', *The Musical Quarterly* 81, no. 1 (1997): 51–63.

8 A representative example can be found in the first movement of Schubert's C major String Quintet, D. 956, whose transition emphatically achieves an i: HC MC.
9 Hepokoski and Darcy, *Elements of Sonata Theory*, 89.
10 Elizabeth Norman McKay, *Franz Schubert* (Oxford: Oxford University Press, 1996). 'Cyclothymia is defined medically as a mild form of manic depression characterized by pronounced changes of "mood, behaviour, thinking, sleep, and energy levels". In adults, periods of depression, hypomania (mild mania), and complete normality alternate, the latter lasting no more than two months at a time. The condition at this level of severity is not debilitating, but the severity is liable to increase with the years, in many cases into full-blown clinically definable manic depression' (138).
11 Susan Wollenberg, *Schubert's Fingerprints: Studies in the Instrumental Works* (Farnham: Ashgate, 2011), 29.
12 *Ibid.*, 30–31.
13 This can be observed in the present work; the 5th Symphony, D. 485, i; and the 8th Symphony, D. 759, i.
14 See Webster 'Schubert's Sonata Form and Brahms's First Maturity', 21; Beach, 'Schubert's Experiments with Sonata Form: Formal-Tonal Design versus Underlying Structure', 17; and Burstein, 'Lyricism, Structure, and Gender in Schubert's G Major String Quartet', 56.
15 Robert Bailey, 'The Structure of the "Ring" and its Evolution', *19th-Century Music* 1, no. 1 (1977): 48–61; and Robert Bailey, Ed., *Prelude and Transfiguration from Tristan and Isolde* (Norton Critical Editions, 1985). See also William Kinderman and Harold Krebs, eds, *The Second Practice of Nineteenth-Century Tonality* (Lincoln: University of Nebraska Press, 1996).
16 See Carl Dahlhaus, 'Sonata Form in Schubert: The First Movement of the G-Major String Quartet, Op. 161 (D. 887)', trans. Thilo Reinhard, in *Schubert: Critical and Analytical Studies*, ed. Walter Frisch (Lincoln: University of Nebraska Press, 1986), 1–12.
17 In Hepokoski's and Darcy's Sonata Theory, their 'Type 3' sonata form corresponds with the textbook model with exposition, development, recapitulation, and optional coda. In their Sonata Theory, Types 1 and 2 are presented as abridged forms, and Types 4 and 5 as Rondo and concerto hybrids respectively.
18 See Slavoj Žižek, 'Fantasy as a Support for Reality', in *The Sublime Object of Ideology* (London: Verso, 2008), 47–50. See also Slavoj Žižek, *How to Read Lacan* (London: Granta Books, 2006), 47–48 and 59: 'Fantasy is the screen that protects us from the encounter with the Real'.
19 By modern, I mean in the era after 1978 when derisory commentary began to decline and become outmoded as new analytical techniques (neo-Riemannian theory and hexatonicism, for example) were rapidly accepted into Schubert scholarship.
20 J.P.E. Harper-Scott, *The Quilting Points of Musical Modernism: Revolution, Reaction, and William Walton* (Cambridge: Cambridge University Press, 2012), 243.
21 An example of this can be found in the finale of Beethoven's Eighth Symphony in which the 'wrong note' in the opening theme is at first ignored, but then returned to and addressed at length in an obscenely long coda that is almost as long as the sonata space that precedes it.
22 Harper-Scott, *The Quilting Points of Musical Modernism*, 243–245.
23 Hepokoski and Darcy, *Elements of Sonata Theory*, 340.
24 *Ibid.*
25 Clark, *Analyzing Schubert*, 219.
26 See Harper-Scott, *The Quilting Points of Musical Modernism*, 139.

27 Clark, *Analyzing Schubert*, 4.
28 Hepokoski and Darcy also use the lens metaphor in their discussion of the sonata types, remarking that nineteenth-century exemplars of the Type 2 form have been viewed through 'the Type 3 sonata-form lenses that the analytical tradition has given us to perceive these later works—the wrong lenses, we would argue' (*Elements of Sonata Theory*, 364).
29 Žižek, *The Sublime Object of Ideology*, 100–101.
30 Harper-Scott, *The Quilting Points of Musical Modernism*, 52.
31 Cohn, *Audacious Euphony*, 2.
32 Slavoj Žižek, *Looking Awry: An Introduction to Jacques Lacan through Popular Culture* (Cambridge, MA: MIT Press, 1991), 86–87.

5 Subjective and objective violence in Taylor Swift's 'I Knew You Were Trouble'

Alexi Vellianitis

Psychoanalysis has become in many ways synonymous with a critique of popular music within musicology.[1] The most extreme example is J.P.E. Harper-Scott's *The Quilting Points of Musical Modernism*, in which the author draws upon a number of different psychoanalytic thinkers, including Jacques Lacan, Slavoj Žižek and Alain Badiou, in order to address what Andreas Huyssen has referred to as the 'great divide' between high and low art.[2] Harper-Scott begins his text with the 'radical contention [...] that the definition of modernism must encompass *all music of the twentieth century*, and not just a privileged group of works by a group of nominated composers'.[3] The basic point is that modernist music articulates a sense of resistance in accordance with an ethical dilemma that is universal; consequently, all other types of music should be held to the same aesthetic standards. In other words, this proposition is radical because, rather than being complicit with the project of bridging the great divide, it collapses the great divide entirely. However, Harper-Scott does not discuss pop music at all in the text, and he repeatedly qualifies his original contention throughout the text by referring to types of music that are distinct from modernism. By the conclusion, modernism is again set up in contradistinction to pop music, which is the most 'successfully marketized' form of music,[4] and Harper-Scott concludes that 'modernism continues to offer the best scholarly locus for an emancipatory musicology to develop'.[5] My aim is neither to disagree with Harper-Scott's original contention, nor suggest that it fails as a sustained argument; but I do wish to apply it more directly to pop music in an attempt to strengthen the radicalness of the original claim.

The terms 'subjective' and 'objective' violence are useful here because they foreground an anxiety about the difference between complicity and resistance present in Harper-Scott's work. Slavoj Žižek has recently made the distinction between 'subjective' violence—acts of 'crime and terror, civil unrest and international conflict'—and 'objective' violence, 'a violence that sustains our very efforts to fight violence and promote tolerance'.[6] At stake here is the difference between the violence inherent in rupture, and the violence inherent in promoting 'normality'—in other words, Žižek is concerned with the way in which true acts of resistance are constituted. In this sense,

Žižek's work follows a long history of societal critique that has been fundamental to psychoanalysis since its inception: from the violent exchanges of power that Sigmund Freud saw as contributing to the formation of society, to Jacques Lacan's interest in the way psychotic subjects functioned outside of or around the neurotic social bond.[7] For Žižek,

> subjective violence is experienced as such against the background of a non-violent zero level. It is seen as a perturbation of the "normal", peaceful state of things. However, objective violence is precisely the violence inherent to this normal state of things.[8]

This is a description that echoes with his better-known approach to ideology, that 'stepping out of it [is] the very form of our enslavement to it': we can never truly inhabit a space of normality without violence being exerted upon us or by us upon another.[9] Viewing contemporary pop music from this angle is interesting since this is a type of music that (following Harper-Scott) functions as an objectively violent, purely marketized, and almost ideologically neutral type of music. Yet, I want to highlight that it is one that constantly distinguishes itself by engaging with other types of non-popular musics that are more appealing because they seem like they have been less marketized: since these are 'outside' pop, they enact a kind of subjective violence onto it, and in so doing, constitute it as popular. In other words, acts of subjective violence are inflicted upon pop music, and these acts contribute to the objective violence of popular music's marketability. Throughout this chapter, I will focus on the way in which pop music is marketized by accepting some of modernism's definitive traits, namely, a sense of difficulty that manifests in different ways.

This is where an example becomes useful. Taylor Swift's song 'I Knew You Were Trouble', from her third studio album *Red*, was released in October 2012. Up until its release, Swift had been seen as mostly a country star who produced radio-friendly songs about simple problems associated with being an affluent white female teenager, set against a predominantly acoustic guitar sound with a limited amount of electronics and vocal alteration. However, 'I Knew You Were Trouble' was much harsher in its sound: as one reviewer wrote, 'the chorus is built around whirring sub-bass, with extra, digitally tweaked vocal hooks, so it's a far cry from traditional country'.[10] The lyrics told the story of a messy breakup, with Swift lamenting that she 'knew [her lover was] trouble when [he] walked in'. Reflecting this, the music video also had a much darker tone, with Swift engaging in a whirlwind romance with a rock star who seemed to draw her down into his seedy lifestyle of sex, drugs, and rock and roll. 'I Knew You Were Trouble' represented a specific sense of resistance, and thus a connection with (apparently subjective) violence: if previously Swift had been known for her country image, then this track seemed to undermine or resist that image, something knotted together through the incorporation of a 'bass drop', a musical device from the underground musical genre dubstep. As Jon Caramanica wrote, a 'dubstep wobble arrives about halfway through like a wrecking ball, changing the course not just of the song but also of Ms. Swift's career'.[11] In other words, this sense of loss and rupture implied in this musical device seemed to articulate a sense of subjective violence against the ideology of pop. Yet what is also interesting is that this song was part of a trajectory from Swift's country music image to a more pop image: in other words, the journey towards being a true 'pop' star involves creating music that also resists a pop image.[12]

The musical language of modernism

The technical features of what would constitute a resistant, subjectively violent music are unclear. Harper-Scott is clear that pop music 'explicitly rejects the musical language of modernism',[13] the emancipation of dissonance, which 'constituted an excess to tonality, the system of musical organization'[14] and in so doing flagged up a 'suppressed third term: a radical redrawing of the current situation, including its official antagonism'.[15] For Harper-Scott,

> the central asseveration of tonality is that a musical configuration is either consonant or dissonant in one of an increasingly varied number of ways [...] in this sense, *tonality is an ideology of music*, which functions in a comparable fashion to a state ideology.[16]

In one sense, this is a familiar proposition: the simplicity of popular culture is reflected in a simplicity in musical language, namely, the ignorance of the ideological rupture represented by the emancipation of dissonance. In Žižek's terms, the emancipation of dissonance provides a true act of subjective violence against the objective violence of the ideology of tonality, which sanctions a fundamental antagonism within music.[17] The main point being made here is that using a broadly diatonic/tonal musical language is seen as a capitulation to market forces. But how does this happen? For Harper-Scott, 'much of minimalism and pop (and most jazz) simply rejects the principle of emancipated dissonance outright. The correspondence between this tendency and its increased saleability is surely not fortuitous'.[18] Perhaps not, but the *nature* of the correspondence bears expanding upon.

Most importantly, it should be stressed that Harper-Scott's point is less about tonality itself than it is about the fundamental antagonism that tonality flags up. This antagonism, however, is also present in other places. Allan F. Moore has made an attempt to link together the musical language of pop with that of modernism by looking at the music of the band Jethro Tull. Yet the question of tonality is moot for Moore, and he suggests that many of the hallmarks of modernist music include metrical syncopation, alienation, a 'disturbed surface',[19] and, most importantly, a general 'unnecessary "difficulty", [which] of course, appears to many lay audiences as an obvious criterion of the "modern"'.[20] So the sense of difficulty or antagonism is separable from tonality itself: any difficult pop music can display it too through, for example, lyrics or other timbral effects (as I will show later through a discussion of the bass drop). Building on this, Chris Atton has written that listening to difficult or *avant-garde* popular music requires a 'disciplined listening', a 'concentrated listening that requires dedication and time',[21] eliding the antagonism with a perseverance, concentration, and desire to put something at stake. I will suggest below that the attraction of dubstep is that it owes its appeal to the lengthening of musical time and the increased attention on the part of the listener. More importantly, however, the way that this disciplined listening links to psychoanalysis needs to be clarified.

Moreover, I want to suggest that it is specifically the *difficulty* of psychoanalysis that makes it appealing as a critical tool, since difficulty is often seen to constitute an act of resistance. Harper-Scott in particular is explicit about the fact that *The Quilting Points of Musical Modernism* uses 'heavyweight theoretical tools' in order to undertake a critique 'so radical that it may constitute for some a challenge'.[22] This focus on conceptual difficulty and its link to modernism is made by Arved Ashby, who uses the Lacanian term *jouissance* to foreground the way in which pain and pleasure come together in modernist music, writing that 'modernist music is the most conflicted we have. More than any other kind of music ... it offers each listener a unique, volatile, high-stakes dialectic of inseparable pleasure and pain, reward and risk'.[23] Yet the appeal of difficulty isn't limited to musicology. This difficulty is also present with Žižek, although it manifests through an anxiety that his use of a broad range of references from popular culture seems to make him complicit with capitalism. Paul Taylor highlights Žižek's anti-capitalist status by reminding us that he is a *difficult* writer, complaining that even sympathetic commentators

> seek to reduce [Žižek] to the conceptual equivalent of pure caffeine. Instead of the finely balanced entity of both form and content that makes good coffee a rich-tasting, palate-challenging beverage to be savoured, constantly on-the-go, capitalist consumers prefer the intellectual equivalent of the sickly sweet quick hit of the high-energy drink.[24]

Here we have a fairly explicit sense of what it might be to be resistant to capitalism: someone who is anti-capitalist enjoys savoring challenging thought, reflecting on and off over a long period of time, limiting or measuring his or her thought, while the capitalist wants it all now, wants it at once, and wants too much of it. It is also remarkable that this is the kind of process that writers on psychoanalysis Julie Jaffee Nagel and Samuel Bradshaw have in mind when they pitch a musical approach to psychoanalysis as a solution to the many problems with contemporary society, including 'popular trends in media reporting emphasize celebrity idealization and instant access to Internet insights which accentuate simplicity, quick answers, and sound bites'. For

Nagel and Bradshaw, 'psychoanalytic and musical knowledge can contribute to many areas that impact human motivation, critical thinking, decision making, and our quality of life while probing beneath external events and simplistic solutions to thorny and complex questions'.[25] So abstaining from immediate satisfaction and instead choosing the more difficult, detailed, and conceptually sophisticated road is positive since it articulates a sense of authentic subjectivity. Yet this same sense of difficulty has become irresistible not only to critics of popular culture, but also to pop music producers, who see it as another way of making the popular music product more desirable. This is what I want to discuss below.

If the sense of difficulty is linked to a savoring of the conceptual coffee rather than a sickly sweet hit of energy drink, then it is also the former (rather than the latter) mode of enjoyment that is generally seen to be synonymous with music. Holly Watkins makes the link between music and psychoanalysis: drawing on Žižek's idea that our contemporary time is characterized by a sense of loss that results in an ongoing searching for a 'home', Watkins writes that

> music, I would propose, renders this homelessness audible. In its very transience, music holds out the promise of home and then withdraws it, moment after moment. In Adorno's terms, music is the ultimate figure of non-identity: as soon as it is, it isn't.[26]

This sense of a gradual, moment after moment unfolding within music has made its way more generally into criticism of pop music. Indeed, one of the most fruitful ways of establishing common analytical ground has been to analyze music in terms of gradual expansion: Victoria Malawey's work on Björk uses a metaphor of 'emergence', which is defined in terms of an increase or dramatic change in texture or development, something drawn explicitly from Schenker;[27] Mark Spicer analyzes rock music in terms of 'accumulative form';[28] and Keith Negus uses temporal metaphors of narrative.[29] Dai Griffiths puts it succinctly and sarcastically: 'there is one clearly established theory for tonal music, that established by Heinrich Schenker [...] Pop music is tonal music, and so there is no need *not* to apply Schenkerian models to pop music'.[30] Whether or not this is an imposition of traditional methods on popular music,[31] this is nevertheless a way in which the sense that music's status as a temporally unfolding artform is seen as being linked to an increase in conceptual difficulty that is also present in psychoanalysis. I will flesh out all of these issues below with a discussion of Swift's song.

'I Knew You Were Trouble'

As mentioned above, 'I Knew You Were Trouble' was remarkable because it incorporated dubstep, a type of electronic dance music (E.D.M.) typically more resistant and antagonistic than the softer, acoustic sound of Swift's pop music. This was part of a more general fascination on the part of pop producers with E.D.M.: Swift's use of dubstep coincided more generally with the 'surprising rise of dubstep, even as the music [got] more extreme and aggressive' against the backdrop of 'unexpected resurgence of rave in America', in which the genre achieved 'a level of mass popularity that dwarf[ed] its previous incursions into the mainstream'.[32] Inasmuch as dance is generally linked to illegal raves, drugs, and general antisocial behavior, E.D.M. represented a general act of subjective violence against an ideology in America and in the UK.[33] The increased intensity of the rave scene in America began leading to drug-related deaths, and yet, notwithstanding the high-profile death of fifteen-year-old Sasha Rodriguez, the popularity of rave increased unabated.[34] On the other hand, it wouldn't be too much to say that this popularity could have been *because of* the obsession with the violence (particularly against young females), since it was generally seen as a sexually violent musical idiom: indeed, the resurgence of dubstep itself attracted a sexually aggressive male audience, and critics began referring to '"thugstep", "cockstep", and "bukkakestep", and they referred to the low-frequency oscillator riffs as "LFO rape"'.[35] So it would be more accurate to describe the fascination with E.D.M. as a terror that this music would enact a kind of subjective violence onto the pop music world. Yet this act of subjective violence never happened: in an article published in 2015 in the *New Yorker*, Carrie Battan reflected upon this moment that 'E.D.M. has not overtaken culture in the way that was feared; instead, it has put a twist on an old model. Rather than smash everything in its wake, E.D.M. has curled itself around finicky pop impulses'.[36] In other words, if dubstep articulated a sense of violent resistance to the mainstream, any threat of subjective violence against pop quickly became absorbed into the objective violence of marketization.

What I want to foreground first is that 'dubstep' is part of a popular avant-garde, a taxing kind of music characterized by the difficulty we now often associate with modernism broadly conceived. One writer on The Urban Dictionary[37] notes that while dubstep now has mainstream appeal, it 'started off as an underground genre'.[38] The 'underground' here has no stable definition within music scholarship, but another writer on The Urban Dictionary defines it as

> a genre in music and other forms of media intended for an elite audience, that is often characterized by its high levels of originality and experimentation, and does not conform to typical standards, trends, or hypes as set by the popular mainstream media.[39]

In other words, if dubstep is underground then it must be challenging and resistant to the status quo. Another, more incendiary definition defines the 'underground' as a term used by pretentious musical elitists to deflect criticisms and to feel superior. Underground Music is simply music that has not yet gained widespread fame and notoriety. Listening to Underground music does not make you elite; it only means you discovered it through channels other than popular mass media. Many fans of artists like to maintain the label of "Underground" even though the band or artist has gained success and notability.[40]

So, listening to difficult, non-mainstream music is paradoxically desirable even after a band has become mainstream and consequently 'pop'. In both cases, the derogatory terms 'popular' or 'mainstream' here are important, because they suggest that dubstep is a form of high art, which leads us back to a problem flagged up long ago by Simon Frith in *Performing Rites*.[41] Frith takes issue with Bourdieu's

> interest [...] in the creation of a taste hierarchy in terms of high and low: the possession of cultural capital, he suggests, is what defines high culture in the first place. My point is that a similar use of accumulated knowledge and discriminatory skill is apparent in low cultural forms.[42]

In other words, Frith argues that there is also 'such a thing ... as popular cultural capital',[43] that the distinction between the high and the low is present within popular music as well, and manifests in a sense of discriminatory skill or separation from the masses. In fact, this is not merely a re-casting of the problem within the sphere of low art, since we can conceive of the 'underground' as discriminating specifically between different levels of marketization that cut across the high/low divide: for example, David Grazian describes the way that underground musical scenes proliferate in urban areas to counterbalance both 'branded pop entertainment and elite cultural attractions'.[44] Yet, if discriminatory skill defines high art, then popular cultural capital becomes an oxymoron, and the whole discussion risks collapsing into a set of tautologies. Stephen Graham gets around this problem by suggesting that 'underground music'

> positions itself resolutely outside the academy, all the while its harsh sonics gnaw and upbraid the ears [...] Popular culture is used and rejected [...the underground] represents a sort of popular avant-gardism where mass culture is mined for material and inspiration, but where an avant-garde sensibility adopted from Dadaists—egalitarian, yet destructive and challenging—places much of the work beyond the ken of the general public.[45]

There is an ambiguous reasoning here. Partly, the sense of challenge is not aligned solely with modernism or with the avant-garde: 'the underground can be understood as a distinct zone of cultural activity existing "below" or "between", but permeated by and permeating, the high and low mainstreams'.[46]

However, for Graham, underground music is still 'organized around some core sense of aesthetic and political innovation and radicalism', and on these grounds, he 'tentatively link[s] this aspect of the underground and its fringes with some notion of the avant-garde and of modernism, without, however, collapsing the underground into a simple continuation of those traditions or sets of ambitions'.[47] None of this is conclusive, but it is nevertheless the case that dubstep, as a type of underground music more generally, is caught up in a sense of resistance against a prevailing popular ideology present in popular music.

It is here that we need again to turn to the technical features of dubstep. The Urban Dictionary has a number of different definitions of these features: the most well-phrased describes it as 'a music centred around bass [which] ranges in style from melodious instrumentals to dark, techy and distorted numbers';[48] another definition simply provides the words 'womp womp womp womp';[49] the top-rated definition defines it as 'the music that is created from transformers having sex',[50] a description that seems to get to the heart of its grating, mechanical, expansive sound. Central to this sound is the 'bass drop', which is defined in the Urban Dictionary as 'one of the best charictaristics [sic] in Dubstep, Drum and Bass etc. its [sic] normaly [sic] when the percussion pauses for a second and then comes back with a heavier bassline'.[51] In other words, the bass drop is a climactic moment of arrival after a long build-up. A *Saturday Night Live* short, premiered in 2014, parodies the moment of the bass drop eloquently: it begins in a club, in which a crowd of dancers are so hooked in anticipation of the bass dropping, and are so obsessed with the DJ, that when the bass finally drops the extreme release of tension causes the clubbers to go fatally insane: heads begin to explode and one clubber suffers internal bleeding.[52] As Simon Reynolds describes it, 'to be in the audience when [E.D.M. artist] Skrillex unleashes the bass drop is like being zapped by seven lightning bolts at once'.[53] What is so interesting about the moment of the bass drop is that we see a regulation of tension present in the DJ's actions, and yet, when the moment of arrival occurs, it is like a sickly sweet hit of high energy drink, a pure moment of violence. However, this is not merely resistance: while members of the audience in the SNL sketch die horrifically, they appear thrilled to do so. In Žižek's terms, this is a moment of false subjective violence that ultimately functions as part of an objectively violent sense of enjoyment. Moreover, dubstep's status as an underground genre of musical resistance is played out in ongoing contestations over the way that the bass drop is perceived. One writer provides the following definition of dubstep on the Urban Dictionary:

> The fanbase mostly consists of people ranging from 14–18 years of age. Most of these "fans" are preppy kids who listen to dubstep not because they like how it sounds, but because they think it's "cool", and that's what all the "cool" kids listen to. Those kids make up about 85% of the fanbase. The other 25% [sic] are actual dubstep fans, who appreciate the rhythm [sic] and basslines and aren't just looking for filthy drops.[54]

This writer implicitly emphasizes listening to rhythms and basslines—the lead-up to the drop—rather than the drop itself, as the site of the music's value. To be a true, discerning dubstep fan, then, is to appreciate it for *more* than just appreciation of the sickly sweet hit of the bass drop, the term 'filthy' suggesting a level of baseness. Yet, the drop exists by virtue of this lead-up. The drop, then, can be both a complex musical procedure that demands sophisticated listening, and a vulgar or disingenuous device that provides instant gratification.

These contestations over pop music should be seen as part of a wider set of processes that tap into the discriminatory skill linked to underground music in order to target the consumer as an individual subject rather than as part of a mass. As Martin Scherzinger puts it,

> the dynamic between corporate desires and listeners' desires is inherently complex and capricious. To cope with this, the music industry, now part of an oligopolistic multibillion dollar mass-culture industry, has differentiated its markets to correspond precisely with the identitarian categories of race, gender, nationality, class and religion.[55]

Adam Krims follows David Harvey in describing this as the 'flexible accumulation' of post-Fordism, which produces 'an industry with more centralized control and greater product diversification at the same time'.[56] Or, as Timothy D. Taylor puts it, 'if we increasingly inhabit a world of commodities, those very commodities seem to be almost like intimates'.[57] These issues have their roots in contestations over modernism: glossing Adorno and Horkheimer, Scherzinger refers to musical moments of 'pseudo-individualisation', a mechanism that functions to instill 'the halo of free choice or open market on the basis of standardization itself'.[58] This is also what Taylor refers to as the commodification of 'creativity', the creation of 'a new capitalism that is more culturalized than earlier ones',[59] or, in other words, more concerned with normalizing subjectivity itself. The status of resistance, of difficulty, of shock value, has consequently become so omnipresent within capitalism that it risks becoming meaningless. In this light, Žižek's distinction between subjective and objective violence is intriguing because the idea of a true rupture to the fabric of ideology seems to contradict Žižek's own idea that 'stepping out of it [is] the very form of our enslavement to it'. Indeed, Harper-Scott acknowledges the same problem when he writes that

> it is clear that the most rebarbatively "modernist" forms of today ... are in fact the most conventional and ideologically collusive form of art of all, each of their "perversions" sucked greedily into the system of postmodern capitalist consumption.[60]

For Harper-Scott, 'the "shock" element is really an index of the buyer's or the viewer's cultural and economic superiority over the mass'.[61] And yet the placement of "modernist" forms in inverted commas here also reinscribes a separation between true and false modernism that reinforces the prestige of true (resistant) modernism.

Reading the media's response to 'I Knew You Were Trouble' in this light is interesting. Reviews were almost unanimously cynical about the incorporation of dubstep into 'I Knew You Were Trouble': for Randall Roberts, the 'bass drop [is merely] the current stylistic signifier of choice among pop stars looking to expand market share and stay relevant';[62] Marc Hogan agreed, writing that 'dubstep breakdowns have increasingly become just another feature of the ever-changing pop landscape';[63] for Amanda Dobbins, the track was 'good news, unless you were super invested in Taylor Swift's E.D.M. reinvention: The dubstep here is limited to a few "wubs" in the (slightly jarring) chorus';[64] and Allison Stewart found the track 'gratuitous and weird, done for the sake of saying you did it, and so tentative they might not have bothered'.[65] In other words, reviewers were cynical about this use of dubstep in order to display yet again a sense of discriminatory skill: this was not true avant-garde underground music, but a mere simulacrum used in order to sell records to the duped masses. Yet Roberts also conceded that the presence of dubstep should be a good thing, writing that 'pop has been sonically conservative for the past half-decade (at least). Any hint at evolution or surprise from the upper echelons of the charts is a welcome development, [since it] serves as a reminder of pop's fluidity'.[66] So, on the one hand, reviewers were all cynical about the incorporation of dubstep, believing that this was merely an attempt on Swift's part to be "cool", and not a true sense of resistance. Yet at the same time, and perhaps paradoxically, it was seen as a mark of pop's increasing fluidity, the subjective violence of underground resistance again blending seamlessly with the ongoing objective violence of marketization.

Moreover, the way in which dubstep is identified as underground happens through its association with a sense of difficulty, which is not so different to the kind of difficulty associated with modernism. Dubstep has its roots in dub, a Jamaican club music, which Paul Sullivan describes as

> a genre and a process, a "virus" and a "vortex": it draws the listener into a labyrinth, where there are false signposts and "mercurial" trails that can lead to the future, to the past [...] or to nowhere at all.[67]

This is the same kind of pleasure felt by the dancing crowd when watching the DJ, paying close attention to his each move, trying to ascertain when he will let the bass drop. For Sullivan, 'the way in which dub pioneers [...] began deconstructing songs into their constituent parts then rebuilding them into alternative compositions—literally turning them inside out to reveal their "seams"—made the music simultaneously avant-garde and hugely popular'.[68] The fact that dubstep gets its popularity from an avant-garde sense of complexity, of deconstruction, of its coolness and detachment from the mainstream, of its "being led on" by the DJ (and the fact that this was incorporated into a mainstream song that achieved wide success), offers a neat point of tension. In another time and place this would have been known as, to quote Rose Rosengard Subotnik, 'structural listening', a 'process wherein the listener follows and comprehends the unfolding realization, with all its detailed inner relationships of a generating musical conception'.[69] To listen to, say, Schoenberg, and to listen to dubstep, is to listen with a discerning ear. Linking this without qualification to the apprehension of the dubstep drop may seem callous, and yet while a member of a club or a listener to 'I Knew You Were Trouble' may not be listening attentively in order to gain an idea of the track's 'musical "idea"',[70] the pleasures of the labyrinth of dubstep are not so different from those more often associated with Schoenberg.

The mixture of dubstep with pop resulted in an interplay of sonic violence (represented by three distinct bass drops)[71] and violent imagery: the song is married with an extremely dark music video, in which the sonic violence of the track is used to accompany a story about an initially naïve and innocent girl (played by Swift) whose infatuation with a rock musician leads her to become sucked into an underworld of drugs and illicit sex. This loss of innocence is signaled sonically through a contrast between an aggressive, growling bassline and a pure, piercing vocal line. During drop sections, notes of the bassline are detached and punctuated, and, as Brunner writes, a 'darkness emerges from the space between beat and un-played beat. Absence signifies a moreness that is open for difference'.[72] The absences between beats are filled in with very high, scream-like vocals, as though the beats of the bassline are causing physical violence to the singer, being felt 'as a vibrating sensation across the entire body'.[73] This is also reflected in the music video. Towards the middle of the song, the two become embroiled in a bar fight in which a group of older men attack Swift's lover; at one point, the point of contact between one of these men's fists and the younger man's abdomen coincides with one of the bass notes, and the next shot is of Swift doubling over in pain, her scream being heard as a note in the vocal line of the song. These moments underscore the 'distinctive power of sound to [...] produce organic damage'.[74]

This violence also manifests through a deformational lengthening of the song's structure. The song begins with a fairly thin texture that increases with the addition of instruments into the first chorus—we assume that a song's chorus will be accompanied by a dramatic filling out of texture, but the first chorus of 'I Knew You Were Trouble' goes against this with an immediate thinning of the texture that creates an air of expectation. In other words, the first chorus functions as a slide into to the first drop, which occurs immediately after it at around 65 seconds in, or just under a third of the way through the song. So, when Caramanica writes that the 'dubstep wobble arrives about halfway through',[75] this overstatement should be read as reflecting the fact that the first section of the song seems to stretch musical time, as well as bifurcating the track. Yet this first is also accompanied by shots of Swift for the first time seeing a rock band on stage, viewing from afar rather than getting entirely caught up. The failure for the drop and the chorus to coincide, as well as the anticipation we feel vicariously through the eyes of Swift's character, results in a kind of failed first attempt at subjective violence that leads the listener to anticipate the second chorus more intensely. The second dubstep drop is aligned fully with the arrival of the second chorus and consequently accompanied by the most violent imagery—that of the bar fight. Yet the textural plenitude of the dubstep drop increasingly saturates the sound world of 'I Knew You Were Trouble', so by the end of the track it has become normalized, and the moment of violence that occurred earlier on in the track is a distant memory.

The sense that the drop enters 'like a wrecking ball, changing the course not just of the song but also of Ms. Swift's career',[76] suggests that this moment of subjective violence is part of a type of objectively violent discourse that sees many singers or women in the public eye enact a performative 'fall from grace' moment.[77] Allison Stewart not only noted the increased focus on turbulent romantic encounters on the album, but also wrote that 'when it comes to intimate details, Swift is as chaste as a Jonas brother. She spends most of *Red* managing to have it both ways—untouchable virgin as serial dater'.[78] Caramanica agreed, suggesting that Swift is 'without precedent: not as a country star looking for something bigger, but as a pop singer trying hard to maintain an air of innocence'.[79] In a more general sense, the album *Red* (on which 'I Knew You Were Trouble' appeared) was itself divided between Swift's original country sound and a more general 'pop' sound. This was mostly reflected in its three singles, produced by pop writers Max Martin and Shellback. For Caramanica, 'each of the three songs written with Mr. Martin and Shellback feel like inside jokes about the squeaky-clean pop of eras past'.[80] This kind of quotation touches on a rhetoric of degeneration, infection, or corrosion:[81] for Allison Stewart, Max Martin and Shellback did not merely import dubstep as a musical signifier, but rather they had made the choice to '*infect* "I Knew You Were Trouble" with a wobble right out of Hot Topic's dubstep department';[82] Caramanica concurred with this, writing that *Red* 'is lighter on starry-eyed anthems than Ms. Swift's past albums. Almost everything here is corroded in some way'.[83] In other words, the act of subjective violence had the effect of strengthening the promise of a pop music sound that was seen as ideologically normative through becoming nostalgic. In a broader sense, Paul Taylor writes that objective violence occurs partly through 'the excessive concentration upon celebrity figures to the exclusion of more politically important issues, and as this form of symbolic violence becomes the predominant background value of the media, it enables objective violence to continue largely unchecked and unquestioned'.[84] The musical violence enacted upon the pop idiom thus functions both as subjective and objective at the same time.

Conclusion

Where does this leave psychoanalysis, music, and musicology? I would suggest that psychoanalysis should only be used as a difficult theoretical tool in the fight against the forces of global capitalism very carefully. My basic point has been that an assumption is often made within writers on psychoanalysis that to be challenging is to be slow, to be measured, to be conceptually taxing; and these things, in turn, are to be resistant to capitalism. This chapter has highlighted the fact that not only is this not the case, but to be resistant is also to capitulate with capitalism—under capitalism, subjective and objective violence are now one and the same. Applied to pop music, this process becomes apparent: when Randall Roberts writes that the use of dubstep in 'I Knew You Were Trouble' reminds us of 'pop's fluidity', there is still no question that the track remains 'pop' rather than becoming 'dubstep' in any real sense; the 'fluidity' is not a reflection of true subjective violence but rather a sense that pop is able to appeal to many different types of consumer. Quoting Peter Sloterdijk, Žižek describes 'capitalism's split from itself, its immanent self-overcoming'.[85] the way in which pop is 'fluid' while remaining 'pop' is a discursive sleight of hand that allows capitalism to keep functioning by incorporating acts of resistance against it.

Žižek admits at the end of *Violence* that 'it is difficult to be really violent, to perform an act that violently disturbs the basic parameters of social life'.[86] For Žižek, however,

> the threat today is not passivity, but pseudo-activity, the urge to "be active", to "participate", to mark the nothingness of what goes on. People intervene all the time, "do something", academics participate in meaningless debates, and so on [....] Sometimes, doing nothing is the most violent thing to do.[87]

Following this, I want to suggest that discussions about different types of resistance should be abandoned, not because resistance itself should be abandoned, but because the idea of an implicit absolute complicity should be abandoned: pop music may be marketized, but the sense of resistance to marketization is so tightly ingrained in the mechanisms of marketization itself that it does not make sense to suggest that resistance is either inside or outside of the scope of pop music, since resistance and complicity are one and the same. If the use of psychoanalytic cultural critique in musicology involves privileging in psychoanalysis the same aesthetic of difficulty that is also prized as a marketing tool for pop music, then it seems preferable to find a different definition of psychoanalysis; perhaps one that does not set it up in opposition to popular culture, but better one that does not view popular culture as obsessed with simple solutions, instant gratification, and sensual overload. Similarly, modernism will only prove to be an emancipatory locus for musicology if both the focus on its distinctness from popular music and its difficulty as a site of resistance are abandoned.

Notes

1 While there is no clear project, and different writers approach the topic in different ways, there is definitely a trend. See, for example, David Clarke, 'Elvis and Darmstadt, or: Twentieth-Century Music and the Politics of Cultural Pluralism', *Twentieth-Century Music* 4, no. 1 (2007): 3–45; and James R. Currie, 'Music after All', Journal of the American Musicological Society 62, no. 1 (2009): 145–203.
2 Andreas Huyssen, *After the Great Divide: Modernism, Mass Culture, Postmodernism* (Bloomington: Indiana University Press, 1986).
3 J. P. E. Harper-Scott, *The Quilting Points of Musical Modernism: Revolution, Reaction, and William Walton* (Cambridge and New York: Cambridge University Press, 2012), xiv.
4 *Ibid.*, 251.
5 *Ibid.*, 252.
6 Slavoj Žižek, *Violence* (London: Profile Books, 2008), 1–2.
7 Sigmund Freud, *Totem and Taboo* (London and New York: Routledge, 2001); Jacques Lacan, *The Seminar of Jacques Lacan, Book III: The Psychoses*, ed. Jacques-Alain Miller (New York and London: Norton, 1997).
8 Žižek, *Violence*, 2.
9 Slavoj Žižek quoted in Petar Ramadanovic, 'No Place like Ideology (On Slavoj Žižek): Is There a Difference between the Theory of Idoelogy and the Theory of Interpretation?' *Cultural Critique* 86 (2014): 119.
10 Marc Hogan, 'Hear Taylor Swift's Dubstep-Tinged "I Knew You Were Trouble"', *Spin*, October 9, 2012.
11 Jon Caramanica, 'No More Kid Stuff for Taylor Swift', *New York Times*, October 24, 2012.
12 Keith Harris, 'Trace Taylor Swift's Country to Pop Transformation in 5 Songs', *Rolling Stone*, September 9, 2014.
13 Harper-Scott, *The Quilting Points of Musical Modernism*, 185.
14 *Ibid.*, 172.
15 *Ibid.*, 173.
16 *Ibid.*
17 *Ibid.*, 172.
18 *Ibid.*, 186.
19 Allan F. Moore, 'Jethro Tull and the Case for Modernism in Mass Culture', in *Analyzing Popular Music*, ed. Allan F. Moore (Cambridge: Cambridge University Press, 2003), 168.
20 *Ibid.*, 169.
21 Chris Atton, 'Listening to "Difficult Albums": Specialist Music Fans and the Popular Avant-Garde', *Popular Music* 31, no. 3 (2012): 360.
22 Harper-Scott, *The Quilting Points of Musical Modernism*, xiii.
23 Arved Ashby, 'Introduction', in *The Pleasure of Modernist Music: Listening, Meaning, Intention, Ideology*, ed. Arved Ashby (Rochester, NY: University of Rochester Press, 2004), 5.
24 Paul Taylor, *Žižek and the Media* (Cambridge: Polity Press, 2010), 141.
25 Julie Jaffee Nagel and Samuel Bradshaw, 'Coda: Psychoanalysis and Music in the Psyche and Society', *International Journal of Applied Psychoanalytic Studies* 10, no. 2 (2013): 147.
26 Holly Watkins, 'Slavoj Žižek: Responding from the Void', *Contemporary Music Review* 31, no. 5/6 (2012): 459.

27 Victoria Malawey, 'Musical Emergence in Björk's *Medúlla*', *Journal of the Royal Musical Association* 136, no. 1 (2011): 143–147.
28 Mark Spicer, '(Ac)cumulative Form in Pop-Rock Music', *Twentieth-Century Music* 1, no. 1 (2004).
29 Keith Negus, 'Narrative Time and the Popular Song', *Popular Music and Society* 35, no. 4 (2012).
30 Dai Griffiths, 'The High Analysis of Low Music', *Music Analysis* 18, no. 3 (1999): 409.
31 Henry Klumpenhouwer, 'Late Capitalism, Late Marxism and the Study of Music', *Music Analysis* 20, no. 3 (2001): 377–378: 'General commentaries on [...] popular performers and technical or structural analysis of popular music (stylistic analysis as well as the interpretation of individual works, being almost always carried out using the analytical methodologies that had earlier been applied to (tonal) serious music) are now common'.
32 Simon Reynolds, *Energy Flash: A Journey through Rave Music and Dance Culture* (London: Faber & Faber, 2012), 685.
33 Christoph Brunner, 'The Sound Culture of Dubstep in London', in *Musical Performance and the Changing City: Post-Industrial Contexts in Europe and the United States*, ed. Fabian Holt and Carsten Wergin (New York: Routledge, 2013).
34 Reynolds, *Energy Flash*, 686 and 689.
35 *Ibid.*, 702.
36 Carrie Battan, 'Past Peak', *New Yorker*, November 9, 2015.
37 The Urban Dictionary is a crowd-sourced public online dictionary of slang and informal words.
38 Lycr, 'Dubstep, n.', The Urban Dictionary, October 22, 2011. www.urbandictionary.com/define.php?term=dubstep Accessed April 10, 2016.
39 Essix, 'Underground, n., adj.', The Urban Dictionary, April 16, 2005. www.urbandictionary.com/define.php?term=Underground&utm_source=search-action Accessed April 10, 2016.
40 Assjuyo Patruyo, 'Underground Music, n.', The Urban Dictionary, April 5, 2011. www.urbandictionary.com/define.php?term=Underground+Music Accessed April 10, 2016.
41 Simon Frith, *Performing Rites* (Oxford: Oxford University Press, 1996), 6.
42 *Ibid.*, 9.
43 *Ibid.*
44 David Grazian, 'Digital Underground: Musical Spaces and Microscenes in the Post-Industrial City', *Musical Performance and the Changing City: Post-Industrial Contexts in Europe and the United States*, ed. Fabian Holt and Carsten Wergin (New York: Routledge, 2013), 128.
45 Stephen Graham, '(Un)Popular Avant Gardes: Underground Popular Music and the Avant-Garde', *Perspectives of New Music* 48, no. 2 (2010): 13.
46 Stephen Graham, *Sounds of the Underground: A Cultural, Political and Aesthetic Mapping of Underground and Fringe Music* (Ann Arbor: University of Michigan Press, 2016), 8.
47 *Ibid.*, 5–6.
48 ukpat, 'Dubstep, n.', The Urban Dictionary, January 12, 2008. www.urbandictionary.com/define.php?term=dubstep Accessed April 10, 2016.
49 turdburgerEarl, 'Dubstep, n.', The Urban Dictionary, December 22, 2010. www.urbandictionary.com/define.php?term=dubstep Accessed April 10, 2016.
50 carsoncb, 'Dubstep, n.', The Urban Dictionary, August 23, 2010. www.urbandictionary.com/define.php?term=dubstep Accessed April 10, 2016.
51 Dubstep.girl, 'Bass drop, n.', The Urban Dictionary, July 23, 2009. www.urbandictionary.com/define.php?term=dubstep Accessed April 10, 2016.

52 The video is available at www.youtube.com/watch?v=DoUV7Q1C1SU Accessed April 10, 2016. Carrie Battan also mentions this in 'Past Peak'.
53 Reynolds, *Energy Flash*, 685.
54 kidwhohasexperiencewiththishit, 'Dubstep, n.', The Urban Dictionary, July 22, 2011. www.urbandictionary.com/define.php?term=dubstep Accessed April 10, 2016.
55 Martin Scherzinger, 'Music, Corporate Power, and Unending War', *Cultural Critique* 60 (2005): 29.
56 Adam Krims, 'Marxist Music Analysis without Adorno', in *Analyzing Popular Music*, ed. Allan Moore (Cambridge: Cambridge University Press, 2003), 136.
57 Timothy D Taylor, *The Sounds of Capitalism: Advertising, Music, and the Conquest of Culture* (Chicago, IL and London: Chicago University Press, 2012), 239.
58 Scherzinger, 'Music, Corporate Power, and Unending War', 36.
59 Taylor, *The Sounds of Capitalism*, 231.
60 Harper-Scott, *The Quilting Points of Musical Modernism*, 184.
61 *Ibid.*, 185.
62 Randall Roberts, 'First Take: Taylor Swift Accents New Single with Hint of Dubstep', *Los Angeles Times*, October 9, 2012.
63 Hogan, 'Hear Taylor Swift's Dubstep-Tinged "I Knew You Were in Trouble"'.
64 Amanda Dobbins, 'Taylor Swift's Version of Dubstep Is a Little Different than Regular Dubstep', *Vulture*, October 9, 2012.
65 Allison Stewart, 'Taylor Swift's "Red" Is Another Winner, But She Needs to Start Acting Her Age', *Washington Post*, October 22, 2012.
66 Roberts, 'First take'.
67 Paul Sullivan, *Remixology: Tracing the Dub Diaspora* (London: Reaktion Books, 2014), 7.
68 *Ibid.*, 8.
69 Rose Rosengard Subotnik, *Deconstructive Variations: Music and Reason in Western Society* (Minneapolis: University of Minnesota Press, 1995), 150.
70 *Ibid.*
71 At 1′05″, 1′55″, and 2′46″.
72 Brunner, 'The Sound Culture of Dubstep in London', 261.
73 *Ibid.*, 258; Likewise, Bruce Johnson and Martin Cloonan write that the voice is a 'tactile phenomenon experienced through vibrations'. Bruce Johnson and Martin Cloonan, *The Dark Side of the Tune: Popular Music and Violence* (Burlington, VT: Ashgate, 2008), 15.
74 Johnson and Cloonan, *The Dark Side of the Tune*, 14.
75 Caramanica, 'No More Kid Stuff for Taylor Swift'.
76 *Ibid.*
77 For a paradigmatic example, see Huyssen, *After the Great Divide*, 44–62.
78 Stewart, 'Taylor Swift's "Red" Is Another Winner'.
79 Caramanica, 'No More Kid Stuff for Taylor Swift'.
80 *Ibid.*
81 Sullivan writes that dubstep is a '"meta-virus" […] it has infiltrated and informed a host of mutant "strains"'. Sullivan, *Remixology*, 7.
82 Stewart, 'Taylor Swift's "Red" Is Another Winner'.
83 Caramanica, 'No More Kid Stuff for Taylor Swift'.
84 Taylor, *Žižek and the Media*, 146.
85 Žižek, *Violence*, 19.
86 *Ibid.*, 174–175.
87 *Ibid.*, 183.

Part II
Situating music and psychoanalysis

6 Does the psychoanalysis of music have a 'subject'?

Samuel Wilson

In his *Foundations of Music History*, Carl Dahlhaus asked a seemingly simple yet far-reaching question: 'Does music history have a "subject"?'[1] In doing so, he brought a reflexive lens to the discourse of music historiography; he also showed that any subject identified in the writing of music history was a subject invested with cultural and philosophical assumptions. Responding to Dahlhaus's question with a playful misreading, I explore, in a similar gesture, the "subjects" recognized, understood—even constituted—through psychoanalytical discourses about music.

It has been said that in psychoanalytic interpretations of art there 'is first the basic question of who or what is to occupy the position of the patient— the work, the artist, the critic, or some combination or relay of all of these?'[2] *Who or what* is the subject of analysis or—more broadly—of interpretation, when psychoanalysis and music are brought together? I ask this question not with a prescriptive answer in mind, but so as to begin to recognize and reflect upon a number of possibilities. Indeed, one may find the subject goes beyond occupying 'the role of the patient'. It goes without saying that *what* is being interpreted differs for psychoanalysis and for music studies. Clinical psychoanalysis gives us the client, the patient, the analysand—a tangible individual to whom interpretive methods are directed or with whom meanings and outcomes emerge. By contrast, interpretations of musical "meaning" likely start from the score and/or listening experiences and— more recently—attend to recordings and specific occasions of musical performances. As Leo Treitler has pointed out, there is an implied relation between the (imagined) stability of the object of interpretation and its subject: 'As the ideology of musical studies demanded a stable object, it had to demand a stable subject, for one depended on the other'.[3] Recent musicology has, of course, challenged the stability of its object of interpretation—and thus also leads us to question where this leaves the subject. So, to rephrase the central question differently: when psychoanalysis and music speak and listen to one-another, where does interpretation begin, and what kinds of conceptual spaces do these open, spaces in which meanings might emerge?

To pre-echo the trajectory of my response to this question: I suggest that one may identify, broadly conceived, three treatments of "subjects" in psychoanalytically inclined discourses about music, which I tentatively label *tangible, fictional,* and *fictive*—although it should be said from the very beginning that an overdetermined distinction between these subjects is necessarily problematic. The *identity* of these subjects, and their "representation", is the focus of the second half of the chapter. Here, I also explicate these subjects' implied relations to one another through processes such as *identification*. The development of these ideas leads from bringing together numerous sources into conversation, from both psychoanalytically inclined musicologists and musically minded psychoanalysts.

Musical and psychoanalytic subjects

Peter Brooks suggests that classic psychoanalytic criticism 'displaces the object of analysis from the text to some person'.[4] These *tangible subjects* are comparable to the client, patient, or analysand of clinical settings: the music tells us about them; it is taken, perhaps, as a symptom, or as the sublimation of some wish, that has taken on an aesthetic, sonic, symbolic guise. This focus reflects what Alexander Stein calls "applied" psychoanalytic thinking, which often attempts to 'deal with the biography of the composer and attempts to understand the composition through his or her life events', and/or to 'present psychoanalytic treatment studies of musicians and composers'.[5] Approaching psychoanalytic theory through literature, Brooks has also reflected on trends in the methodologies of traditional psychoanalytic criticism. As he puts it: 'Traditional psychoanalytic criticism tends to fall into three general categories, depending on the object of analysis: the author, the reader or the fictive persons of the text'.[6] While "the author" in literature provides a musical parallel, the composer, the reader of musical situations is multiplied—most obviously, as performer(s) and listener(s). The fictive "persons" of a text—or a musical work—can be clear in some cases, as in Opera, which provides us fictional characters. What is less clear is the status of "the subject" in music that lacks these represented persons, such as absolute music. The implications of this issue are discussed in detail below.

Within musical contexts, one may continue to focus his or her attention towards some "tangible" subject, a subject somewhat identical with an observable individual: a composer, a performer, an audience member; in all, one may observe psychological processes taking place in the cause of or response to music. For each of these subjects, music—creating, playing, and listening to music—may enact or enable some psychological function. A classic example of this is the role of *sublimation* in artistic creation, whereby in creating music, and art more generally, the artist expresses in symbolic form some repressed wish or impulse. As Freud puts it, sublimation enables "excessively strong excitations arising from particular sources of sexuality to find an outlet and use in other fields [....] Here we have one of the origins of artistic activity [...]".[7] This interpretational attitude invites an interest in 'the dynamics' of the processes of creating hidden meanings, through which the artist "moulds his [sic] pleasures into a new kind of reality".[8]

Applied psychoanalytic studies of musical individuals are numerous and varied in approach.[9] One example is provided by *psychobiographical* studies, in which the principle aim is gain insight into the psychology of the artist (the composer) through their works, writings, and biographical details. The best-known early example of psychobiography is provided by Freud's 1910 essay 'Leonardo da Vinci and A Memory of His Childhood'.[10] Max Graf's 1911 study of Richard Wagner is the earliest example of a musical psychobiography. Stein calls it 'the first distinctly psychoanalytic inquiry into music and musical creativity'.[11] (Notably, Graf's son was Herbert Graf, "Little Hans", famously analyzed by Freud. He went on to become a successful opera director, including at the Metropolitan Opera in New York.[12]) Edward Hitschmann, in 1915, completed a short study of Franz Schubert. Hitschmann's goal was clear, given his subject of interpretation: the artist and their inner world. The author asked rhetorically, 'What were the inner conflicts which had already made the boy so deeply sensitive and highly impressionable and which had determined his urgent need for release through music?'[13] Hitschmann analyzed a short story written by Schubert, based on one of his dreams, drawing on biographical details in doing so, and concluded that the dream may have, at least in part, functioned to 'succeed in winning to himself [Schubert] the virgin goddess of music [St. Cecelia] and in addition his father's approving love'.[14]

Psychobiographies provide instances when individuals are focused on explicitly as the subjects of analysis. There exist, however, other methods whereby tangible individuals become the subjects of study. As noted above, multiple persons are involved in musical practices of production and consumption. Each provides a tangible subject for psychoanalytic study. One could ask of a performer, for instance, why they chose that profession. What lies behind their choice of instrument: is it the physical relationship offered by it (the feeling of 'cradling the violin under the chin', 'of the reed in the mouth'); how does their life as a performer relate to their upbringing (starting training young); how do they navigate a musical 'object world of teachers, mentors, parents, siblings, idols, rivals, [...etc.]'? What psychological sustenance does performance offer—exhibitionism, a position of control, of even 'omnipotent fantasies of control and/or merger'?[15] Such questions have been asked with regard to musical styles and types of performer, as, for instance, in C. Glenn Cambor, Gerald M. Lisowitz, and Miles D. Miller's 1962 study into thirty American "Jazz Kings", an attempt to profile and 'clarify their personality structures and their interpersonal relationships'.[16]

Similarly, one could ask of listeners their musical preferences, practices of listening, musical identifications, and so on, and what these imply about their mental life past and present. The psychoanalyst Theodor Reik extended this logic beyond the boundaries of concert halls and performance events as such and to moments *after* the act of listening to music had passed.

He asked, 'What does it mean when some tune follows you, occurs to you again and again so that it becomes a haunting melody? [...] when a melody occurs to you in the middle of thoughts of a quite different kind?'[17] His answer was that these tunes opened up hidden meanings and enabled for the subject the disguised expression and release of some thought or feeling that was otherwise repressed. For individuals, certain melodies held clear associations with important moments from their childhoods or their past more generally; Reik cited, by way of example, melodies that haunted him, and that these held hidden connections to his past life in Vienna.[18] The listener would carry away from the concert hall or the opera house musical memories that furnished their mind with musical material to be later deployed and heard internally as a disguised expression of something otherwise repressed or unacknowledged consciously. Reik extended his thesis beyond the listener to the performer—who is, of course, *also* a listener—when he noted that the inner compulsion to hear a melody could elicit its being sung or played. He provided an example of a case study in which, after an intense argument with his wife, a husband—unconsciously and unironically—selected to play on the piano the title song from *I Married an Angel*, a musical (object) choice that constituted a reconciliatory or even confessional musical act.[19] These musical renditions, both on the piano and in the mind's ear, 'fulfil a certain psychological function'. It is for this reason, Reik suggests, that the 'analyst has to listen to the whisper of their meaning while until now he did not give them a second thought, if he gave them any'.[20] Indeed, tunes might also occur to the analyst in their listening to the patient. These also express something disguised in them. In noting this, Reik also recognized that these melodies could be useful in inviting analytic reflections in that they articulated unexpressed feelings and opened associative connections.[21] Reik provoked such questions not only through attending to the tangible subject that is the client, but also by relating this to the position of the analyst, and hence to the intersubjective relation between the two encountered in clinical practice. Music and the discourses that surround it are here opened up as intersubjective spaces negotiated by more than one tangible individual.

By contrast, others look not to a tangible subject—in whose psychical world music functions as an object—but for a subject "in" the music itself. Some music is well suited for this interpretational point of entry. Opera, mentioned earlier, provides us with protagonists and definable subjects, fictional though they are. Hence, I will refer to these as *fictional subjects*. However, looking toward a subject in the music does not meaning forgetting more tangible subjects. The 'listening subject', to borrow a phrase from David Bard-Schwarz, may identify with aspects of an operatic character, and the musical representations of this character's psychological drama (an idea further explored below).[22] Similarly, the "composing subject" may express his or her own wishes and anxieties operatically, with an opera's protagonist standing as an image (an imago, an ideal-I, or even an abject image) of the composer himself or herself.[23] The narrators provided by some lieder similarly offer fictional subjects that are *identifiable* (a word considered in detail below) within the music and/or its text.

Notably, while the tangible subject appears as a relatively autonomous entity, the subject-in-music is readily recognized as fluid in nature—a character in an opera, for instance, is defined by musical material that is related to and permeated by the music of other characters and the (musical) "world" that stages them. A leitmotif may identify a character in Wagner's *Ring* cycle, for instance, but it will unfold in fluid interconnection with other leitmotivic materials. An operatic character, a subject-in-music—like the "musical subject" of the sonata and other musical forms—is an entity defined by what surrounds and penetrates it, sharing harmonic, melodic, and rhythmic content with other material in a given musical work. Indeed, this may serve to remind us, more generally, that the internal world of a subject (be it fictional or tangible) is always related to and interpenetrated by a world around it. Music is perhaps best placed among the arts to remind us of this, given its often-cited ability to transgress ego-boundaries and to breakdown the inner-outer threshold of subject and world, self and other.

Specific characters, protagonists, or images of subjects provide—the listener, the interpreter, the psycho- and music-analyst—a subject towards which attention is focused, and from which meanings, connections, and associations may emerge. Yet, of course, this cannot be the case for all music, as not all music has explicit "subjects" to be taken as the first interpretive points of call. So-called "absolute music", for instance, does not present an image of a subject, at least in the same way that something like opera might. That said, aspects of what could be described as "fictive" musical subjects have been evoked in a number of musicological discourses. These discourses vary extensively, though they have the common feature of acknowledging the apparent presence of a subject, or the articulation of a subject, in music that is without any explicit protagonist. Some examples of *fictive subjects* include: Beethoven's "Heroic" subject (perhaps the paradigmatic example), as described by Scott Burnham in his classic *Beethoven Hero*, and developed more recently by Janet Schmalfeldt and others.[24] Gustav Mahler's music provides a contrasting example: Theodor W. Adorno saw Mahler's symphonies as "novel-symphonies", in which characters and character functions were evoked;[25] Julian Johnson has more recently identified the diverse *voices* that exert subjective presences within these same symphonies.[26] Fictive subjects are thus diverse, and the basis of their appearances operate differently: in the music of Beethoven's Heroic period, the musical work as a totality performs a subject undergoing self-determination; Mahler's musical subjects, by contrast, offer up a plurality of dialogic voices—something more akin to a fragmented totality.

These fictive subjects point us to another feature of music's relationship to subjectivity: music's immanent occasioning of broader cultural, ideological, and historical issues, which are themselves bound up with our view of the subject in question. The classical sonata provides a clear case in point. It does not offer us an explicit protagonist, as in opera and in some Lieder, but instead gives us "musical subjects" that are stated, developed, and synthesized. These musical subjects attend to aspects of subjectivity—and by organizing these aspects thusly, their cultural and ideological implications become apparent. Speaking in the broadest terms, in the sonata, the first thematic area often brought with it associations of masculinity and strength, the second, of a lyrical femininity. *Aspects* of subjectivity—not an auditory image of the subject as whole—were re-presented and, in the course of the musical dialectic, were negotiated. Compromises were sought harmonically and thematically between these two "subject areas", manifesting a compromise between the cultural connotations that these areas performed, including notions of masculinity and femininity, and evocations of rationality and sensuality. It is in their synthesis—through this musical phantasy—that one may finally be offered an audible image of a subject as unitary whole.[27]

Identity, identification, and identifiability

In these terms, musical works offer opportunities for identification and projection for composers, performers, and listeners; these tangible subjects may find—in or through the music—features that resonant with aspects of their own selves. Yet the relation between the tangible subject and that with which, or to whom, they identify is not self-evident. Hence, another question may be posed: *who* or *what* is the object to which the audience member, composer, or performer (unconsciously) relates? Different thinkers provide various answers to this question. What is notable, however, is that many seek implicitly to answer it.

This relation has been understood in terms of subjects identifying with one another, in part or whole: via musical mediation, the listening subject identifies with or projects onto their perception of the composer or performer. Ernst Kris's view of the arts typifies this perspective: as he saw it, the audience member identifies with aspects of the artist him or herself. Here, one tangible subject identifies with another via a relation that is mediated by the artwork. This artwork was, for Kris, a cathected object whose meaning arose in the relation between the artwork's creator and its audience. As Kris wrote in 1952, "We started out as a part of the world which the artist created; we end as co-creators: we identify ourselves with the artist".[28] Here, the artist is the object of identification, and the artwork facilitates this process. Considering our relationship to these subjects, the psychoanalyst, the interpreter, may also ask why they are interested in the life and music of one artist, as opposed to any other. Theodor Reik did just this, and asked himself why he was so interested in researching the life and music of Gustav Mahler: why choose him as his subject of study, how did he as researcher identify with the composer and his music, and what desires or needs did this identification fulfil for him symbolically?[29]

Fictional subjects provide similar opportunities for acts of identification. In music with clearly defined protagonists, fictional subjects in the music may resonate unconsciously with (aspects of) of the listening subject. Richard Rusbridger has noted this in relation to Mozart's *Don Giovanni*. As he puts it, the dark themes explored in the opera, which tell us something about the psychology of the eponymous character, also evoke 'in us [the listener, the interpreter] our own abandonment, and our own sexual violence, our oedipal claims and our own remorse'.[30] Yet the operation of the listener's acts of identification and projection is less clear where a subject articulated musically—be this tangible or fictional—is not readily discernible, as for instance in the case of absolute music.

This music still, arguably, provides places for fictive subjects or musical representations of aspects of subjects that might be unconsciously identified with by the listener, performer, or composer. Melody and musical themes provide excellent examples. There is a longstanding association of these musical features with subjective presence—with a sublimated voice that seems to be expressing itself.[31] While the concept of the fictive subject, introduced above, is not reducible to melody or theme, its subjecthood is often foregrounded at such moments of presence: this presence can go on a harmonic journey and find itself thematically changed and transformed over its course, as is the fictive subject in accordance with this. In these terms, themes provide instances where musically sublimated voices are speaking up, voices that arise from, give form to, or are traces of one subject or many. Correspondences between theme, melody, voice, and subjecthood are made explicit in psychoanalytic accounts such as Desiderius Mosonyi's 1935 study. Monsonyi celebrated melody as music's most individualistic and developed feature. As he put it, melody is "the only musical form of individual discharge, since rhythm is motoric, premusical, and harmony beyond the individual".[32] Melody here provided an articulation of the ego and gave shape to the self; it lifted music above the rhythmic gesticulations and release demanded by the id and a state of bodily plenitude.

This act of "identification" can be read in another, supplementary way. The (tangible, fictional, fictive) subject is not only *identified with* in a number of ways (by the listener, analyst, interpreter…): it is also *identifiable as* a subject in so far as "there is" a subject that is symbolically recognizable—in as much as this subject can be said to "have" or "articulate" an identity in the first place. These subjects are in some sense "represented" musically such that they can be identified as possessing some kind of symbolic presence, *of* "being subjects" as such. The former situation—*identification with*—functions for a listener (to give one example) where he or she finds the symbolic fulfilment in the music of something for oneself. The latter—the condition of being *identifiable as* a subject—exists (or at least seems to exist) inherently, as an autonomous identity that is "simply there" as an aspect of the music: it is *present* as a melody, as a theme, as an operatic character, as a song's implied narrator. This perhaps recalls Julia Kristeva's suggestion that the subject is knowable and identifiable only in so far as this is articulated symbolically; as she puts it in *Revolution in Poetic Language*, 'Signifying systems alone allow us to deduce that the subject is a fixed point'.[33] However, that this symbolic existence always leaves something in remainder. Indeed, it is notable that music which seems to lack a melody or, more broadly, some focal point of articulation (for example, some minimalist music) often also connotes a state that is somehow "pre-subjective" or "subjectless", in that the boundaries of a discernible subject seem to have become dissolved, evoking what Freud labels an "oceanic feeling" of limitlessness.[34] This music apparently lacks a sublimated voice that is identifiable, that which marks the presence of speaking/singing subject, or at least its trace.

It has been commonly suggested that aspects of music may enable our mastery of the (sonic) world around us—or, broadly, that music diversely *fulfills* psychological desires and need. "Identifying" subjects, subjects that may be identified with, seems to imply some terms or other through which subjects become identifiable. Music has been said to "*represent*", however abstractly, psychological states and processes, to—in our terms—represent subjects or aspects of them such that they are (unconsciously) identifiable on these terms. It should be acknowledged immediately that the word "represent", while useful for our purposes, is liable to being easily misunderstood; it could be perhaps taken to imply authorial intention on the part of the composer—the idea that the composer consciously decided to sonically depict *the mirror stage* or the infant's *fort-da* game. This is not the case. "Representation" may here be understood better through a psychoanalytic frame of reference: something as deep-seated as oedipal conflict (for example) may be *symbolically worked through* time and time again in dreams and waking life— and in music and art—without conscious authorial intention. Dramas such as these, it has been argued, are shared, prototypical experiences, recognized and intuitively explored unconsciously, and ever partially, by composer, performer, and listener alike. Furthermore, they are not the only, "true" meanings of given musical works and experiences of music; however, they do still remain one source, among others, of meaning and significance.

The apparent opposition between fulfilling and representing can be immediately problematized on the basis that doing (fulfilling psychological functions such as our need for mastery of our world) and depicting (representing psychological functions and processes) both serve some psychological need on the part of the subject: musical representations of "psychic turmoil", for example, can enable its symbolic or imagined working through. Music might fulfill or represent psychological needs of various subjects—tangible, fictional, and fictive—and it might thus be interpreted in part through interconnections between these subjects. For example, through processes of identification (and/or projection), the psychical processes of a fictional operatic character—represented musically and *identifiable as* a subject—may be *identified with* by the listener, such that the representation of the former may symbolically meet something of the latter's psychological needs.

The view taken of the subject profoundly affects our view of fulfilment and representation, or of doing subjectivity and of identifying it. With a "tangible" subject in focus, the analyst-interpreter foregrounds the functional: they ask, even where representation is at work, "what does this do for the subject?" Some forms of the representational (taken psychoanalytically) are foregrounded most evidently in neo- and post-Lacanian studies that focus on those symbolic systems that exceed an individual for whom music acts functionally. As explored below, Lacanian interests into transindividual systems such as language manifest this most obviously. Although, again, one should be careful not to separate doing and depicting too vehemently. Indeed, language itself is not reducible to representation, and involves other (functional, performative, material, structural...) aspects.

Hence, doing and depicting subjectivity in music are different registers that are not mutually exclusive. They instead might be switched between in the act of analysis-interpretation; one could, for example, talk of Schubert the man, his music's meaning, and, in the same discussion, regard these facts in light of his compositions' context in a symbolic universe.[35] Put another way, his music could be said to serve the psychological needs of the composer and his listeners (it *does* things for them), while also "representing" psychological states and processes in a more abstract sense (it *"depicts"* things). Ravel's opera, *L'enfant et les sortilèges* may represent an infantile anxiety-situation while simultaneously functioning to evoke now sublimated memories of this situation in the listener.[36] As David Bard-Schwarz has written, music can '"remind" us of something we can only imagine', connecting fantasies with 'a wide variety of theoretical, historical, and personal contexts'.[37] Cutting across these registers, one need not situate music's significance in any of these contexts exclusively; yet, at the same time, it is prudent to identify these different registers and the interpretational possibilities, limitations, and the methodological priorities implied through the foregrounding of any one over the others.

The "depiction" of subjectivity is clearest in accounts where musical works, or passages from these works, have been interpreted as staging or symbolically manifesting specific psychological processes or developmental dramas. Here, music has provided what one could describe as a kind of auditory "subject image", if one that is only partial or particularized. Instances of this kind of account are numerous and varied, although excellent examples are provided by Bard-Schwarz's interpretations, in his *Listening Subjects,* of songs from the Beatles to Schubert that, he argues, invoke psychoanalytic "plots". In *Winterreise,* for example, 'the composer constructs a fantasy of a male narrator who wanders in a winter landscape in search of a subjectivity he imagines to have resided in desire for a female object'.[38] Also reflecting on music's "representational" qualities, Ellen Handler Spitz reads George Crumb's *Ancient Voices of Children* as a work that echoes or engages early experiences of separation and individuation of the child from the mother. The work musically dramatizes the role of the voice in the mediation of this process—this echoes those psychical mechanisms that underpin separation and individuation, and the pleasures and anxieties associated with these processes.[39] Sarah Reichardt has explored aspects of Shostakovich's string quartets as embodying problematic relationships to the Lacanian Real—this is observed, for instance, in the musically dramatized relation to death, and the gap between death and its symbolization, expressed through the treatment of closure in the Seventh Quartet.[40]

In all cases such as these, the "music itself" seems to act as the locus of psychological drama; subjective states and/or processes are staged, manifested—and sometimes symbolically worked through—in the musical treatment of fictional subjects (as in the Schubert and Crumb examples) or fictive subjects (as in the case of Shostakovich's quartets). That said, these musical representations of psychological states and/or processes nonetheless relate to or affect tangible listeners. As Reichardt herself puts it in respect to her focus on the crises of subjectivity manifested in Shostakovich's quartets, 'In Shostakovich's music listeners find articulations of their own anxieties'. Indeed, 'the ambiguities in the music allow the listeners to redeploy the signifying act such that it reflects how they experience existence'.[41]

Thus, music's ability to "represent"—however abstractly—can be put to work in the psychological roles it may play for tangible subjects. Indeed, the cultural, "extra-musical"—and, as such, "public"—meanings attached to pieces of music relate to our (apparently) private, interior hearings of them. Theodor Reik's "haunting melodies" provide clear instances in which one may observe music's mediation between public and private spheres. Reik argued that music depicting, for example, mockery and irony could arise from the unconscious of the (tangible) subject when they needed to internally express, in a disguised form, an impulse to mock another; these were moments at which 'hostile and defiant impulses crossed the threshold of preconscious thinking in the disguise of familiar tunes'.[42] Similarly, Reik demonstrated how the reoccurrence of a sad and mournful melody (from Tchaikovsky's Fourth Symphony) occurred to a patient at a time when they felt they "should" be happy and joyous, when their life was going well—this Reik called a 'tuneful paradox'. This enabled 'a breakthrough of an unconscious emotion' associated with the guilt of the patient's finding himself to be happy, a guilt rooted in the patient's upbringing.[43] Reik argued that one should recognize the analytic and therapeutic relevance of these often reoccurring tunes. Their appearance for individuals negotiates meanings that are both publicly "represented" (sadness, mockery) and rooted in the personal experiences of these individual subjects.

Through positioning tangible subjects as the subject of one's focus, music has been commonly understood as a symptom of something unsaid. Such is the case with Reik's haunting melodies, which enable the disguised expression of something otherwise (consciously) unsayable. The idea of "music as symptom" was incorporated into clinical practice as early as 1923, when Van der Chijs 'reported on two patients whose compositions were analysed in the course of analytic treatment'.[44] Summarizing a view of art held widely by psychoanalysts of the early and mid-twentieth century, Richard Sterba wrote in 1940 that, the 'fundamental dynamic force at the root of a work of art is an unfulfilled wish of the artist; just as in dreams and fantasies the work of art represents this wish as fulfilled'.[45] But, as Gilbert J. Rose has pointed out more recently, music's ability to abstractly "represent" in aesthetic form some inner turmoil, desire, or need also invites an act of self-reflexion on the part of the subject. The creation of art and music as an externalization that enables a nuanced concretisation of something felt: 'Attempting to objectify thoughts and feelings in whatever form discloses them more fully to oneself.'[46] One could extend this idea by saying that musicking forges an object with which the subject has an intimate link—it is "a part" of them—but that may be regarded simultaneously as autonomous, concretized thing that stands "apart" from them.

The recognition of music's ability to represent something of or for the subject has taken vulgar forms. It has been noted that early Freudian criticism tended to be overtly symbolic. It took the artwork

> as if it were a dream to be decoded in terms of a latent message hidden behind a manifest content: "This is not a pipe; it is really a penis" [....] In such readings the artist is the ultimate source to which symbols point: the work is taken as his symptomatic expression.[47]

This is a clear instance in which a tangible subject, the artist or the composer, is the ultimate interpretational referent. With regard to literature, Peter Brooks has likewise suggested that orthodox Freudian criticism advocated 'that all that appears is a sign, that all signs are subject to interpretation and that they speak messages that ultimately tell stories that contain the same *dramatis personae* and the same narrative functions for all of us'.[48] This mode of criticism opens the possibility that readers—or, in the case of music, listeners—might also be the subjects of interpretational focus; allegedly "universal" psychological themes and functions are brokered by a text (i.e. musical works and performances), and composers, performers, and listeners are all "subject to" these forces. The composer unknowingly manifests aspects of the (e.g.) Oedipus complex, which bear pressures on the compositional act; the listener unconsciously "recognizes" these same forces on hearing the musical work in performance, and these psychological dramas are correspondingly stirred in them. Of course, this view presumes tangible subjects as the focus of one's investigation, a certain relation between them and, indeed, it implies a certain formulation of subjectivity as such—as subject to the Oedipus complex, if one were to entertain that example.

Thus, it is not only *who* constitutes the subject of interpretation that I want to draw attention to, but also the manner in which this focus implies a particular conception of subjectivity. One might ask, of a psychoanalytic study, if the subject is presumed to function through universalized principles (say, oedipal conflict) or, alternatively, if the study documents the particularities of a specific kind, moment, or model of subjectivity (one that is perhaps argued to be culturally or historically contingent); indeed, a study might explore some dialectic between the universal and the particular. Furthermore, one might ask: what normative or ideological assumptions are implicit in presuming universality or particularity? This question not only affects tangible subjects, as observed, for instance, in the orthodox Freudian view, but also those that are fictional and fictive. As Maud Ellmann has pointed out, the analysis of fictional subjects can fall into a presumed and unproblematized generalization about the nature of subjectivity. Ellmann writes of Ernest Jones's *Hamlet and Oedipus* that Jones

> makes the fundamental error of treating Hamlet as a real person, vexed by unconscious impulses unfathomable even to the text itself [....] Unlike a real analysand, he cannot lie down on the couch and free associate about his dreams or recapitulate the traumas of his infancy.[49]

Most importantly, argues Ellmann, 'Hamlet *never had a childhood*', leading Jones to overlook 'the verbal specificities of Shakespeare's text to focus on its universal archetypes'.[50] The universalism assumed in an act of interpretation such as this erases the particularity of the text under scrutiny; this interpretation paradoxically leads to a loss of meaning where the "same old psychoanalytic story" (Oedipus!) is merely uncovered once again.[51]

Peter Brooks contrasts orthodox Freudian perspectives with approaches that offer 'the refusal of any privileged position in analysis', as developed by some poststructuralists.[52] Brooks ultimately concludes that productive psychoanalytic criticism enables us to appreciate that meaning is not either "in the text" or in its readers: it is 'in the dialogic struggle and collaboration of the two, in the activation of textual possibilities in the process of reading'.[53] I would like to suggest that this view is concordant with the status of subjects as explored here: the sense that psychoanalytic perspectives on music can and do productively navigate multiple interpretational registers that pertain to subjects that are tangible or "real" (in the everyday rather than Lacanian sense of the word), fictional, and fictive, while simultaneously embracing heteronomous transubjective or transindividual concerns that, potentially, call into question the autonomous identity of any given subject as such.

In this view, music is taken as a discourse, one indicative, constitutive, or performative of different modalities of sociality and ideology. In his editor's introduction to *Discourse in Psychoanalysis and Literature,* Shlomith Rimmon-Kenan writes that 'The word "discourse" [...] shift[s] the emphasis away from the personality of the artist, the creative process or the psyche of the fictional characters'.[54] This word also invokes a focus on the 'rhetorical structures and textual strategies' of the work, and their capacities to convey and be invested with 'desire, power, and other aspects of subjectivity'.[55] I suggest that the fictive musical subject can be understood in its discursive constitution, and that within this it coheres broad social and philosophy issues that exceed the boundaries of the naïvely taken "subject itself". This subject unfolds in social and philosophical contexts, contexts on which, conversely, its very identification is reliant.

Looking to the *processes* that underpin given manifestations of the subject accords with some recent trends in neo- and post-Lacanian musicology (although it is not solely in Lacanian thought that one may locate such theoretical connections). These perspectives have explored necessarily partial musical "representations" of subjects and of processes constitutive of subjectivity. The autonomy of the subject—and the autonomy of the music—is often challenged on these terms; the autonomy of both relies on practices of representation that go beyond the self-referentiality of either—these are practices that, put another way, are heteronomous by their very nature. Indeed, such approaches have often engaged a theoretical richness that draws in ideas from philosophy, hermeneutics, Critical Theory, and elsewhere.

Intermingling with ideas that trace diverse intellectual lineages, Lacanian concepts have provided focal lenses for the observation and interpretation of musical phenomena—these concepts include the *mirror stage,* the *objet petit a*, and the *point de capiton*.[56] In the terms outlined here, I would argue that these concepts enable us to better understand music's "representation" and "doing" of the subject(s) in process. The notion of the *objet petit a*, for instance, has been brought into dialogue with ideas from outside of parochial psychoanalytic-theoretical discourses. As Kenneth Smith has noted, this concept is central to the functioning of desire, which is 'inscribed in linguistic systems'. He takes music in as one such system, as "language" in the Lacanian sense, in that it is a 'discontinuous system of signifiers' that take on meaning through their interrelation.[57] J.P.E. Harper-Scott is likewise interested in the functioning of desire within musical language and deploys the *objet petit a* as part of his philosophical-psychoanalytic-interpretative conceptual arsenal. Pointing to Wagner's prelude to *Tristan und Isolde*, and to Britten's *Death in Venice*, he notes how harmonically one can desire a harmonic resolution via an object that is not present yet implied. At the same time, were this object to be present, we would realize that this does not meet our needs: 'We feel a passionate desire for something we feel we can name [...] yet if we were presented with it we would know immediately that we had been mistaken'.[58]

This understanding of the musical subject accords with some recent trends in psychoanalytic criticism. As Tim Dean has written,

> Whereas traditional psychoanalytic criticism decoded the neurotic conflicts of individual artists (finding in writers' and painters' characters the surrogates of warring parts of their selves), contemporary

psychoanalytic criticism demystifies the transindividual struggles (whether social or ideological) that the work of art is understood to encode.[59]

A focus on "fictive subjects" speaks to latent yet already present interests in transindividual or transubjective modalities of criticism and interpretation. Indeed, this transubjective focus is not a "fourth" subject as such—one added to a roster of *tangible, fictional,* and *fictive*—but instead provides grounds for questioning the integrity of these subjects' perceived autonomy and solidity; the existence of term "trans-" denies these subjects' discreteness from one-another and points rather to the ongoing process of subject formation. The boundaries of tangible subjects (this or that individual "outside of" the music) and fictional and fictive (subjects "in" the music) are blurred where this individual's sense of self is shaped through engagement with musical subjects undergoing dynamic acts of transformation. Appearances of these subjects are thus now recognized to obscure elements crucial to their very constitution: the unconscious, non-identical processes that drive the possibility of variegated appearances of any subject imagined to be stable, self-identical, and—as explored above—*identifiable* as such. Indeed, music, owing to its often-cited ability to blur the boundaries between itself and the listener that it envelops, is well-placed to call attention to the meaningful interrelation of subjects that characterizes the arts more generally.[60]

Psychoanalytic theory, in these terms, does not finally show us what the music "really means".[61] Instead, it gives us nuanced and far-reaching modalities of listening to and thinking about music and subjectivity. This is one respect in which psychoanalytic tools are valuable to critical music studies. Bringing music and psychoanalysis together implies often unacknowledged ideas about what the subject of study constitutes in the first place. To ask if the psychoanalysis of music has a subject is also to inquire into the political and philosophical cartographies that make its position identifiable in the musical and musicological discourses that chart it. In invoking the terms *tangible, fictional,* and *fictive,* I have suggested a nominal legend for this map. I do this with the important caveat that none of these positions maintains absolute autonomy from the others—something that is apparent once one considers the heteronomous transubjective processes that underpin and undermine these subjects' perceived stability.

With this in mind, I suggest two questions, to be carried as tools of inquiry when advancing though this terrain: First, in psychoanalytic interpretations of music, what is considered identifiable as the subject of focus (what is its identity)—and how are other subjects presumed to relate to it though, for example, acts of identification and projection? Second, if the subject is an unvoiced hermeneutic center, what kind of subject is this presumed to be? Or, to put this second question slightly differently: what is left

Psychoanalysis of music 133

unsaid, hidden—even repressed—when one imagines and speaks of musical meanings and subjectivities?

Notes

1 Chapter 4: 'Does music history have a "subject"?', in Carl Dahlhaus, *Foundations of Music History*, trans. J.B. Robinson (Cambridge: Cambridge University Press, 1983). My thanks to Stephen Downes for his insightful comments on an early version of this chapter.
2 Hal Foster, Rosalind Krauss, Yve-Alain Bois, and Benjamin H.D. Buchloch, *Art since 1900: Modernism, Antimodernism, Postmodernism* (London: Thames and Hudson, 2004), 18.
3 Leo Treitler, 'Reflections on the Communication of Affect and Idea through Music', in *Psychoanalytic Explorations in Music: Second Series*, ed. Stuart Feder, Richard L. Karmel, and George H. Pollock (Madison, CT: International Universities Press, 1993), 57.
4 Peter Brooks, 'The Idea of a Psychoanalytic Literary Criticism', in *Discourse in Psychoanalysis and Literature*, ed. Shlomith Rimmon-Kenan (London: Methuen, 1987), 2.
5 Alexander Stein, 'Psychoanalysis and Music', in *Textbook of Psychoanalysis*, ed. Glen O. Gabbard, Bonnie E. Litowitz, and Paul Williams, 2nd edition (Washington and London: American Psychiatric Association, 2012), 553.
6 Brooks, 'The Idea of a Psychoanalytic Literary Criticism', 2.
7 Freud cited in Pinchas Noy, 'The Psychodynamics of Music—Part 1', *Journal of Music Therapy* 3, No. 4 (1966), 128.
8 Freud cited in Foster et al., *Art since 1900*, 20.
9 A selection can be found in part 'III. Studies of Composers and Compositions' in Feder et al., *Psychoanalytic Explorations in Music: Second Series* (Madison, CT: International Universities Press, 1993).
10 Sigmund Freud, *Leonardo da Vinci and a Memory of His Childhood*, ed. James Strachey, trans. Alan Tyson (New York and London: W.W. Norton and Company, 1961).
11 Stein, 'Psychoanalysis and Music', 552.
12 Julie Jaffee Nagel, *Melodies of the Mind: Connections between Psychoanalysis and Music* (London: Routledge, 2013), 16–17.
13 Edward Hitschmann, 'Franz Schubert's Grief and Love' [1915], *American Imago* 7 (1950), 68.
14 Hitschmann, 'Franz Schubert's Grief and Love', 74.
15 Stein, 'Psychoanalysis and Music', 556–557.
16 Noy's summary of the study. 'The Psychodynamics of Music—Part 5', *Journal of Music Therapy* 4, No. 4 (1967), 117. See C. Glenn Cambor, Gerald M. Lisowitz, and Miles D. Miller, 'Creative Jazz Musicians: A Clinical Study', *Psychiatry* 25 (1962): 1–15.
17 Theodor Reik, *Haunting Melody: Psychoanalytic Experience in Life and Music* (New York: Da Capo Press, 1983), vii.
18 *Ibid.*, 16–19.
19 *Ibid.*, 15–16.
20 *Ibid.*, 122. In this spirit, Lawrence Kramer develops Freud's thoughts about a case explored in *The Interpretation of Dreams*, and considers how music material from *Fidelio* and Beethoven's Ninth became material suitable to represent erotic content in the dream of one of Freud's patients. See Kramer's *Opera and Modern Culture: Wagner and Strauss* (Berkeley, Los Angeles, and London: University of California Press, 2004), 32–36.

134 *Samuel Wilson*

21 Reik, *Haunting Melody*, 19–24.
22 David Bard-Schwarz, *Listening Subjects: Music, Culture, Psychoanalysis* (Durham, NC and London: Duke University Press, 1997).
23 In Zemlinsky's *Der Zwerg* (1919–1920), for example, 'it was plainly understood' that "the Dwarf" represented the composer himself, enabling him to give aesthetic form to his desires and anxieties about his own self-image'. See Kenneth Smith, 'Lacan, Zemlinsky, and Der Zwerg: Mirror, Metaphor, and Fantasy', *Perspectives of New Music* 48, No. 2 (2010), 78–80.
24 Scott Burnham, *Beethoven Hero* (Princeton, NJ: Princeton University Press, 1995); Janet Schmalfeldt, *In the Process of Becoming: Analytic and Philosophical Perspectives on Form in Early Nineteenth-Century Music* (Oxford: Oxford University Press, 2011); see also Samuel Wilson, 'After Beethoven, after Hegel: Legacies of Selfhood in Schnittke's String Quartet No. 4', *International Review of the Aesthetics and Sociology of Music* 45, No. 2 (2014): 311–334.
25 Theodor W. Adorno, *Mahler: A Musical Physiognomy*, trans. Edmund Jephcott (Chicago, IL: University of Chicago Press, 1992).
26 Julian Johnson, *Mahler's Voices: Expression and Irony in the Songs and Symphonies* (New York and Oxford: Oxford University Press, 2009).
27 By contrast with the classical sonata, and Beethoven's Heroics, one could take Mahler's fragmented totality as enacting anxieties over the irreconcilability of different aspects of the subject at that later historical moment. Here, one could make productive connections with both the Freudo-Lacanian 'split subject', as well as Adorno's claims about the impossibility of dialectical synthesis between subject and object in twentieth-century modernity, as explored in his *Philosophy of New Music,* ed. and trans. Robert Hullot-Kentor (Minneapolis: University of Minnesota Press, 2006).
28 Kris cited in Pinchas Noy, 'The Psychodynamics of Music—Part 2', *Journal of Music Therapy* 4, No. 1 (1967), 20.
29 Reik reflects also on the writer's block he experienced after completing the research for his book on Mahler. See in particular Reik, *Haunting Melody*, Chapter XXV, 'Last Movement', 355–376.
30 Richard Rusbridger, 'The Internal World of Don Giovanni.' *International Journal of Psychoanalysis* 89, No. 1 (2008), 192.
31 On the idea of "voice" as subjective presence in non-vocal music, see Johnson, *Mahler's Voices*.
32 Mosonyi cited in Noy, 'The Psychodynamics of Music – Part 2', 21 (Noy's translation). Originally from Desiderius Mosonyi, 'Die Irrationalen Grundlagen der Musik', *Imago* 21 (1935): 207–226.
33 Julia Kristeva, *Revolution in Poetic Language*, trans. Margaret Waller (New York: Columbia University Press, 1984), 94–95.
34 Indeed, some have explored musical representations of subjects *becoming* identifiable, of the move towards their symbolic (re)presentation. See for example David Bard-Schwarz's discussions of the acoustic mirror stage and the sonic formation of identity in Chapter 1: 'Music as Sonorous Envelope and Acoustic Mirror', in his *Listening Subjects* and Chapter 2: 'Voices', in his *An Introduction to Electronic Art through the Teachings of Jacques Lacan: Strangest Thing* (London and New York: Routledge, 2014).
35 As Bard-Schwarz does regarding Schubert's *Winterreise*. See his *Listening Subjects*.
36 See Melanie Klein, 'Infantile Anxiety-Situations Reflected in a Work of Art and in the Creative Impulse', *International Journal of Psychoanalysis* 10 (1929): 436–443.
37 Bard-Schwarz, *Listening Subjects*, 14–15.

38 *Ibid.*, 37. Another example is provided by Ryan R. Kangas' article on Mahler's "Resurrection" symphony. He outlines similarly identifies a psychoanalytic "plot" whereby the work charts a move from melancholia to mourning. See his 'Mourning, Remembrance, and Mahler's "Resurrection"', *19th-Century Music* 36, No. 1 (2012): 58–83.
39 Ellen Handler Spitz, 'Separation-Individuation in a Cycle of Songs: George Crumb's Ancient Voices of Children', *The Psychoanalytic Study of the Child* 42 (1987): 531–543.
40 See Chapter 3: 'The Space Between: Codas, Death and the Seventh String Quartet, Op. 108 (1960)' in Sarah Reichardt, *Composing the Modern Subject: Four String Quartets by Dmitri Shostakovich* (Aldershot: Ashgate, 2008).
41 Reichardt, *Composing the Modern Subject*, 13.
42 Reik, *Haunting Melody*, 77.
43 *Ibid.*, 211.
44 Pinchas Noy, 'The Psychodynamics of Music—Part 3', *Journal of Music Therapy* 4, No. 2 (1967), 45.
45 Richard Sterba, 'The Problem of Art in Freud's Writings', *Psychoanalytic Quarterly* 9 (1940), 258.
46 Gilbert J. Rose, *Between Couch and Piano: Psychoanalysis, Music, Art and Neuroscience* (Hove and New York: Brunner-Routledge, 2004), 154.
47 Foster et al., *Art since 1900*, 19.
48 Brooks, 'The Idea of a Psychoanalytic Literary Criticism', 3.
49 'Introduction', in *Psychoanalytic Literary Criticism*, ed. Maud Ellmann (London: Longman, 1994), 3.
50 Ellmann, 'Introduction', 3–4 (emphasis in the original).
51 *Ibid.*, 2–4.
52 Brooks, 'The Idea of a Psychoanalytic Literary Criticism', 3.
53 *Ibid.*, 14.
54 'Introduction', in *Discourse in Psychoanalysis and Literature*, ed. Shlomith Rimmon-Kenan (London: Methuen, 1987), xii.
55 Rimmon-Kenan, 'Introduction', xii.
56 As Kenneth Smith points out, there are numerous discussions of music in which Lacanian ideas are 'employed on an ad hoc basis in order to explicate compositional ideas [within particular musical works]'. Smith, 'The Tonic Chord and Lacan's Object *a* in Selected Songs by Charles Ives', *Journal of the Royal Musicological Association* 136, No. 2 (2011), 354. Smith argues that some Lacanian ideas might become relatively generalisable, with regard to some specific features of music.
57 *Ibid.*, 354.
58 J.P.E. Harper-Scott, 'Britten and the Deadlock of Identity Politics', in *Masculinity in Opera*, ed. Philip Purvis (New York and Abingdon: Routledge, 2013), 159.
59 Tim Dean, 'Art as Symptom: Žižek and the Ethics of Psychoanalytic Criticism', *Diacritics* 32, No. 2 (2002), 29.
60 For a discussion of the idea that music might blur boundaries of the self, see the Introduction to this collection.
61 Roy Schafer summarized in Nagel, *Melodies of the Mind*, 22.

7 Jung and the transcendent function in music therapy

Rachel Darnley-Smith

In his seminal essay, 'The Transcendent Function', published in 1957 but originally completed during the First World War, Carl Jung advocated the ideal of an inner dialogue taking place between the conscious and unconscious, at best like 'between two human beings with equal rights'.[1] He extended the metaphor with the following comment: 'the present day shows with appalling clarity how little able people are to let the other man's argument count, although this capacity is a fundamental and indispensable condition for any human community'.[2] Jung repeatedly stated that 'any psychological theory is in the first place the expression of its author's subjectivity', and 1916 is considered by one commentator as 'certainly a very special year in Jung's own life marked as it was by the solution of the severe crisis which followed his rupture with Freud and the psycho-analytic movement'.[3] Jung's determination to make sense of both his own inner turmoil, his 'psychic situation', and the 'concrete reality of the outer conflict', of war in Europe, is made explicit in his autobiographical writings, where he describes intense fears that he experienced in the forms of extended fantasies, visions, and dreams.[4]

It is not insignificant, therefore, that the major theme of the chapter is the expansion of Jung's notion of the psyche as a synthesis of conscious and unconscious influences and the process in analytic treatment of the holding *together* of what might be understood as "opposites". To this end, Jung set out a radical idea. He suggests that emotional disturbance, both psychoses and less severe disturbance and unhappiness, 'could be dealt with, not by clarifying it intellectually' but also by giving the 'mood' an external, 'visible shape' through art media such as painting or drawing, as a way of giving fantasy free play.[5] Jung distinguished between active and passive fantasies: passive fantasy making was a process in which the conscious did not participate, dreams being a prime example.[6] Alternatively, the active fantasy was evoked by a conscious waking attitude 'directed to the perception of unconscious contents'.[7] It was the giving rein to active fantasy through art-making that was advocated by Jung as being so productive, he wrote, for here the conscious and unconscious personality of the subject flow together into a common product in which both are united. Such a fantasy can be the highest expression of the unity of a man's *individuality* [...], and it may even create that individuality by giving perfect expression to its unity.[8]

To this end, the process of free art-making was facilitated by the imagination or what Jung later called 'active imagination' a way of 'dreaming with open eyes'.[9] The psychological 'transcendent function' referred to the way in which conscious and unconscious tendencies could be mediated and engaged simultaneously. He wrote that it was 'called "transcendent" because it makes the transition from one attitude to another organically possible, without loss of the unconscious'.[10]

In this chapter, I examine Jung's notion of the transcendent function and his method of using art media to create and to freely fantasize in the context of analytic treatment. While Jung did not consider the possibilities of using music in this way except very briefly and much later on in his life—nor indeed did he consider music in his writings at any length—for some clinical practitioners, it has made sense intuitively to extend his ideas in the context of music therapy practice.[11] As Chodorow has commented 'Jung's analytic method is based on the natural healing function of the imagination, so there are obviously many ways to express it. All the creative art psychotherapies (art, dance, music, drama, poetry) as well as Sandplay can trace their roots to Jung's early contribution'.[12] I will present some historical background to approaches to music-making in music therapy and show how there is a parallel to be found in Jung's idea of free art-making as a way of accessing the unconscious.[13] I consider Jung's understanding of the distinct art "product" that is created within therapy as embodying both the conscious and unconscious. I discuss this within the context of current music therapy practice and consider the role of free improvisation in Jungian terms as a dynamic experience of the unconscious, 'the Unknown [sic] as it immediately affects us'.[14]

Art-making as transcendent function

In the months after his break with Freud, Jung discovered for himself the emotional power and creativity unleashed in freely using art materials.[15] During this time, he suffered greatly, and experienced disturbing visual phenomena and dreams that set him in pursuit of gaining ever deeper knowledge of his own unconscious. He felt driven to understand the meaning of 'the incessant stream of fantasies' released and was reminded of how, as a child, he would play 'passionately with building blocks'.[16] It was in the making of this link with his childhood self that prompted him to experiment with stones and mud from the lake near his house, and to build 'cottages, a castle, a whole village', and that convinced him of the efficacy of play in pursuit of healing.[17]

It might well have been this experience of self-healing that convinced Jung of the value for his patients to work 'imaginatively' both between sessions as well as following the end of analysis.[18] However, this poses a question: while the insights of the patient during their analysis are naturally integral to the process, how does the individual gain access to unconscious material after the analysis is over, without the mediation of the analyst in person? While the dream is a 'pure product' of the unconscious, Jung suggests that the difficulties of analysing one's own dreams are too great and too emotionally demanding.[19] There are also problems with other recognised sources of the unconscious, including those that appeared 'in the waking state, ideas "out of the blue", slips, deceptions and lapses of memory, symptomatic actions, etc.', the content of which Jung considered 'too fragmentary' and lacking in continuity between the conscious and unconscious.[20] Similarly, allowing the spontaneous fantasy free rein, as a means of accessing the unconscious, not only needed 'practice' in terms of 'eliminating critical attention', but the individual also needed the emotional availability and strength to process the fantasy on their own. Even to access fantasy in the first place, the raw content needed sufficient 'libido charge [...] actually lying ready'.[21] Where this 'libido charge' is not available, where the individual is too depressed, Jung suggests that an alternative approach is needed:

> He must make the emotional state the basis or starting point of the procedure. He must make himself as conscious as possible of the mood he is in, sinking himself in it without reserve and noting down on paper all the fantasies and other associations that come up [.... T]he depression was not manufactured by the conscious mind but is an unwelcome intrusion from the unconscious, the elaboration of mood, as it were, a picture of the contents and tendencies of the unconscious that were massed together in the depression. The whole procedure is a kind of enrichment and clarification of the affect, whereby the affect and its contents are brought nearer to consciousness, becoming at the same time more impressive and more understandable.[22]

It is at this point that Jung suggests the moving away from 'intellectual clarification' and into the domain of art, whereby the 'emotional disturbance' might be given a different kind of clarification through the act of giving it 'visible shape'. This might emerge through media other than words, namely: visual images, 'inner words' from an 'inner voice', plastic media, those shaped by the hands, bodily movement, and automatic writing.[23]

While there is no mention of music, Jung's proposal can, without difficulty, be extended to include all art forms and practice. The process of making art within this analytic context served the purpose of elaborating the unconscious in conscious form, not in order to interpret specific feelings or meaning, but through the experiencing of a creative tension between the two domains; 'embodying the striving of the unconscious for the light [or meaning] and the striving of the conscious for substance [or, it might be said, concrete form]'.[24] The following comments in a lecture on poetry, which he gave towards the end of his life, provide further clarification:

> Art by its very nature is not science, and science by its very nature is not art; both these spheres of the mind have something in reserve that is peculiar to them and can be explained only in its own terms. Hence when we speak of the relation of psychology to art, we shall treat only of that aspect of art which can be submitted to psychological scrutiny without violating its nature. Whatever the psychologist has to say about art will be confined to the process of artistic creation and has nothing to do with its innermost essence. He can no more explain this than the intellect can describe or even understand the nature of feeling.[25]

For Jung, therefore, the availability of "psychological" meaning of the emergent art "object" had limits and lay in considering and engaging with the process of its making.

The subject/object distinction made here suggests a parallel with a line of enquiry in nineteenth-century musical aesthetics. Eduard Hanslick advocated a penetrating distinction to be made in the criticism of music, between the formal musical object and the feeling experience of the listening subject, together with the emotional expressiveness of the performer. Hanslick's perspective enables us to construe one way in which Jung might have approached an account of music and the unconscious. Our relationship to the unconscious through music can be conceptualised not through a projection of meaning into the musical object, but instead through our felt experience of that same music, whether as performer or listener.[26]

Mary Priestley, a music therapist who was among the first to integrate psychodynamic thinking into a music-based clinical practice, expresses this synthesis in similar terms: 'The patient explores new pathways symbolically in the world of the imagination but with the bodily expressed emotion in sound which gives her a safe toe-hold in the world of everyday reality'.[27] While Jung is rarely accredited as an influence upon contemporary music therapy, it is noteworthy that the year in which he finally published 'The Transcendent Function', 1957, was following a brief single meeting with the American music therapist Margaret Tilly.[28] After the meeting, he expressed that

> this opens whole new avenues of research I'd never even dreamed of. Because of what you have shown me this afternoon—not just what you've said, but what I have actually felt and experienced—I feel from now on music should be an essential part of every analysis. This reaches the deep archetypal material that we can only sometimes reach in our analytical work with patients.[29]

At the same time that the practice of improvised music as therapy was beginning to emerge in the UK; the Society for Music Therapy and Remedial Music was founded one year later in 1958.[30]

Towards contemporary practices of music therapy

Music therapy, music healing, or music as medicine refer to a myriad of therapeutic practices, past and present, which intentionally provide help to people in different ways through music. The development of the modern practice of music therapy that is being considered in this chapter, recognised in the UK, can be traced back to the 1950s and 1960s.[31] Pioneer music therapists such as Juliet Alvin, Paul Nordoff, and Mary Priestley were principally musicians and composers, rather than medical professionals, and so had begun their professional lives as "creators", outside of a framework of treatment outcomes. This factor may well have contributed to the way in which, during the formative years of the practice, an approach developed that was principally derived from the musicality and intuitive inter-personal sensibility of the individuals undertaking the work. Like the emphasis Jung gave to the making of art, this was an approach that emphasised process. However limited the resources of the client might be, the work entailed live music-making with both therapist and the client improvising music together across a range of musical styles, tonal and atonal, in some form or other. Additionally, many therapists composed music especially for their work with clients.

In broad terms, this improvisatory approach to music therapy in the early years of contemporary practice had both a musical and psychoanalytic context.[32] That is to say, by the late 1960s, when the first formal training in music therapy began in the UK at the Guildhall School of Music and Drama in London, there was already a well-established aesthetic for the free music-making that might emerge during a clinical session. For these early cohorts of students, in addition to their studies in improvisation, a familiarity with free sounds may well have been gained from the aleatoric and chance-derived music of the vanguard of experimental composers, including Stockhausen, Cage, and Cardew, together with improvisers such as Derek Bailey, Barry Guy, and Keith Tippett. Another source of influence, for some who had had previous careers in education, was likely to have been the graphic scores of composers who were writing for children in schools such as John Paynter, Bernard Rands and R. Murray Schafer.[33]

Juliette Alvin, who founded the training at the Guildhall School, provides a snapshot of this musical context:

> Music therapy benefits from the fact that musical means are becoming richer and more available to all. Musicians use new techniques, unthought of some years ago. Contemporary composers of the avant-garde act as explorers in a world of sounds and often provide us with

strange experiences related to the modern scene [....] We are referring to the method of free improvisation by the individual or by a group, a technique sometimes called 'instant music' or 'collective improvisation' according to the circumstances and for which no specific musical ability is needed when used in therapy.[34]

Against the background of this soundworld, there was, at least in theory, little need for the music therapist to feel concern as to whether or not they were playing 'music', and no difficulty for the therapist or client in freely creating all kinds of sounds and consonant or dissonant harmonies. One description of the work of Paul Nordoff and Clive Robbins can serve as illustrative here:

In the initial sessions, each child was brought to the music room and was given simple percussion instruments to play such as drum, cymbal, tambourine and bells. While Robbins facilitated or encouraged the child's participation, Nordoff improvised at the piano and with his voice, reflecting and responding to whatever sounds and reactions the child made, whether it was playing, dancing and singing or screaming, crying and rocking.[35]

Not only did this open up the possibilities of music-making to clients with limited or no previous practical experience of playing an instrument, but it also enabled the client to lead the expressive content of the music, however minimal or sparse their contribution might be.[36] Furthermore, an approach to improvised music-making that was not dependent upon a specific genre or sound world could reflect with immediacy the sociocultural identity of the client, it could enable the therapist to engage at an emotional level through such musical elements as volume, intensity, and tempo. Mercédès Pavlicevic conveys the musicality of what she calls the 'dynamic interplay' between clients and therapist:

When using clinical improvisation techniques with adults, the therapist usually asks the patient to begin playing. She listens carefully to the patient's musical utterances: tempo, rhythmic structure (or lack of it); melodic shape, phrasing, the quality of pulse or beat (is it regular, irregular, intermittently regular and irregular?) [...] The therapist then joins in, improvising in a manner which reflects or confirms aspects of his playing. Thus she will match the tempo and dynamic level, play in the same metre and pulse, if this is regular, or attempt to match or meet the pulse if it is irregular. The therapist's first goal is to meet the patient's music, thereby providing a shared musical environment within which both players' improvisation can make sense to one another.[37]

This freedom of music-making, led by the therapist's felt sense of the client, who in turn might respond in kind, enabled an experience in music of shared communication between the two. The intuition that in free music-making an inter-personal relationship can be formed began to be substantiated in the observational research that began to emerge during the late 1970s, in which it was observed that parents and their infants demonstrated the musical components of early communication.[38] In particular, such research came to demonstrate a human capacity for 'communicative musicality', as defined in the 'dimensions' of '[shared] pulse, quality [for example, musical imitation or variation of an infant's pitches by the parent] and narrative [for example a sequence of changes in pitch together with changes in energy or excitement]'.[39] Colwyn Trevarthen and Stephen Malloch write how the 'rhythms, forms and affective qualities in mother-infant vocal communication [...] could be "favourably observed" in early parent-infant communication where the words cannot play a role and [are] due to the infant's and parent's desire to attune to one another'.[40] In recent years, the principle that improvisation in music therapy can be understood as a kind of parallel form of communication has developed further and become central to the approach described here.[41] In describing her work with adult clients with learning disabilities, Watson writes how

> the musical medium is used to establish relatedness between therapist and client, and to communicate something of the client's internal experience. The therapist's role is to enable, receive and digest these communications, and to help the client to find and explore their meaning. She does this in sessions through her musical, verbal and thinking processes and interventions [....] She works to enable meaning to emerge and be understood, and patterns of relating to be recognised and modulated; thus change and progress may be possible for the client.[42]

I have shown how Jung's theory and practice of free art-making foreshadow the developments that led to a contemporary practice of music therapy. Recent developmental theorists in psychobiology have supported the intuitive experience of music therapists in demonstrating how a therapeutic practice of free improvisation has intersubjective meaning also, with roots in the communication between infants and their caregivers: this lends further weight to Jung's original suggestion with regards to the use of art-making.[43] In this next section, I show how Jung speaks to some of the issues of aesthetics that arise in the use of an art form as therapy. Namely, the clinical problem of the client developing 'a purely aesthetic interest' in the art-making and how this suggests a diverse aesthetic to be discerned between art-making in therapy and art-making 'for its own sake'.

Art-making as free fantasy: a diverse aesthetic

It is worth noting that 1916, when Jung originally wrote 'The Transcendent Function', was the same year in which, in response to the war, the Dada "anti art" movement was founded in Zurich, Jung's home and country of birth.[44] Jay Sherry writes how

Jung's preference for "visionary" over "psychological" art led him to oppose modernist experimentation with its rejection of ornamentation and historical references, its preference for fragmentation, and its celebration of meaninglessness. He would make clear his antipathy for what he considered the nihilistic trends in such modernist icons as Dada, Picasso, and *Ulysses*.[45]

However, alongside his method of free art-making centered upon 'play', referred to earlier, it was possibly the freedom inherent in Dada that provided an aesthetic context for this particular development within analytic work. Jung's conception of art-making, like Dada, entailed an alternative aesthetic to conventional ideas of beauty and form. Unlike Dada, however, the driving aesthetic for Jung's art-making was oriented towards a particular kind of integrity. He writes, 'It is not important for the picture [in analytic work] to be technically or aesthetically satisfying but merely for the fantasy to have free play and for the whole thing to be done as well as possible'.[46]

How is it possible to understand the distinction Jung makes here? In terms of music therapy, one route into this aesthetic diversity is via a consideration of notions of "value", the question of what would constitute a "good improvisation" in what might be termed a performance setting, and a "good improvisation" in a therapeutic setting. Is there an aesthetic diversity to be conceptualized between improvising "for the sake of therapy", and improvising "for the sake of music"?[47]

Gary Peters has encapsulated a flavor of this distinction in terms of Heidegger's account of 'care', *sorge*. In *Being and Time*, care is encapsulated in a number of ways. There may be the care for something, *besorgen*, or, care for the welfare of people, *fürsorge*, the latter translated as solicitude.[48] Peters explicitly and deliberately takes the meaning of solicitude, however, to refer to both care for the [improvisatory] work and care for others. Peter's argument is that improvisation has become caught up with 'solicitude' only in the sense of 'care for others'.[49] Put simply, for Peters, it would seem, a good improvisation is one that is concerned with 'care for the work'. For the music therapist whose approach is rooted within a psychoanalytic paradigm, a good improvisation is concerned with 'care for others', in this case, care for the therapeutic quality of the relationship. This is an important shift of emphasis between distinct approaches to music-making.[50] Listening to the saxophonist and free improviser Evan Parker and his group, for example, it is possible to hear the players giving each other opportunities to "solo" one moment and play in parallel or together at other moments. New musical ideas emerge that might or might not be taken up by another player.[51] A similar account could be given of the improvisation in a music therapy group: indeed, the very purpose of such a group might be to provide individuals with an experience of being heard and listening to others, being supported in a solo, or alternatively supporting another group member. However, while there might be a convergence of aesthetic attitude in both settings, whereby value is placed upon the intensity of relationships in music, a diversity can be identified in the coherence of the overall musical outcome. For example, in music therapy a client might play repetitively over a long period of time without variation; the therapist might support this musically and engage with both the musical aspects of the repetition and the felt *experience* of relating in that same music, without necessarily extending the ideas or transforming the repetition into an aesthetic feature in and of itself. For the music therapist, there is an emotional meaning in the repetition, rather than a purely *musical* meaning.

Brown writes about repetition in work with a five-year-old boy with Autism:

> He chooses to play the small glockenspiel and plays each note consecutively from left to right and back again in a two-note stop/start pattern. I improvise on the piano, picking up the rhythm of this, matching the volume, speed and quality of his playing, singing 'hullo', as David plays on in left/right pattern. After a minute or so, I begin to alter the speed, slowing down. David, however, continues in the same manner, showing no awareness of my change. I rejoin his speed and then, a little later, try moving faster. At this point he says 'um', stops playing and reads the letter names of the bars of the glockenspiel.[52]

From this description, it is possible to glimpse how the focus of the music-making is upon therapist's close listening to the young client's particular quality of response to her rather than necessarily (instinctively even) seeking to create an overall coherence to his music by, for example, transforming it through rhythm or melody. The music-making remains as process, or, in Jung's terms, as 'active fantasy'. The repetition in Parker's playing, it may be conjectured will be taken up by his colleagues, imitated, or transformed, or deliberately ignored, but in this instance, this will be in the service of the overall improvisatory event. As Jung describes the creative process of the poet,

> he submits his material to a definite treatment with a definite aim in view; he adds to it and subtracts from it, emphasising one effect, toning down another, laying on a touch of colour here, another there, all the time carefully considering the over-all result and paying strict attention to the laws of form and style. He exercises the keenest judgment and chooses his words with complete freedom.[53]

It is notable, however, that so far this discussion has assumed that the client shares and understands this view of aesthetic diversity where the emphasis in the music-making is to be upon what might now be termed as therapeutic work in contrast to art work. Furthermore, it was stated above that improvisation in music therapy emerged during a period of great musical freedom and that this contributed to a sound world within the clinical setting where it was generally acceptable that anything might happen. It is possible to speculate that this appreciation of freedom does not necessarily extend to every client. What does this mean for the adult client who approaches the music therapy session expressing the wish to play particular pieces of music, already composed? How does the music therapist approach this in the context of free play within an improvisatory culture of no right or wrong?

For Jung, the use of art media was supposedly a means to circumvent a sterility occurring in the therapeutic work, to provide a constant means for the new.[54] However, he identifies this same problem: where media are used in the pursuit of free fantasy,

> [whilst] authentic contents may be produced, the patient evinces an exclusively aesthetic interest in them and consequently remains stuck in an all-enveloping phantasmagoria so that [...] nothing is gained [.... T]he patient is sidetracked into purely aesthetic problems of artistic expression.[55]

One common scenario, which can feel like an obstacle for the music therapist, is to find themselves working with a client who wishes solely to be taught an instrument, such as the guitar or piano. For a client to be invited into a room where there are musical instruments to play and a musician therapist to play the instruments with, it is not surprising, for example, that some people ask to be taught the guitar or piano so that they can play the song they have always wanted to perform. For some clients, this might be extremely worthwhile and constitute the sum of both the content and meaning of their work with a music therapist.

For other clients in music therapy, the learning of a tune could be conceptualized as the conscious form of the therapeutic work, while the unconscious content may be immersed within the experience of the music-making. Working within this psychoanalytic framework, it might be thought that lessons are somehow a "defence" against the more challenging freedom of improvisation. However, to paraphrase Jung, it is not the 'historical antecedents' but the metaphorical *purpose* of this wish for lessons that is important in seeking understanding.[56] This points to Jung's concern with overly reductive methods of understanding clinical material per se, that something of the fantasy, artistic or otherwise, in itself, gets "lost in translation", so to speak. Indeed, as Patricia Skar writes, there may be therapeutic gain to be had in the receiving of piano lessons outside of the clinical setting:

> In my piano teaching, many of my students were adults who were returning to the piano after studying it as children. The decision to confront the instrument again after many years of not playing often symbolized the facing of an important aspect of themselves which had been neglected. Often, I saw that the actual, physical process of playing

the piano was a potent catalyst to facing long repressed feelings from childhood [...] somehow, later in life, their original desire to make music had returned. Now it was necessary to do this with someone who could hold their attempts with love and in the spirit of play.[57]

A similar tension may arise where the client doesn't wish to improvise but instead to sing romantic songs with the much younger female therapist. The form of the music therapy sessions can be understood as being defined through the singing of pre-composed songs, whereas the unconscious content—which might be given the name "longing"—in this instance manifests in the countertransference of the therapist.[58] As Jung writes, 'Consciousness puts its media of expression at the disposal of the unconscious content. In giving the contents form, the lead must be left as far as possible by the chance ideas and associations thrown up by the unconscious'.[59] In following our clients' direction, we have the greatest hope of gaining understanding of their inner worlds.

In addressing this question, I suggest that Jung provides a way in which to approach the tension between conscious and unconscious intention in improvisation, a problematic tension which pervades clinical thinking in music therapy. That is to say, issues of aesthetics are usually not far off, even where the agenda is therapeutic. In all, as was asserted at the outset of this chapter, in 'The Transcendent Function', Jung identifies in the activity of free fantasy a means of apprehending the unconscious through art-making. He not only asserts a concordance between the improvisatory/play-orientated processes of accessing the unconscious through the spoken word, art, music, and movement, but also addresses the matter of what happens when art media are put to use in this way. As suggested above, central to an understanding of Jung's principle of the transcendent function is the way in which both of these tendencies, towards the aesthetic on the one hand, towards fantasy on the other hand, may be bound together in a 'compensatory' relationship of conscious and unconscious, with the one needing the other.

Conclusion

In this chapter, I have emphasized some key themes in Jung's account of the unconscious and the activity of free fantasy in the form of art-making as transcendent function. In doing so, I have suggested some areas of Jung's thinking that may be considered as his legacy to the contemporary discipline of music therapy. While Jung did not include music in the art forms that he experimented with, I have demonstrated the way in which some of the issues he raises are equally applicable to music-making. Finally, I demonstrated how Jung identifies a distinction to be made between a formal aesthetic and what might be termed a 'therapeutic' aesthetic in art-making. While Jung perceives a concern with aesthetic ideals, such as beauty for its own sake, as getting in the way of a therapeutic process, his synthetic understanding of the unconscious lends the need for 'conscious substance' or form.

At the start of this chapter, I presented the idea that 'The Transcendent Function' was written during World War I and that Jung's dialectical notion of conscious and unconscious was in part a response to this fragmentation of international relations that was taking place across Europe one-hundred years ago. I have also implied throughout this chapter that music-making, both inside and outside therapy, is inherently intersubjective. Jung adeptly links these matters where he writes that

> everyone who proposes to come to terms with himself must reckon with this basic problem [of relationships]. For, to the degree that he does not admit the validity of the other person, he denies the "other" within himself the right to exist—and vice versa. The capacity for inner dialogue is a touchstone for outer objectivity.[60]

Notes

1. Carl G. Jung, 'The Transcendent Function', in The Collected Works, Vol. 8, *The Structure and Dynamics of the Psyche*, ed. Herbert Read, Michael Fordham, and Gerhard Adler, trans. R.F.C. Hull, 2nd edition (London: Routledge Keegan and Paul, 1969), 67–91.
2. Jung, 'The Transcendent Function', ¶ 187.
3. Jef Dehing, 'The Transcendent Function', *Journal of Analytical Psychology* 38, No. 3 (1993), 225.
4. 'Towards the autumn of 1913 the pressure which I felt was in *me* seemed to be moving outward, as though there were something in the air. The atmosphere actually seemed to me darker than it had been. It was as though the sense of oppression no longer sprang exclusively from a psychic situation but from concrete reality [...] In October while I was alone on a journey, I was suddenly seized by an overpowering vision: I saw a monstrous flood covering all the northern and low-lying lands between the North Sea and the Alps. When it came up to Switzerland I saw that the mountains grew higher and higher to protect our country. I realized that a frightful catastrophe was in progress. I saw the mighty yellow waves, the floating rubble of civilization, and the drowned bodies of uncounted thousands. Then the whole sea turned to blood. [...] On 1st August [1914] the world war broke out. Now my task was clear: I had to try to understand what had happened and to what extent my own experience coincided with that of mankind in general'. Carl G. Jung, *Memories, Dreams, Reflections*, ed. Aniela Jaffé, trans. Richard Winston and Clara Winston (London: Collins/Font Paperbacks, 1983), 199–200.
5. Jung, 'The Transcendent Function', ¶ 168.
6. Carl G. Jung, 'Definitions', in *The Collected Works*, Vol. 6, *Psychological Types*, 16th edition, trans. R.F.C. Hull and H.G. Baynes (Hove and New York, NY: Routledge Keegan and Paul, 1971), ¶ 715.
7. Jung, 'Definitions', ¶ 712.
8. *Ibid.*, 714.
9. Andrew Samuels, Bani Shorter, and Fred Plaut, *A Critical Dictionary of Jungian Analysis* (London and New York: Routledge, 1986), 9.
10. Jung, 'The Transcendent Function', ¶ 145.

11 See William McGuire and Richard Francis Carrington Hull (eds), *C.G. Jung Speaking: Interviews and Encounter* (London: Picador, 1980), 261–63. For examples of Jungian influenced accounts of music therapy, see: Mary Priestley, *Music Therapy in Action* (London: Constable, 1975); Diane S. Austin, 'The Role of Improvised Music in Psychodynamic Music Therapy with Adults', *Music Therapy* 14, No. 1 (1996): 29–43; Sandra Brown, 'Some Thoughts on Music, Therapy, and Music Therapy: A Response to Elaine Streeter's "Finding a Balance between Psychological Thinking and Musical Awareness in Music Therapy Theory—A Psychoanalytic Perspective"', *British Journal of Music Therapy* 13, No. 2 (1999): 63–71; Johannes Th. Eschen, *Analytical Music Therapy* (London: Jessica Kingsley Publishers, 2002).
12 Carl G. Jung and Joan Chodorow, 'Introduction' in *Jung on Active Imagination: Key Readings Selected and Introduced by Joan Chodorow* (London: Routledge, 1997), 1.
13 For the purpose of this chapter, where 'art' or art-making is specified, I shall be using 'art' in the collective sense meaning all art forms, including music.
14 Jung, 'The Transcendent Function', Prefatory Note, 68.
15 Jung, *Memories, Dreams, Reflections*, 194.
16 *Ibid.*, 197.
17 *Ibid.*, 198.
18 Jung, 'The Transcendent Function', ¶ 144–46.
19 *Ibid.*, ¶ 153.
20 *Ibid.*, ¶ 154–65. Compare with Freud's essay 'The Unconscious', published the previous year in 1915, see especially 166–71. Many of Jung's comments with regards to technique are explicitly directed in criticism of Freud's method of Free Association. Sigmund Freud, 'The Unconscious', in The Standard Edition, Vol. 14, (1915–1916), *On the History of the Psycho-Analytic Movement, Papers on Metapsychology and Other Works)*, trans. James Strachey (London: The Hogarth Press, 1957), 159–215.
21 Jung, 'The Transcendent Function', ¶ 155.
22 *Ibid.*, ¶ 167.
23 *Ibid.*, ¶ 168–71.
24 *Ibid.*, ¶ 168.
25 Carl G. Jung, 'On the Relation of Analytical Psychology to Poetry', in *The Collected Works*, Vol. 15, *The Spirit in Man, Art and Literature*, ed. and trans. Gerhard Adler and R.F.C. Hull (London: Routledge Keegan and Paul, 1966), ¶ 99.
26 Eduard Hanslick, *On the Musically Beautiful: A Contribution towards the Revision of the Aesthetics of Music*, trans. Geoffrey Payzant (Indianapolis, IN: Hackett Publishing, 1986).
27 Mary Priestley, 'Linking Sound and Symbol', in *The Art and Science of Music Therapy: A Handbook*, ed. Tony Wigram, Bruce Saperston, and Robert West (Amsterdam: Harwood Academic Publishers, 1995), 130.
28 Margaret Tilly, 'The Therapy of Music', in McGuire and Hull (eds), *C.G. Jung Speaking*, 261–63. This short account was originally prepared as a contribution to a memorial booklet compiled by the Analytical Psychology Club in San Francisco in 1961. As it is probably a unique indication of any commentary from Jung regarding music therapy practice, and probably his sole meeting with a music therapist, Margaret Tilly's description of this encounter is frequently quoted. See also Dorinda Hawk Hitchcock, 'The Influence of Jung's Psychology on the Therapeutic Use of Music', *Journal of British Music Therapy* 1, No. 2 (1987), 17; Patricia Skar, 'The Goal as Process: Music and the Search for the Self', *Journal of Analytical Psychology* 47 (2002), 631.
29 Margaret Tilly, 'The Therapy of Music', 263.

30 Helen M. Tyler, 'The Music Therapy Profession in Modern Britain', in *Music as Medicine: The History of Music Therapy since Antiquity*, ed. Peregrine Horden (Aldershot: Ashgate, 2000), 375–93.
31 Since 1996, music therapy has had legal status as a profession allied to medicine: it is recognised by the Health Care Professions Council.
32 Rachel Darnley-Smith, 'Improvisation as Transcendent Function: The Role of the Unconscious and Jung's Active Imagination in Twentieth-Century Music Therapy' (In Review).
33 See John Paynter, *Hear and Now: An Introduction to Modern Music in Schools* (London: Universal Edition, 1972).
34 Juliette Alvin, *Music Therapy* (London: Hutchinson, 1974), 104–105.
35 Tyler, 'The Music Therapy Profession in Modern Britain', 387.
36 This is not to say that all music-making at this time in music therapy was atonal: one of the two trainings to have been established by the mid-1970s was inspired and taught by the American composer and pianist, Paul Nordoff. Nordoff brought to bear on the new 'clinical improvisation' a deep affinity with the nineteenth- and early twentieth-century repertoire for piano.
37 Mercédès Pavlicevic, 'Dynamic Interplay in Clinical Improvisation', *Journal of British Music Therapy* 4, No. 2 (1990), 7.
38 Stephen Malloch and Colwyn Trevarthen, 'Musicality: Communicating the Vitality and Interests of Life', in *Communicative Musicality: Exploring the Basis of Human Companionship*, ed. Stephen Malloch and Colwyn Trevarthen (Oxford: Oxford University Press, 2009), 2.
39 *Ibid.*, 4.
40 Colwyn Trevarthen and Stephen Malloch, 'The Dance of Wellbeing: Defining the Musical Therapeutic Effect', *Nordisk Tidsskrift for Musikkterapi* 9, No. 2 (2000), 6.
41 *Ibid.*, See also Mercédès Pavlicevic and Gary Ansdell, 'Between Communicative Musicality and Collaborative Musicing: A Perspective from Community Music Therapy', in *Communicative Musicality*, ed. Stephen Malloch and Colwyn Trevarthen (Oxford: Oxford University Press, 2009), 357–76.
42 Tessa Watson, 'Music Therapy with Adults with Learning Disabilities', in *The Handbook of Music Therapy*, ed. Leslie Bunt and Sarah Hoskyns (Hove: Brunner-Routledge, 2002), 103.
43 Trevarthen and Malloch, 'The Dance of Wellbeing'.
44 Jay Sherry, *Carl Gustav Jung: Avant–Garde Conservative* (New York: Palgrave Macmillan, 2010), 47.
45 *Ibid.*
46 Jung, 'The Transcendent Function', ¶ 168.
47 See Rachel Darnley-Smith, 'What Is the Music of Music Therapy?: An Enquiry into the Aesthetics of Clinical Improvisation' (PhD diss., Durham University, 2013) for an extended discussion of this this topic.
48 Michael J. Inwood, *A Heidegger Dictionary* (Oxford and Malden, MA: Blackwell Publishers Limited, 1999), 35–6; Martin Heidegger, *Being and Time*, trans. John Macquarrie and Edward Robinson, 7th edition (Oxford: Blackwell Publishing, 2002), 157–58 (¶ 121), see also *n*.4, 157. Gary Peters, *The Philosophy of Improvisation* (Chicago and London: University of Chicago Press, 2009), 58.
49 Peters, *The Philosophy of Improvisation*, 58.
50 Some music therapists, especially perhaps those working outside of a psychoanalytic framework, would not share this view. See Kenneth Aigen, 'In Defense of Beauty: A Role for the Aesthetic in Music Therapy Theory: Part I: The Development of Aesthetic Theory in Music Therapy', *Nordic Journal of Music Therapy* 16, No. 2 (2007), 115.

51 In recognition that each improvisation is 'unique', the following event is referred to: Evan Parker, John Russell and John Edwards, at the Rose and Crown, Walthamstow, London, UK. Friday, 23 January 2015.
52 Sandra Brown, '"Hullo Object! I Destroyed You!"', in *The Handbook of Music Therapy*, ed. Leslie Bunt and Sarah Hoskyns, 84–96 (Hove: Brunner-Routledge, 2002), 86.
53 Jung, 'On the Relation of Analytical Psychology to Poetry', ¶ 109.
54 Jung, 'The Transcendent Function', Prefatory Note, 68.
55 *Ibid.*
56 *Ibid.*, ¶ 146.
57 Patricia Skar, 'The Goal as Process', 631.
58 For a case study account see: Rachel Darnley-Smith, 'Music Therapy with Elderly Adults', in *Music Therapy and Group Work: Sound Company*, ed. Alison Davies and Eleanor Richards (London: Jessica Kingsley, 2002), 77–89.
59 Jung, 'The Transcendent Function', 85.
60 *Ibid.*, ¶ 187.

8 Symbolic listening
The resistance of enjoyment and the enjoyment of resistance

Jun Zubillaga-Pow

We often express our preference for or disgust with certain music, but the reasons behind such aesthetic selection are little understood. Our cognitive and sensory ability or inability to appreciate a wide range of music including the traditional and the experimental have more often than not been attributed to generic or cultural differences.[1] Yet, any reservation towards these differences in musical reception, one can argue, is most likely a result of something more psychologically innate than the perennial cultivation of taste. To achieve a common consensus, aesthetic judgments, according to the Kantian school of thought, have to be predicated on the cognitive capacities that are shared not only by everyone, but also by the condition that these faculties are pleasurable and unconstrained by rules.[2] In other words, the act of making sound choices relies on the normative functioning of one's 'cognitive capacities', and the invariable criterion that these senses are able to experience and enjoy pleasure. A physical sign of a good judgment, in the Kantian sense of the word, would then be the satisfaction of one's senses to the extent where cognitive responses attain maximum amount of sensorial and psychological pleasure.

Such a persistent want to obtain pleasure and avoid displeasure is aligned with what Sigmund Freud calls the pleasure principle. While cognitive perception is certainly not reducible to a single criterion of pleasure, the psychoanalytic mechanism operates at least on a multitude of levels and orders. By applying this theory to the sense of hearing, or musical cognition in particular, both psychological and philosophical examinations of the human phenomenon become necessarily more critical. However, researchers of the two disciplines seldom engage with each other's research, so one of my motivations behind writing this chapter is to deliberate over the mutual coherence of their findings. By juxtaposing psychoanalytic theories and empirical results derived from experimental psychology, the main objective of my argument is to situate psychic resistance, or its lack thereof, among various psychological processes of musical listening. In contrast to conventional wisdom, I contend that aesthetic enjoyment is itself a mode of resistance against one's desire for pleasure and disdain of displeasure.

152 *Jun Zubillaga-Pow*

This chapter is organized in three sections. I first provide an exposition to the current state of psychological theorization within music studies through an analytical criticism of a single experiment. After an extensive discussion of the principle of resistance in the second section, I apply the psychoanalytic concept on the same experiment. I go on to propose that the act of listening, itself a process of interpretation, neither prioritizes the cognitive over the affective nor disregards the entire agency of the latter. Enjoyment qua resistance operates in tandem with both the desired and the undesired.

Music psychology and psychological theories

Since the 1980s, music psychology has gained academic popularity and eventually become a major field in its own right. There are major research laboratories founded in North America, Western Europe, and Japan. Most experimental work focuses on the cognitive, sensory, or affective aspects of musical perception, and a smaller number of psychologists specialize in cross-cultural or infant-related research.[3] The general findings conclude that musically trained and untrained adults respond differently to musical cues, as do listeners with different auricular abilities; infants' perception of music is also dependent on the familiarity of the person making the sound, its directedness, and certain ethno-cultural characteristics.[4]

Given the wide range of psychological interests and directions, including recent ventures into neuroscience and cochlear implants, contemporary scholars have developed several theories of musical perception. Rather than offering a straightforward explanation of their respective ideas, I will analyze a single experiment with three of these systematic methodologies, namely, Jerrold Levinson's *concatenation*, Eric Clarke's *affordance*, and David Huron's *expectation*, to show the congruity of each theory with the empirical outcome. I will then discuss the fortes and weaknesses of each proposition before arguing in the final section that the principle of resistance is epistemologically more superior for our purpose in apprehending musical understanding and enjoyment.

Music in recent musicological discussion has expanded beyond the scores and lives of their producers. The analysis of music now encompasses performances, recordings, and their distribution to airports, coffee clubs, hotels, and personal devices.[5] As their equivalence, music played in a psychological setting should also be perceived similarly as a form of functional music to elicit responses of the participants. This is a stark point that has been vastly ignored by many a musicologist; that if music used in classrooms and hospitals are deemed worth of research, what about those created in experimental contexts?

My arguments for this chapter are based on the work of a group of scientists led by Emmanuel Bigand, who investigates the psychological strength between the sensory and the cognitive processes of musically trained and untrained students listening to harmonic sequences ending in either a tonic or subdominant chord.[6] In two separate tasks, the target cadence and speed of the chord sequences were manipulated. The time taken for participants to identify the target cadence—perfect or plagal, correctly or incorrectly— was recorded as they attempted the two experiments, where one harmonic sequence had its final cadence altered while the other sequence was played either at an acceleration from 300ms per chord to 150ms and 75ms per chord, or vice versa. For reasons unexplained, a feedback signal was also sounded whenever an incorrect response was received. Except for the decelerating sequence that drew sensory responses, the cognitive aspect of processing the musical sequence remained the more salient component for most of the listeners, whether musically trained or not. In order to understand the empirical reactions in a contingent manner, I will rely on the three above-mentioned theories as analytic tools to decipher the multiple meanings of the musical material used in the tests.

For Levinson, basic musical understanding is achieved via three forms of intuition, that of following, reproducing, and experiencing the music, all in a concatenated fashion.[7] Via a temporal appraisal of the listener's aural adeptness, the subject grasps the musical meaning of the work by attending to every 'moment', as well as reproducing aspects of the music without prompting in their mind. In addition, the music at each particular moment evokes certain emotions from the listener via its 'residential' expressivity. If we apply the Levinsonian analysis to explain the empirical results by Bigand and his team, the test subjects are deemed to have 'followed' each chord in the sequence and 'reproduced' the sequence in their mind when asked to determine the final harmonic cadence. Their innate 'experiential' intuition of the music's expressive quality permits them to make a final grasp of any possible musical meaning when the extract becomes too complicated for their cognitive capability. For Levinson, this model of musical listening and understanding via concatenation is aimed to invoke 'an image of music as a chain of interconnected and interpenetrating links'.[8] In the context of this thesis, Levinson's theory of listening 'moment-by-moment' is probably overly tenuous and rigid a methodology for the listener. Paying *total* attention to every instance within the music and reproducing what one has heard chronologically would be extremely regimental. If this theory is to be enthroned as the *right* way of listening, the listener would be accused of being incompetent upon any lapse in auditory attention. To expect any listener to attend to every moment, say, of a Bruckner symphony or a Stockhausen opera would also be rather unrealistic.

Clarke, in contrast, proposes an ecological approach to musical listening with the aim of a proper contextualization of musical meaning. Appropriating James Gibson's theorization of the ecological, Clarke believes that the musical material itself already allows for limited affordances to semantic interpretation. Affordances, while being 'the product both of objective properties and the capacities and needs of organisms that encounter them', impose categorical restrictions upon musical material, which,

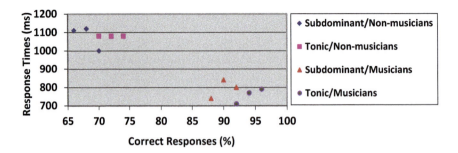

Figure 8.1 Speed and accuracy of harmonic recognition by musicians and non-musicians.

unless otherwise stated, are meant to be distinguished from structural semantics.[9] Citing parallel interpretations of Beethoven's late music by Tovey ('heavens on fire') and McClary ('murderous sexual rage'), Clarke outlines a musical hermeneutics based on an essentialist rule that is only credible if it follows an assumed set of cultural conventions.[10] Semantically speaking, this brand of musical understanding continues to invest in a binary system of constructing cognitive apartheid—logical/illogical, true/false—as far as these attitudes can be justified empirically. Clarke has inevitably overlooked the fact that Tovey and McClary have so arrived at their musical readings due to the socio-psychological situations in 1930s British and 1990s American history, respectively. More precisely, should an ecological understanding of music encompass a subjective perception of musical meaning, it will have to be extrapolated from both within the musical material as well as the listener's life experience. That is, the affordance of a certain musical passage must widen to include the socio-historical understanding of music by the listening subjects in question.

Appropriately, an ecological analyst, in contradiction to Levinson's triple-prong methodology, would treat the entire chord sequence from Bigand's experiment as "affordable" for an interpretation leaning towards the tonic or the subdominant region.[11] Given that test accuracies hover around 70% for non-musicians and 90% for musicians (as shown in Figure 8.1), it is highly possible that Bigand and his team deliberately ensured that both conditions of sequence and speed were potentially "affordable" in these terms.[12] That is, experimental criteria could have been constructed so that about 70% of the expected results can afford to be right and 30% can afford to be wrong for non-musically trained listeners. Although statistical results have not been provided for a more detailed review, a more systematic explanation for this allowance could be that the tonic triad and subdominant triad shares the tonic note, thus creating *ecologically* a one third probability of getting a false response. The law of affordance seems to be useful in this context, but, for psychological experiments conducted in tempered laboratories, this methodology grounds musical meaning objectively to the material and fails to differentiate a listener who listens with his or her senses from one who listens cognitively.

As opposed to the concept of affordance, Huron's theory of expectation performs better as a first principle for musical cognition than Clarke's because it is based on subjective responses elicited via heuristic means. Huron's starting point is biological, and by dividing the listening process into five response systems—imagination, tension, prediction, reaction, and appraisal—Huron attempts an explanation of the listener's cognitive mechanisms when any musical stimulant is presented to them.[13] This theory is strongly relevant and applicable to Bigand's experiment where test subjects do enact the five responses upon hearing the chord sequences, given that they were tasked to decipher the final harmonic situation at the end of the extract. Chronologically, put in Huron's terms, the listeners imagined the harmonic progression that was about to unfold, felt a sense of aural 'tension' at any point of harmonic inception, and, as fast as their cognitive ability allowed, made intuitive 'predictions' upon the hearing of the cadence, before 'reacting' to express their opinion of the harmony. The 'appraisal' step is internalized when the correct answer is revealed to them, cohesively enhancing their musical understanding of the extract.

Huron's methodology appears to be founded on Darwinism; this being evident from the desired effects anticipated from within the defense of the system: 'beneficial', 'protective', and 'adaptive'.[14] This approach can obscure different responses to aural stimuli, which are less determined by our evolutionary history. There is without doubt the existence of passive listeners, who are oblivious to musical semantics and are artistically unimaginative; they do not react or feel any cognized tension to certain sounds, musical or otherwise. This criticism challenges the relevance to listening models of Huron's assumption that 'all the world's peoples share a common biological heritage' and that representation, memory and inductive learning are cognitive fundamentals for the acquisition of knowledge.[15] His is a theory that would have to be further subjected to cross-cultural scrutiny, especially within ethnomusicological epistemology. Some readers may have intimated that Huron's theory parallels that of Husserlian phenomenology. Accordingly, the Freudian-Lacanian psychoanalytic concept of resistance—with its subcutaneous treatment of the act, listening or otherwise—would appear to present itself as a theoretical antithesis to Huron's phenomenological appraisal. Correspondingly, I will examine the notion of resistance from the idealist and psychoanalytic perspectives in the next section.

The principles of resistance

Resistance as a phenomenon exists on many levels and in different domains, such that it can be derived from social, ideological, and biological processes. It can also present itself as an effect of a psychological disorder. One of the definitions cited in the Oxford English Dictionary is a person's *'ability not to be affected by something undesirable*'.[16] This definition appears relevant to the psychoanalytic argument pertaining to the effect of resistance during the act of listening to music. There are some key points pertinent to this discussion that can be extrapolated from this definition. That is, the 'ability' of a person to undertake an action, the 'affect' of the subject, and the agency of 'desire'.

The first point relates resistance to the capability or power of a person to act or to do things. Within Lacanian philosophy, both the actor and the person who triggers or intervenes in the action are accountable for the deed.[17] Psychoanalysis enables a review of every aspect of the deed vis-à-vis its consciousness and time. Following Freud, the act, whether intentional or unintentional, whether conscious or unconscious, can be subjected to psychoanalytic analysis, and interpreted for the reason that a process of working-through is necessary to account fully for one's action. Coming before them was the Idealist philosopher, Johann Gottlieb Fichte (1762–1814), who considered the action of a person to be determined solely by one's consciousness of oneself, or more specifically, the act of one's self-positing (*sitzen*). Fichte formulates the principle of *Tathandlung* or deed-action as the first principle of all philosophy and as a more pervasive alternative to Karl Leonhard Reinhold's principle of consciousness (*Bewusstseins*) and Gottlob Ernst Schulz's principle of contrast (*Widerspruch*).[18]

Juxtaposing the theories of Freud and Fichte, a work of psychological interpretation would only be successful when an action can be explained through its genesis within the unconscious to its revelation in the conscious mind. In essence, this psychic movement from the unconscious to the conscious is a form of self-positing, that is, the conscious deed of situating an initial unconscious self. The reflexive act occurs only during the process when one becomes aware of the existence of oneself before acting upon one's consciousness and also, paradoxically, when one acts upon one's consciousness before realizing the existence of oneself. More importantly, it is this original unity of the acting self as the empirical and the knowing self as the theoretical or intellectual that, accordingly to Fichte, allows reasoning to be of practical use and instrumental to critical understanding. In other words, the intellectual deed and the empirical action are correlated and contemporaneous with one determining the other.[19]

To extend this into Lacanian psychoanalytic discourse, the reflexive act that associates one entity with another can be deemed as a process of signification. Such is the case where conscious content, in adherence to Fichte's first principle of deed-action, are referred to those in the unconscious. To the extent that the aim of psychoanalysis is to locate meaning to different physical or speech acts, the 'possession' (*besitzen*) of a single meaning by a single act is analogous to Fichte's positing (*sitzen*) of the I by oneself. To put it another way, the positing of the I as a reflexive act already takes on a structure of signifying what the I is or is becoming. There is an a priori process of signification in any interpretation of action. To act is to signify, and to signify is to act: a reflexive process.[20]

In the absence of any reflexion, resistance can be redefined as the 'ability' of the subject to *not* act, physically or linguistically, or to *not* engage in the symbolic process of revealing the meaning behind his or her action. In Freud's own words, 'resistance is acting as an *agent provocateur*', one that expends a psychic force and possesses the ability to hinder the act or action of the subject.[21] With resistance, the act of self-positing and the making conscious of meaning via signification get interrupted. To maintain resistance is thus to bear the ability to remain unconscious and uphold the indifference between the I and the not-I. To resist is to go against the reflexive process of the symbolic order and accept a state of being.

The final point arising from the Oxford English Dictionary's definition of resistance pertains to the subject's or the analyst's 'affect' acting as a form of resistance during psychoanalytic work. Theoretically, affect or emotions are ascertained to be analytically deceptive in general with anxiety as the only exception.[22] According to Lacan, affects are mere signals to analytic content and not the actual signifiers themselves, the latter of which come with pronounced meaning for interpretive work.[23] In these terms, signifiers and affects lie on the opposite ends of the latent-manifest spectrum. While signifiers are real, repressed, and unconscious, affects are imaginary and observable through feelings and emotions.[24] For Lacan, affects are by themselves not conducive to psychoanalytic interpretation and have to be treated as extraneous to the subject.[25] That is not to say that feelings are to be ignored totally, but to recognize the expression of enjoyment as highly desirable by the psychoanalytic subject.[26]

Slavoj Žižek, for instance, compares and contrasts the respective absence and presence of enjoyment in the courtly love songs of the Troubadours in the high middle ages with the invention of modern operatic arias. While the medieval Lady is 'being posited as the inaccessible Thing' depriving herself and others of enjoyment, the dramatic soprano 'puts herself entirely into the voice' and partakes in the act of *jouissance*, where the 'sheer self-consuming enjoyment of the voice eclipses meaning'. During this moment of surplus enjoyment, the singer 'has it in herself, *objet petit a*, the voice-object, the cause of desire'.[27] From Poppea to Kundry, the figure of the feminine hysteric arose from this externalized feeling of excess and meaning and became an epitome of the division between the I and the not-I. Enjoyment, musical or otherwise, thus works alongside a desirable thing or object.

To redefine resistance with the new understanding of enjoyment as a desirable affect, resistance becomes the ability not to be affected by the unaffected. In short, resistance keeps affects in check. While desire or enjoyment subsists as an unconscious act of acting, signifying, and partaking in the reflexive process that displaces the signifier onto other semantic objects, resistance persists to counter-act the extension of the deed-action. In the final section, I investigate the applicability of affects and the principle of resistance on the act of listening in general and through the psychological experiment conducted by Bigand and his colleagues.

Symbolic listening

The phenomenon of listening is an active one; it is an act as well as a signifying process. In contrast to passive auditors, active listeners inhabit the desire to make sense of what they have heard and their emotions serve as arbitrators of their cognitive capabilities. The act of listening shares mechanical similarities with the Fichtean reflexive act, where the subject only assumes the position of the listener when he or she participates in the act of listening and subsequently realizes himself or herself as a listening self. Within the experimental setting, listening to chord sequences, for example, is deemed as an empirical action, while the subject realizing that he or she is listening to musical harmonies becomes an intellectual deed. While one phenomenon determines the other—that is, one has to listen to know and to know to listen—both phenomena occur within the single subject, the one self. To recognize oneself as a listening self is an adherence to the principle of the original unity between the empirical and the theoretical consciousness of a listening self. This psychological duplicity is most apparent when one becomes aware of oneself as both someone who does the listening (the I) *and* the object of listening (the not-I); I am listening *and* the I to whom one is listening.[28]

For the analytical philosopher Thomas Nagel, an 'objective self' is appropriately both subjective *and* objective because the self as such is the subject from an objective point of view.[29] To contextualize this theory within music psychology, the objective listener's comprehension of the sonic object is said to constitute both his or her subjectivity upon the object *and* his or her subjectivity upon his or her self as a subject. In other words, a listener should be able to understand the auditory aspect of himself or herself with the aid of an external object, by subjecting his or her comprehension of the external object upon himself or herself—an action earlier termed the 'self-positing' of one's thoughts or self-consciousness. By introducing the notion of thinking about one's self from this particular philosophy of the mind into the psychology of music, musicologists are given further scope to explore the phenomenon of listening. The listening self in this case arrives at the transcendental moment with the sonic object acting as a catalyst. This act of self-positing results in psychical changes in the subject's listening patterns and affects the individual subjectivity of the listening self.

While the music qua sonic object triggers a reflexive process in the listening self, the affect evoked and sustained in the listening subject acts as a form of resistance, deceptive or otherwise. Within a psychoanalytic framework, the emotions conjured up during the act of listening are more symbolic of the self than of any autonomous musical meaning.[30] Therefore, these feelings, which vary from person to person and from time to time, as experienced during the act of symbolic listening, are extraneous to the music itself. I suggest that they manifest themselves as a counterforce against the

Symbolic listening 159

desires and disdains of the listener, especially for someone who is not musically trained. Precisely because resistance is the ability to be unaffected by the undesirable, the emotions generated posterior to the encounter with the sonic object appears to be experiential manifestations of resistance. These feelings obstruct what is referred to in Fichtean terms as the 'free, outward striving, practical activity' of the self embodying an affective form of resistance or, by extension, counter-resistance.[31]

Applying this principle of resistance to this act of symbolic listening, there is no contradiction in stating that feelings or emotions are defense mechanisms when listening to sounds or music. Conversely, I argue that the determination to cognize certain musical elements is an attempt to resist the very consciousness of one's feelings as a listening subject. This sensorial resistance acts as an obstacle to the self-positing of the listening self. The listening subject feels limited by the music and, as a result, gains an impetus to know the music only to be hindered yet again by the subsequent emotive experience. Especially for listeners who are not musically trained, *feeling* the music may then be the more resistible mode of gaining musical knowledge as opposed to *knowing* the music, because the limitation of the self reveals its inability to resist.

Resistant or symbolic listening therefore addresses some of the methodological limits of the three aforementioned theories of concatenation, affordance, and expectation. Symbolic listening provides the listening self with an awareness of oneself with each passing moment of the music regardless of the listener's ability to 'reproduce' that which had happened as being in accord with the concatenated musical experience. Instead, the psychical mechanics of resistance reject the dissonant-sounding chord as undesirable and mediate its effect through a repressed or expressed emotional response. Symbolic listening demands total attention much more upon one's own psychological and affective states than the integral apprehension of the musical artifact, as required of a concatenated way of listening.

In addition, resistant listening takes into consideration both the inherent properties of the musical object as well as the epistemological capacity of the listening subject. This criterion is akin to the ecological approach. However, by stipulating the nature of either thing or person as fixed, the concept of affordance overlooked the plasticity and performativity of the music and the listener, who, for one, bears the reflexive trait of imagination. That is, music can be repeated or reinterpreted with different technologies, while the human faculty of imagination enhances or distorts the composition of the sound or musical object. Understanding resistance as the ability not to be affected by something undesirable provides us with the predetermined condition to calibrate the changing circumstances of both the object and its desirability, and the mind and its affectability.

Huron's theory of expectation fares better by taking imagination as one of five active processes towards the generation of musical meaning. Both the theory of expectation and the principles of resistance share the adaptive and defensive nature of the anthropological enterprise in knowledge acquisition. In terms of differences, expectant listening focuses solely on the cognitive responses, while resistant listening constitutes the affective and the aesthetic in tandem. Listening with psychical resistance engenders a symbolic comprehension of the subject-object relation, one that encompasses the positing of the self through the signifying of the other and vice versa. A brief but concise application of symbolic listening to Bigand's experiments would exemplify the comprehensiveness of the theory.

Correspondingly, the most likely explanation for the irregularities in response time and accuracy for the non-musicians (Figure 8.1) when listening to the musical stimuli at varying speeds in the experiment by Bigand and his fellow scientists would then be attributed not to their sensorial resistance, but to their psychical resistance with or without the arbitration of affect. I claim that their allowance for musical enjoyment has effected the slowing down of their self-consciousness vis-à-vis their response to the aural stimuli. It also effects an infinite but simultaneous objectification of their sensory experiences, which, by way of confusing the acting and signifying processes, results in the high rate of inaccurate observations. Naturally, the feedback sound signals affixing consonance and dissonance with emotional connotations and judgements such as 'correct' or 'incorrect' would have caused further delays and uncertainties in their sensory responses to signify the consonant and dissonant chords as aurally pleasurable or undesirable symbols respectively. The binary of sonic signifiers—either causal or effectual—seems rather arbitrary and even imperative for they restrict the listening subjects to engage and associate their desires with value judgments. It is only when the listeners self-posit themselves (the I) against the aural stimuli (the non-I) and 'imagine' the feelings and disregard their prior preference or taste that the subjectivity of the self can assert greater resistance and autonomy.

Conclusion: enjoyment/resistance

In contrast to the standing psychological theories of *concatenation*, *affordance* and *expectation*, semantic resistance is neither intuitive nor teleological. Instead, it is reflexive and affected. Rather than bearing the conservative ethics of the ecological or phenomenological approaches, resistance disrupts the signification process through actions and affects. The act of self-positing (or in our case, self-listening and also self-feeling) creates an original duplicity that can only be resisted by the seepage and stoppage of emotions.

While most psychologists have attributed empirical differences to cognitive abilities or cultural characteristics, my arguments in this chapter posit the centrality of resistance, especially that of affective resistance, in accounting for the responses of the listening subject. Given that Lacan has called for the subject 'to name, to articulate, to bring this [unconscious] desire into existence', my contention has been to consider in tandem the emotions welled up in the non-acting self as well as those elicited in the listening self.[32] It is through the act of symbolic listening that musical meaning gets realized not only through the enjoyment of the resistance, but also through the resistance of enjoyment.

Notes

1 For example, see Kofi Agawu, *Representing African Music: Postcolonial Notes, Queries, Positions* (New York and London: Routledge, 2003).
2 Paul Guyer, 'Kant, Immanuel', in *Routledge Encyclopedia of Philosophy*, ed. Edward Craig (London: Routledge, 2004). Online at www.rep.routledge.com/article/DB047SECT12, Accessed 14 May, 2011.
3 Patrik N. Juslin and Daniel Västfjäll, 'Emotional Responses to Music: The Need to Consider Underlying Mechanisms', *Behavioral and Brain Sciences* 31 (2008): 559–621; Klaus R. Scherer, 'Which Emotions Can Be Induced by Music? What Are the Underlying Mechanisms? And How Can We Measure Them?', *Journal of New Music Research* 33, No. 3 (2004): 239–51.
4 Sandra E. Trehub and Erin E. Hannon, 'Conventional Rhythms Enhance Infants' and Adults' Perception of Music', *Cortex* 45 No. 1 (2009): 110–18; Gaye Soley and Erin E. Hannon 'Infants Prefer the Musical Meter of Their Own Culture: A Cross-Cultural Comparison', *Developmental Psychology* 46 (2010): 286–92; Yasuyo Minagawa-Kawai et al., 'Prefrontal Activation Associated with Social Attachment: Facial-Emotion Recognition in Mothers and Infants', *Cerebral Cortex* 19, No. 2 (2009): 284–92; Maude Beauchemin et al., 'Mother and Stranger: An Electrophysiological Study of Voice Processing in Newborns', *Cerebral Cortex* 21, No. 8 (2011): 1705–11.
5 Cf. Anahid Kassabian, *Ubiquitous Listening: Affect, Attention, and Distributed Subjectivity* (Berkeley and Los Angeles: University of California Press, 2013).
6 Emmanuel Bigand et al., 'Sensory Versus Cognitive Components in Harmonic Priming', *Journal of Experimental Psychology: Human Perception and Performance* 29, No. 1 (2003): 159–71.
7 Jerrold Levinson, *Music in the Moment* (Ithaca, NY: Cornell University Press, 1997), 22ff.
8 Jerrold Levinson, 'Concatenationism, Architectonicism, and the Appreciation of Music', *Revue Internationale de Philosophie* 238 (2006): 506.
9 Eric Clarke, *Ways of Listening: An Ecological Approach to the Perception of Musical Listening* (Oxford: Oxford University Press, 2005), 36ff.
10 *Ibid.*, 203–204.
11 Emmanuel Bigand et al., 'Sensory versus Cognitive Components in Harmonic Priming'.
12 The combinatorial results in the graph are derived from Bigand, 'Sensory versus Cognitive Components in Harmonic Priming'. I have plotted the response time and accuracy against each other when, in the original experiment, they were separated into two graphs. Each further point on the y-axis corresponds to the temporal increment of the musical stimulant.
13 David Huron, *Sweet Anticipation: Music and the Psychology of Expectation* (Harvard, MA: MIT Press, 2008): 15–18.
14 Giorgio Biancorosso, 'Whose Phenomenology of Music? David Huron's Theory of Expectation', *Music and Letters* 89, No. 3 (2008): 396–404.
15 Huron, *Sweet Anticipation*, 376.
16 *Oxford English Dictionary*, 3rd edition (Oxford: Oxford University Press, 2010).

17 Dylan Evans, *An Introductory Dictionary of Lacanian Psychoanalysis* (London and New York: Routledge, 1996), 2.
18 Johann Gottlieb Fichte, 'Review of Aenesidemus', in *Fichte: Early Philosophical Writings*, ed. and trans. Daniel Breazeale (Ithaca, NY: Cornell University Press, 1988), 59–77.
19 Although Fichte has also deliberated on the idea of the 'original duplicity', which Günter Zöller has discussed in length, it philosophical implications are beyond the scope of this chapter. See Günter Zöller's 'Original Duplicity: The Ideal and the Real in Fichte's Transcendental Theory of the Subject', in *The Modern Subject: Conception of the Self in Classical German Philosophy*, ed. Karl Ameriks and Dieter Sturma (Albany, NY: State University of New York), 115–30.
20 This reflexive process occurs, for Lacan, on the theoretical order of the symbolic. Whether the initial element is a sign, signal, signifier, symbol, or symptom, the task of psychoanalysis is to interpret these entities. It is thus logical for Lacan to describe psychoanalysts as the 'practitioners of the symbolic function'. Jacques Lacan, *Écrits*, trans. Bruce Fink (London and New York: W.W. Norton, 2006), 235.
21 Sigmund Freud, 'Observations on Transference Love', in *The Freud Reader*, ed. Peter Gay (London: Vintage, 1995), 381.
22 Evans, *An Introductory Dictionary of Lacanian Psychoanalysis*, 5.
23 Jacques Lacan, *The Seminar of Jacques Lacan Book, VII: The Ethics of Psychoanalysis*, ed. Jacques-Alain Miller, trans. Dennis Porter (London and New York: Routledge, 2008), 126–27.
24 That said, Lacan deems affects as displaceable onto other symbolic forms and are thereby transposed strategically into comprehensible knowledge for psychoanalytic work. *Écrits: The First Complete Edition in English*, trans. Bruce Fink in collaboration with Héloïse Fink and Russell Grigg (New York and London: W.W. Norton, 2006), 598.
25 Lacan coined the neologism 'extimacy' to connote the relationship of 'an external, contingent, found element, which simultaneously stands for the subject's innermost being'. Slavoj Žižek, 'Robert Schumann: The Romantic Anti-humanist', in *The Plague of Fantasies* (London: Verso, 1997), 205. Cf. Elisabeth Bronfen, 'Extimate Violence. Shakespeare's Night World'. www.bronfen.info/writing/writing-2006/extimate-violence-shakespeare-s-night-world, Accessed 14 October, 2016.
26 Žižek has a larger thesis in which he compares Fichte's *Anstoss* (as feelings) with Lacan's *objet petit a* (as object-cause of desire and as surplus enjoyment). For reasons of space I am unable to elaborate this thesis here. See Markus Gabriel and Slavoj Žižek, *Mythology, Madness and Laughter: Subjectivity in German Idealism* (London: Continuum, 2009), 142: '*Anstoss* is closer to *objet petit a*, to the primordial foreign body that "sticks in the throat" of the subject, to the object-cause of desire that splits it up'.
27 Slavoj Žižek, *The Metastases of Enjoyment: Six Essays on Women and Causality* (London: Verso, 1994), 156–57.
28 This follows Lacan's theorization of the gaze, with *one seeing oneself see oneself*. Jacques Lacan, *Seminar XI: The Four Fundamental Concepts of Psychoanalysis*, ed. Jacques-Alain Miller, trans. Alan Sheridan (London and New York: Routledge, 1998), 80–83.
29 Thomas Nagel, *The View From Nowhere* (Oxford: Oxford University Press, 1989).
30 This individualised semantic subjectivity is congruent to the polysemic theory of Jean-Jacques Nattiez as well as the absolutist expressionism of Leonard Meyer. See Jean-Jacques Nattiez, *Music and Discourse: Toward a Semiology of Music*, trans. Carolyn Abbate (Princeton, NJ: Princeton University Press, 1990) and

Leonard Meyer, *Music and Emotion* (Chicago: University of Chicago Press, 1956).
31 Daniel Breazeale, 'Check or Checkmate? On the Finitude of the Fichtean Self', in *The Modern Subject: Conception of the Self in Classical German Philosophy*, ed. Karl Ameriks and Dieter Sturma (Albany, NY: State University of New York, 1995), 88 and 94.
32 Jacques Lacan, *The Seminar of Jacques Lacan: Book II: The Ego in Freud's Theory and in the Technique of Psychoanalysis 1954–1955*, ed. Jacques-Alain Miller, trans. Sylvana Tomaselli, with notes by John Forrester (New York: Norton, 1991), 228.

9 Masochism and sentimentality
Barthes's Schumann and Schumann's Chopin

Stephen Downes

This essay deploys the relationship between masochism and sentimentalism as the basis of interpretative thoughts on Schumann's depiction of Chopin in his piano cycle *Carnaval* (1834). It does so by bringing artistic and psychoanalytical ideas of masochism into critical dialogue with Roland Barthes's self-confessed 'sentimental' approaches in works such as *Camera Lucida* and *A Lover's Discourse* and with his writings on Schumann's music.

One of Barthes's most famous ideas is the 'punctum', a lacerating, wounding moment or detail felt by the observer of an artwork. This notion of punctum highlights parallels between the structures and expressions of sentimentalism and masochism. Sentimentalism is based upon sympathic response to spectacles of suffering, the adopting of the other's agony as one's own and, through feeling that pain, seeking to come into some state of union (or reunion) with that other. The sentimentalist yearns for a consonance achieved through sympathetic resonance. The masochist stages their own suffering as a mode through which to achieve some desired, altered state.

In his writings on Schumann, Barthes famously hears the 'beating' of the music in the body and its fragmentation into heightened moments. The punctum and the beats that, with Barthesian ears, we might hear when Schumann adopts the mask of Chopin in his *Carnaval*, are suggestive of a sentimental and masochistic identification with Chopin as a pained and suffering figure, an identification that can also be heard, through the symbolic and psychological status of Robert's painful right-hand finger, as a masked musical evocation of the beloved Clara during their period of enforced separation. The figuration in this piece is therefore a valuable case study in how to move, in a Deleuzian manner, between clinical and critical discourse.

First, a necessarily condensed and partial outline of some key aspects of masochism will be necessary before exploring its parallels and connections with sentimentalism.

Masochism

Masochism is a contentious and shifting notion. It moves from an origin in nineteenth-century romantic fiction to a range of developments as a psychoanalytic concept. In his overview of the term's history and varieties, William I. Grossman considers it controversial when used beyond a literary designation for any phenomenon in which sexual pleasure is associated with physical or mental pain. For Grossman, masochism's imprecision means that its value is 'descriptive and evocative'.[1] In such a view, the usefulness of the term in the psychoanalytical realm seems problematic. Its artistic source, however, makes it especially seductive as a psychoanalytical notion in the interpretation of art and responses to artistic stimuli.

As is well known, the source literary text is Leopold von Sacher-Masoch's *Venus in Furs* (1870). Psychoanalytic use of the term was initially developed by Richard Krafft-Ebing in his *Psychopathia Sexualis*, first published in 1886 and subsequently revised through twelve editions, with masochism gradually integrated into the sixth and seventh editions (1891). Krafft-Ebing saw masochism as an extreme, pathological version in men of 'normal' female behavior, female because he deemed the subordination characteristic of the masochist to be associated with women's views of the sexual relationship. This is diagnosed on the basis of interpreting descriptions of inner subjective feelings rather than observing external behavior. The term was not his invention, but one suggested to him by an anonymous Berlin correspondent who found consolation for his fantasies of torture and humiliation at the behest of powerful women in reading Sacher-Masoch's novella. By contrast, the later attempts physically to realize this fantasy with a prostitute were disappointing.[2] Masochism in Krafft-Ebing's text thus emerges from literary, aesthetic phenomenon into clinical case studies.

Stirred by Krafft-Ebing and Havelock Ellis, among others, masochism became an important aspect of fin-de-siècle sexual anxieties and the discourses of perversion and degeneracy that were prominent in medical and psychiatric works of the emerging science of sex as well as the erotic end of popular fiction.[3] The milestone psychoanalytical essay of the inter-war period is Freud's 'The Economic Problem of Masochism' (1924). Freud sustained Krafft-Ebing in arguing that the masochistic subject is in a 'characteristically feminine situation'. Freud ties the masochist's desire for punishment to his well-known theory of the Oedipus complex, in which Freud located the source of individual morality. For Freud, the male masochist invests in a fantasy of castration and guilt, of injury and punishment (often as the naughty child). In 'moral masochism', where the connection with sexuality is loosened, suffering is what matters, and the cause need not be the desired, beloved other but something we might consider impersonal.[4]

Deleuze disagreed with Freud, in particular with Freud's positing of masochism as an internal 'residue' of the 'primal sadism' that Freud considered to be its 'counterpart in instinctual life' in which the libido seeks to defuse the destructive death instinct by diverting it outwards to external objects, but which then might be once more turned inwards to produce 'secondary masochism'.[5] We need not expand on this dispute, but note that Deleuze also disagreed with Freud's Oedipal basis for understanding the masochist's desire for punishment and emphasized the role of the mother as replacing that of the law of the father. More pertinent to my essay is the extent to which Deleuze emphasized the significance of the artistic origins of masochism in Masoch's short story. Deleuze, noting that Masoch worked in the 'grand tradition of German Romanticism' and drew his inspiration from the 'cultural and aesthetic', argued that 'it is when the senses take works of art for their objects that they become masochistic for the first time'. In Masoch's story, significantly, the power of the woman in furs is first revealed in the viewing of a Renaissance portrait.[6]

Deleuze fully explored these themes in his influential text, *Coldness and Cruelty* (1967). Emphasis is placed on Masoch's romanticism, evident in his use of dreamscapes, nocturnal park scenes, evocative paintings, and the metaphor of travelogue to Italy. The main characteristics of masochism—excess, cultivated anxiety, exhibitionism of pain, suffering and martyrdom—are all described in a romantic literary style. Crucially, the masochistic moment is not found in physical realization but in artistic representation, in paintings, sculptures, and dreamscapes. Masoch's text is steeped in aestheticism. The masochist's body is poised in an expectant, tantalized state, anticipating the desired suffering in a condition of endless waiting, held in a moment of heightened sensibility. This suspense, performed as a series of hesitations and lingerings, is captured in artistic tableaux. The pure state of waiting that defines masochism for Deleuze in what he calls 'supersensuous sentimentality'—an inner feeling, a superior, transubstantiated counterpart to the cold cruelties that are imagined to be inflicted on the body. It is performative, contractual, aestheticized.[7] Artistic representation is therefore a 'necessary part of masochism's constitution'.[8]

The central role of suspense—so important for Deleuze—was identified by Theodor Reik in his *Masochism in Modern Man* (1941), where the three main characteristics are 'phantasy', 'suspense', and the 'demonstrative'—imagination, anticipation, and display. Reik also devoted considerable space to discussion of the femininity of masochism.[9] The consequence of this gendered focus, as Kaja Silverman notes, is that avowing masochism questions the masculinity of the subject as it is a pathological rather than 'normal' or accepted subjective position; as Reik noted, the masochist man leaves the accepted social subject behind, either that or this subject is shattered.[10] The aestheticized practice of masochist suspense appears politically and culturally subversive; it seems to perform a reversal of culturally and politically endorsed gender roles, confirming the 'constructedness of gender relations'.[11] It is fascinating that, contemporaneously with the cultural and sexual challenges of masochism, there arose a parallel ambivalent challenge to the (similarly gendered) denigration of sentimentality. Sentimentalism and masochism both appeared to challenge the dominant, culturally acceptable constructions of male subjectivity through the adoption of supposedly 'feminine' positions in which subjective suffering is willingly pursued.

Sentimentalism and masochism

In sentimental literature, the 'feminine' is associated with supposedly 'natural' feeling. In late nineteenth-century modernism, by contrast, the feminine becomes associated with artifice and superficial details, with a preoccupation with style over substance. Through the aestheticization of the erotic by various artistic forms in which narrative expectations are subverted by a play of suspension, ritual, allusion, and parody, the aesthetic itself becomes viewed as the realm of the feminine. In these terms, Sacher-Masoch's *Venus in Furs* shares stylistic and thematic commonalities with Oscar Wilde's *Picture of Dorian Gray* (1890). Both seek a level of sophistication and refinement above the vulgar sentimentality of the masses. For Wilde and Sacher-Masoch, the woman serves feeling only, while the male aesthete uses his feeling—so the paradox is that the apparent subversion in adopting a feminine position reinforces culturally reified power relations. Decorporialized, she, the cold other, becomes an aesthetic image, and it is his desire which actually controls the scene; she is his double, a projection of his fantasy, speaking his words. Apparent subversions of dominant masculinities only in the end serve to 'reinscribe divisions and deep-seated anxieties' in particular through the 'strenuous repudiation' of a specific, debased kind of sentimental aesthetic.[12] The ambiguities here are obvious; the subversive qualities of masochism are deceptive: the rejection of sentimentalism is partial, ambivalent.[13]

Krafft-Ebing reads *Venus in Furs* in the tradition of the novel of sensibility. In the opening section of *Psychopathia*, he describes sentimentalism as the immature love of the 'feeble-minded' and how in male submission the enslavement to the beloved becomes more apparent as the sentimental lover becomes weaker and yields to sensualism. This kind of love, Krafft-Ebing tells us, is self-destructive (when unrequited love often leading to suicide). The characterization irresistibly recalls Goethe's sorrowful young Werther.[14] The sentimental literary tradition emerges in one of his case studies of masochism (no. 57), which cites the act of reading descriptions of scenes of torture in Stowe's *Uncle Tom's Cabin* (1889), a classic of American sentimental literature, as a source of masochistic fantasy. Krafft-Ebing considered masochism to be an extension of the literary preoccupation with romantic agony.[15] Stowe's novel is also cited by Freud in 'A Child is Being Beaten' (1919); for Freud, as for Krafft-Ebing, the masochist gains erotic stimulus from reading a literary evocation rather than from first hand physical experience of suffering, from the perverse identification with a character's sufferings, in this case in scenes of physical punishment.[16] This reading for perverse erotic pleasure lies not only in projecting fantasies on to scenic description but also finds them in tantalizing disruptions to narrative progression and connection. Masochism is an investment in literary themes and techniques characteristically found in sentimental literature, particularly of suspension and other types of temporal or narrative disturbance, in the tensions between moment and plot.[17]

Freud's 'A Child is Being Beaten' and Stowe's *Uncle Tom's Cabin* are important texts in Mariane Noble's analysis of the 'parallel structures' of sentimentalism and masochism. The sympathetic pain of the observer at the spectacle of the misery of the imperiled or vulnerable beloved, the making of their agony one's own, are, of course, notions at the heart of the eighteenth-century cult of sensibility (influentially shaped by Shaftesbury and Smith, among others). Sentimental literature idealized such sympathetic figurations and its aim is for readers to identify with them, to adopt the sympathetic position and its attendant co-option of the suffering subject's pain. The sentimental aim is some kind of union of object and subject—a yearning of consonance achieved through sympathetic resonance. Tears, real or imaginary, are a marker of loss and yearning for the restoration of unity.[18]

Laura Hinton has similarly explored how 'sadomasochistic desire underlies the experience of sympathy, through the perverse narrative spectator who creates and reflects sentimental image-making'. Yet she also notes how a pejorative view of sentimentalism, as overindulgent, excessive, inauthentic, becomes prevalent in modernism.[19] This modernist rejection of the sentimentalist is lamented by Barthes in *A Lovers Discourse: Fragments* (1977). Barthes writes: 'discredited by modern opinion, love's sentimentality must be assumed by the amorous subject as a powerful transgression which leaves him alone and exposed; by a reversal of values, then, it is this sentimentality which today constitutes love's obscenity'. In an historical reversal, it is no longer the sexual that is considered indecent, it is the sentimental. It is 'obscene' because it is deemed 'anachronistic'. In this climate, 'everyone will understand that X has "huge problems" with his sexuality; but no one will be interested in those Y may have with his sentimentality'. In the 'history of tears', Barthes asks, 'why was "sensibility", at a certain moment, transformed into "sentimentality"? When was it taboo for big boys to cry, but not for women?'[20]

Yet modernism's relation to sentimentalism is complex. The tensed coexistence of the sentimental and anti-sentimental has been explored in the work of a wide range of poets and novelists identified with romanticism and modernism.[21] A fruitful illustrative example is the critical and psychoanalytical reception of that sacred cow of modernist literature, James Joyce's *Ulysses* (1922).[22] Its relationship to the tradition of the sentimental novel, discussed by Jay Michael Dickson, is embodied in Leopold Bloom, the novel's most sentimental figure but also, because he seeks the pleasures of vicarious suffering, one who adopts the position of a masochist. Bloom's feminized sensibilities lead to his position as an outsider, marginalized and ridiculed. Dickson argues that Joyce's novel offers the continued promise of sentimentality, even as it remains the subject of stigma.[23] This is the converse to Carl Jung's identification of the 'coldness' of *Ulysses* as anti-sentimental, as the necessary modernist antidote to the still-prevailing sentimental hoax. Jung, viewing Joyce as victim of Catholic authoritarianism, considers sentimentality to be 'the superstructure erected upon brutality'.[24] In a time of intense suffering, such as that caused by modern warfare, sentimental responses are raised to salve the conscience of the observer.

A key text for Noble's exploration of the parallel structures of sentimentalism and masochism is Barthes's *Camera Lucida* (1980). Barthes declares that 'as *Spectator* I was interested in photography only for "sentimental" reasons; I wanted to explore it not as a question (a theme) but as a wound: I see, I feel, hence I notice, I observe, and I think'.[25] The key progression here is the move from initial wound, through feeling to the final stage, 'I think'. The famous distinction underlying Barthes's contemplation of photographic images is that between 'studium' and 'punctum'. The former is a contract between artist and consumer; culturally coded and educationally conditioned, pleasurable but neither painful nor delightful; the latter, unintended by the artist, is that which breaks or 'punctuates' the former, it 'shoots out like an arrow' and 'pierces', 'pricks', 'bruises', 'wounds' the observer. The studium and the punctum exist in a 'co-presence' in which there is no established or consistent rule of connection. The punctum is an addition, something that the observer brings to the photograph, and yet it is already there. It is a detail in the artistic space, one that has 'a power of expansion' and that is 'often metonymic'. Brief, undevelopable, only repeatable, the effect is 'certain but unlocatable, it does not find its sign, its name'. Yet it inspires in Barthes a series of questions—the move from feeling to thought: where is this disturbance that pricks me? The book's most famous example (and the crucial one for Noble) is the Winter Garden photograph of his deceased mother. Unlike preceding examples, this image is not reproduced in the book because for the reader, unlike the author, there would be no comparable wound; the punctum is Barthes's own. (It is always the observer's own; just as sentimentality is also in the eye or ear of the beholder. But this is an intensely personal example. And for this reason, we can strongly sympathize, in sentimental fashion, with the grieving Barthes.) In front of this photograph, Barthes cannot transform his grief, his suffering, into mourning. It 'was for me like the last music Schumann wrote before collapsing, that first *Gesäng der Frühe* Op. 133, which accords with both my mother's being and my grief at her death'. This is something he declared inexpressible except through 'an infinite series of adjectives'.[26] It's not difficult, however, to suspect that Barthes was drawn to the comforting, religious qualities of Schumann's piece, achieved through its hymn-like textures, its contrapuntal passages and long pedal points, all of which suggest the piano imitating an organ played in sentimental *religioso* mode. Even, perhaps, in the way in which the final cadence is prolonged by these pedal points, in a gesture that can be heard as expressing an inability to let go, or to leave the scene of spiritual comfort, to achieve the closure that mourning facilitates.[27]

In his foreword to a recent re-issue of *A Lover's Discourse*, Wayne Koestenbaum (who identifies Barthes's text as a 'whimsical seminar' on

Goethe's *Sorrows of Young Werther*, and hence as an anachronistic commentary on the sentimental literary tradition) is equivocal. For Koestenbaum, Barthes is not a masochist, though he identifies 'laceration' as the 'key word' and argues that Barthes understood 'agony and ravishment' and chose a 'femininized position, or a wounded one': all of which seems remarkably close to the defining characteristics of masochism in the tradition of Krafft-Ebing and Reik. Koestenbaum lauds Barthes as a 'miniaturist' and writer of 'fragments', which is where he most resembles Schumann: the 'stutters, hesitations and refinements, even lacerations', the 'love of nuance' and diversion by 'stray interpretative detail'.[28] In 'Loving Schumann' (1979) Barthes argues that Schumann's music is out of fashion because of the devaluation of 'interiority, intimacy, solitude' in modern society; 'Schumann is truly the musician of solitary intimacy, of the amorous and imprisoned soul that *speaks to itself*'. His music consists of brief moments and interruptions, encapsulated in the term "intermezzo", now applied to *all* music and the source of which is the 'literary theme of Carnival'. In this musical space 'pain', and its associated 'madness', can assume especially powerful guises:

> In this fragmented world, distorted by whirling appearances (the whole world is a Carnival), a pure and somehow terribly motionless element occasionally breaks through: pain. "If you ask me the name of my pain, I could not tell you. I think it is pain itself, and I could not designate it better." This pure pain, without object, this essence of pain, is certainly a madman's pain; we believe that only the mad (insofar as we can name madness and demarcate ourselves from it) quite simply *suffer*.[29]

In 'Rasch' (1975) Barthes explains how in Schumann's *Kreisleriana* Op. 16 (1838) he hears 'beats in the body, what beats the body, or better: I hear this body that beats'. In the music, he hears a body moving, knocking, extending, shuddering, a restless 'pulsional body' that is 'intoxicated, distracted and at the same time ardent'. These beats can assume less violent, pacifying, figures when they are 'linked to subtle movements of the body'. The beating of the heart, which stands for 'sensuous emotivity', is the 'paradoxical' site for beating 'in' the body, one both 'pulsional and moral' for 'heart' is romantically equated with "soul", and "feeling", romantic names for the body—these are the moral terms. Barthes urges a restoration of the body to the romantic text, so we can hear how tonality serves the body, through dissonance, and modulation, to redress the imbalance of the emotive romantic tradition. Yet his primary attraction seems to lie in Schumann's 'interiority', the beats that move from body to feeling, from physics to psyche. Tellingly, Barthes acknowledges, without commentary, that 'beat' is an emblematic word in psychoanalysis by reference to the title of Freud's 'A Child is Being Beaten'.[30] And in his admission that metaphors and images are the only (inadequate) way to describe this beating he also chimes with the aesthetic and performative character that defines the masochistic scene. Music's effect on the body as suffering and wounding also lends its power as a vehicle for sentimentalism. Schumann's music offered comfort to Barthes in his sorrowful pain aroused by the punctum he perceived in the photograph of his mother. Schumann's own critical writings offer comfort for those who sympathize with Barthes, the sentimental Schumannian. These contexts for the interpretative elaboration of Schumannian masochism/sentimentality are now worth considering.

Reading and listening to Schumann

Sentimentalism's cultural heyday in the late eighteenth century was well on the wane by the time Schumann lent his pen to the topic. As Melina Esse has described, ambivalence over the 'sensible body', over the body's capacity for 'tender sentimentalism', was entwined with the suspicion of sensationalism in the 1820s. Sentiment was seen as now debased, vulgarized, by its appropriation by the middle and lower classes. Its value and sincerity was now open to question, and its effects were often placed in ironic or overtly performative contexts.[31] In artistic expressions overtly evoking gendered dynamics, 'physical distress' was portrayed through musical figures imitating the suffering (feminine) character's sobs, sighs, hesitations.[32]

Schumann's writings of the 1830s were an important source of the critical engagement with sentimentalism, especially his descriptions of Chopin's music. For example, in 'The Editor's Ball' (1837), essentially a review of a selection of newly published piano music, listening to a performance of Chopin's *Polonaises* Op. 26 inspires sympathetic images of heroic but suffering Poland: Chopin's music cannot be heard "without weeping". A Chopin waltz is a vehicle for amorous seduction, with Chopin (jealously) described as a "charming heart-breaker". In several reviews, the phrase "*à la* Chopin" occurs as reference to the sentimental aspect of his performative style. "Cannons buried under flowers", as Schumann famously put it, in an encapsulating image of suffering and sentiment conjured up in an 1836 review of Chopin's concertos.[33]

Chopin's relationship with sentimentalism can vex critics. While acknowledging that 'fashionable sentimentality' was an important aspect of Chopin's 'urbanity', Charles Rosen is determined to resist the sentimental character of Chopin's music, or at least to transform it into something he considers to be more aesthetically valuable. He finds a sentimental tone to be especially prominent in the nocturnes, unsurprisingly so as this is a genre of the salon, which Rosen calls sentimental music's 'most prestigious home'. Rosen is at pains to point out how Chopin's nocturnes transcend the restrictions of 'light, social entertainment' and thus 'overwhelm the modest expectations' of both the genre and the milieu. Chopin accomplished this act of aesthetic escapology through the 'transformation of the vulgar into something aristocratic', a turning of the commonplace into the refined and sophisticated, of bad taste into good. Rosen argues that in some of the more intense moments of the nocturnes, Chopin 'evaded the sentimentality of the salon style more ambiguously—by magnifying and exaggerating it, by forcing it to the point of morbidity'.[34] (This 'morbidity' can be readily—*à la* Schumann—related to culturally emphasized aspects of the composer's biography: the familiar tropes of sickness and the effeminate, and of Polish '*żal*', that supposedly special form of melancholic yearning generated by Poland's history of tragic national suffering.)

Rosen is trying to rescue Chopin's music from its fate in the kind of criticism exemplified by Friedrich Niecks's discussion, after Hans von Bülow, of the accusation of Schumann's sentimentality, an 'affected sensibility' that he thought Schumann had misguidedly gleaned from the worst aspects of Chopin.[35] As we shall see, however, the sense that Schumann turns to Chopin for sentimental effect is perceptive. Barthes, too, is consistently sentimentalist, and a romantic one in the Schumann tradition. He seeks, anachronistically and amorously, to rescue Schumann's reputation as sentimental bedfellow.[36] Kevin Kopelson, a self-confessed and conflicted sentimentalist, emphasizes that Barthes's 'body' is a soulful one, and that Barthes 'transcends modernist antisentimentality'. This is exemplified for Kopelson by the contrast with André Gide's anti-sentimental rejection of rubato; for Barthes, rubato is an extremely mediated, highly artful expression of "bodily" desire and sentimentality—'one even pianists who want to come across as desirous and sentimental (in Barthes's case, as *transgressively* desirous and sentimental) won't attempt for fear of coming across badly'.[37]

As we have seen, in 'Loving Schumann' Barthes refers, without discussion, to a key text on masochism. It's a tantalising name-drop. Andrew Brown has sought to pursue the 'sadomasochist' implications in Barthes's notion of beating bodies.[38] He takes his cue from Peter Ostwald's psychoanalytical study of Schumann, in particular the view there may be an association between auditory sensitivity and the fear of being beaten, and, continues Ostwald, 'people who are sensitive to sounds sometimes store memories of harsh sounds—such as crying and screaming—in unconscious regions of the mind, whence they may emerge in fantasies but not as articulated words'.[39] Ostwald and Barthes are both salient late examples in the history of interpreting Schumann's music through notions of the 'intimate', 'madness' in which Schumann's music is heard as especially 'confessional' with a profound unity of life and work, which the composer himself promotes in the critical writings and in the voluminous and frank self-scrutiny of his relationship with Clara in the diaries. Biographical listening turns to autobiographical listening as the listener sympathetically identifies with the 'suffering' figure of the composer. Intimacy can turn to sentimentalism through the amorous musical expressions associated with Clara and the relationship with the expressions and techniques of salon music. Yet sentimentality also flourishes in the posthumous diagnosis of mental illness, in our sympathy for the suffering artist.[40]

The history of the retrospective diagnosis of Schumann starts with Paul Julius Möbius's *Über Robert Schumanns Krankheit* (1906) in which Schumann is described as possessing 'feminine traits' of 'passivity' manifest in a 'surrendering of oneself to sentiment', indeed, of 'excessive sentimentality'.[41] Möbius believed that all this could be discerned through listening to the music. The tradition has recently been sustained and scrutinized by the psychoanalyst Jacques Mauger, who points out that because of the nostalgic, romantic image of Schumann as a melancholic madman, 'finding evidence of Schumann's suffering in his music becomes easy… we are ready to suffer empathetically with him, even finding some pleasure in it'. Sentimentalism turns to masochism. Yet Mauger is keen to make a crucial distinction between suffering and pain: 'suffering has to do with what is representable, nameable', suffering is part of the subjective self, and one can become attached to it, unwilling to be relieved from it. Pain, by contrast, is impersonal, makes the subject disappear; 'but the problem is that one's own ego cannot consider pain without naming it, even though pain is incompatible with the mode of representation characteristic of the ego'.

> Primordial masochism is first and foremost a constituting disposition of my ego that allows me to integrate a painful and traumatic event by transforming it into suffering, into something that is part of my representational network, under the control of the pleasure/unpleasure principle, where unpleasure and pleasure are as inseparable as the two faces of the same psychic experience.[42]

Thus 'only suffering can be domesticated, even sometimes caressed like one's own nostalgic object'. By contrast, pain is sudden and disturbing, and it's only possible to begin to describe it after the event, by 'referring to all sorts of disruptive moments—moments of discontinuity, of dissonance, of dismemberment, of disharmony even in the most harmonious passages, when the most familiar suddenly turns into the strangest experience'.[43]

In 'Loving Schumann', Barthes makes a strikingly similar distinction when he notes that 'absolute', 'un-nameable' pain 'cannot be expressed musically; music can only express the pathos of pain (its social image), not its being'.[44] Mauger's ideas on how music might be heard to express this suffering—fragment, discontinuity, defamiliarization, dissonance—chime with Barthes and are highly suggestive of how one might translate the notion of lacerating punctum into musical terms.

Schumann's 'Chopin'

How to move between pathological clinical symptom and artistic forms, to analyse the clinical in a critical text: what, as we move from pathology is the new artistic content, its origin and its stylistic motivation? What is the

174   *Stephen Downes*

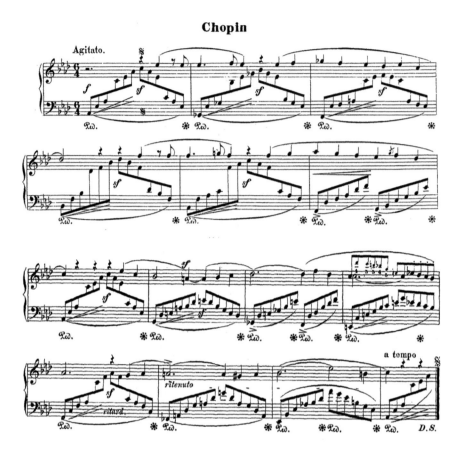

Example 9.1 Robert Schumann, 'Chopin' from *Carnaval*, Op. 9.

device allowing this expression? Be it an enunciative 'quiver, murmur, the stutter', the 'tremolo, or the vibrato' it is something marked and reverberative, asking us to make connections between its points and echoes.[45] Masoch's trembling German syntax in which stammering leads to suspension, the motivating force of masochism;[46] the 'stutters' which Koestenbaum considered so characteristic of Barthes's texts and Schumann's music—both are such devices, and they have potent musical parallels.

So how might one hear masochism and sentimentalism in Schumann's 'Chopin' (Example 9.1), and what characters and implications might accrue and arise through such a hearing? The piece's place and function within the cycle immediately offers a fertile context. In a pursuit of the meanings and subjective identities in Schumann's *Carnaval*, Lawrence Kramer highlights the freedoms of 'cross dressing' in the carnivalesque that allows appropriation of qualities conventionally ascribed to the other, qualities that would in normal social discourse be hidden or denied. Kramer mentions masochism as one such possibility, but not in this piece (he describes it in Schumann's *Frauenliebe und -leben*) and does not mention sentimentalism at all.[47] Yet both, of course, are 'feminine' positions the male subject may adopt only against the prevailing social constructions of gender: carnival offers the space to explore these roles and expressive modes. It is an ideal scenario for playing out masochistic and sentimental fantasies. Kramer describes Schumann's 'Chopin' as a 'faux-nocturne', a fake specimen of that genre of the salon that focusses Rosen's mind on Chopin's sentimentalism, and that was identified with 'feminine' arts of performance and expression.[48] If this *is* all artifice and simulation—faux—then it plays into the hands of both sentimental and masochistic practice. When we hear the sentimental in music we might linger positively upon versions of sweet and possibly vicarious expression and so recuperate expressive and aesthetic types elsewhere too swiftly rejected.[49] We also might hear a sophisticated probing of the problem of aesthetic autonomy and the related issue of artistic sincerity through overt constructiveness and reflectiveness.[50] As we have seen, a masochist will seek to play out his desire, suspending 'reality' through role play, pretense, and fantasy.

For Kramer, Schumann is 'satirizing and imitating the supposed effeminacy of its model' and 'impersonates' Chopin in 'drop-dead note-perfect style'. Yet the impersonation actually only becomes especially close with the ornamental figure in the right hand at bar 10, a poignant and 'punctuating' moment. The piece opens with arpeggiations supporting a lyrical tune that, if it were not for the title, might be heard as comparable with a romantic 'song without words' by a number of Schumann's contemporaries. Two balanced statements of this tune make for a stable section imbued with melancholic charm, particularly the $g\flat$ in bar 3 which, along with the ornamental $g\natural$ in bar 6 might plant the seed to the listener who doesn't know the title and that Chopin is the possible model. The *sforzandi* in the left hand and the performance indication 'Agitato' also suggest, from the start, a pointed anxiety, but it is the $a\natural-b\flat$ semitone in the left hand in bar 8 that really punctures the musical fabric and pricks up the ears. The *a* (as chromatic lower neighbour to $b\flat$) is the first dissonant note within the arpeggiations, a disturbance which immediately sends repercussions in the right hand, significantly as its first *sforzando*, as the $a\natural-b\flat$ is picked up in melody. The functions of the hands and the registers established in the opening have been destabilised.

The "Chopin" figure of bar 10 is an elaboration of $c-d\flat-b\flat-a\flat$, a decorative sequential repetition of the previous bar as well as a second echo of the closing melodic line at the cadence on the tonic in bars 6–7 (the melody after this cadence picks up the falling third-tone motive from the cadence). All of this is connective. Yet bar 10–11 also sounds like an interpolation in F minor, an addition, and therefore a suspense. The descending chromatic bass from bar 7 speeds up in bar 9, but the $e\natural$ in bar 10 is a neighbor to the f, not a passing $f\flat$ and so it slows the descent down to allow the decorated sequential repetition. The moment is composed out structural rubato (the marker of the sentimental which Gide abhorred and Barthes adored). The ambiguity of this suspended moment in the movement to closure is made more piquant by the last four quavers of bar 10: the diatonic descent from $e♭$ to $a♭$ is a miniature version of the structural closing line of the whole piece ($\hat{5}$–$\hat{1}$); but it is made painfully dissonant by the placement of the $e♭$ over the dominant of F minor. Furthermore, the new character of the hands is telling: the right hand loses the legato (which is already imperiled by the fourth and fifth finger of the filigree beforehand) to semi-staccato, and the left hand, for the only time in the piece, offers melodic support an octave below.[51] Textural consistency is broken; notably, the pedal is lifted a beat before the end of the bar to make the change clearer. The image of Chopin, a femininized persona, is evoked at the moment of greatest instability, the pointed moment of heightened expressivity. The resolutions of chromatic lines in the final bars attempt an integrating of this figure of 'otherness', a closing of the wound, in a manner that compares with Slavoj Žižek's hearing of how in Schumann's romantic music

> a foreign body is first intruded as a meaningless trace, a trauma interrupting the flow of the "proper" melodic line; gradually, however, this intruder is "perlaborated", fully integrated into the composition's main texture, so that at the end it loses its external character and is reproduced as something generated by the inner logic of the composition itself.[52]

The experience of listening to this moment is suggestive of Fernand Khnopff's *Listening to Schumann* (1883) (Figure 9.1). Richard Leppert interprets this painting as anti-Barthesian, because for him it suggests 'disembodied', meditative listening in which bodies are 'unfortunate necessities' in the performance and hearing of Schumann's music. For Leppert, the pianist's body is an 'intrusion, a penetration into the picture's space'.[53] We can turn this observation around for Barthesian purposes and see this hand as the punctum (Leppert's 'intrusion' and 'penetration' are close to this effect). In the painting, all we see of the pianist is the right hand, set against the black of the piano, reaching for high registers, as if performing Schumann's 'Chopin' moment. The listening woman's right hand, almost precisely central in the frame and the gesture which focusses our sympathetic observation of her suffering, is correspondingly set against her dark dress. Her hand covers her face in a gesture of private suffering, though we see her ear: the orifice into which the music penetrates the body. The chair in which she sits is a parallel magnification of the ear's shape. She is surrounded by the aural experience, but turned away from the musical source of 'pain'; she can escape but is, it seems, willfully sitting in suffering.[54] The pianist's hand, which seems to reach out towards her, to stroke, caress, to comfort, lies gently upon the

Figure 9.1 Fernand Khnopff, *Listening to Schumann* (1883).
Source: © Royal Museums of Fine Arts of Belgium, Brussels / photo: J. Geleyns - Ro scan.

upper reaches of keyboard as the woman's right hand covers her face, touches her brow. Through Schumann's music, selected as 'an agent of dread and unbearable intensity',[55] there is sentimental identification in which we absorb her pain, take it into ourselves. Central to all this is the pianist's performance of Schumann's fingering, '*à la* Chopin', of filigree figures in the upper register.

Rosen hears Schumann 'parodying' Chopin's technical fingerprint of exploiting the individual characteristics (smaller, 'weaker') of the fourth and fifth fingers of the right hand for performing delicate chromatic figures.[56] This aspect of Chopin's touch relates to the salon styles of delicate sentimentalism, the caressing of keys by moving along them, reluctant to let go, a touch associated with Chopin's melancholic and sensitive 'soul' and expression of a certain type of 'sentiment'.[57] This emphasis on the fingered features move us to further potential masochistic resonances, for the 'Chopin' figure can also be heard as a premonition of, or maybe inspiration for, the ornamental figures in Clara's *Notturno* (1835–1836) her sophisticated adaption of Chopin's recent innovations in the genre in which the right hand filigree is strikingly similarly shaped. In the final *Novelletten* (1838), Schumann incorporated the theme of Clara's nocturne as the most precious of her pieces for him, as a 'distant voice' which interrupts the piece's progression, and is subsequently twice recalled.[58] The repetitions may be heard to reinforce feelings of separation, loss, and inward suffering. In its last evocation, the music comes to a virtual halt in melancholic descending chromatic lines; and significantly, Schumann's performance indication for this moment is "Innig, *con intimo sentimento*". There are numerous examples of Robert's identification of Clara with Chopin: in a letter of September 1836, for example, he declared that her performances 'imbue Chopin's compositions with almost more meaning than he does.'[59] Chopin's music was an imaginary meeting ground, a fantasy of amorous expression, for the separated lovers during the 1830s, in which pain and suffering performed central roles. After the notorious self-induced injury to a finger on Schumann's right hand (most probably the middle finger, though the debate still rages), his painful hand became another aspect of the fantastic figuration of Clara: 'You are my right hand', he wrote to her in December 1838.[60]

So we move back and forth from critical to clinical text. Mauger, after the psychoanalyst Michel Schneider, argues that Schumann could control, and thereby express, his madness 'as long as [he] could call *his* pain Clara', 'spell' it in musical shapes symbolic of her.[61] Tell it, we might add, in fantastic fragments. In a sense, he can express it only by faking it. In this hearing of Schumann's 'Chopin', the right hand is feminized—it is a double identity, Clara-Fréderic, physical pain transformed into a symbol of psychological suffering, one that emerges as a performative, carnivalesque gesture aroused by a pointed disturbance (punctum) in the supporting left hand. It is a specific example, imbued with masochistic and sentimental tones, of the lacerations and elaborations that Barthes desired us to hear in Schumann, the beatings that move through the body into interior spaces of feeling and out again, translated into the metaphorical imagery that might encode subjective suffering.

Deleuze proposed a radical move, a breaking out from interiority (the restriction that masochism is really only Masoch's problem; or, we can add, Schumann's) in order to understand the 'world-historical situation', the 'milieus and moments' to which artistic representations of masochism are response.[62] We can evoke a similar move, of course, for sentimentalism. The painful vulnerability of the sensitive body, particularly in conditions of listening to music that move the subject between sensuality and inwardness, between physical and psychical, are vital in the interacting figurations of Schumann, Chopin and Masoch. And for Barthes, these figures of romanticism were reminders, against the fashion of his day, of the power of music to move us through the sufferings and sympathies of life.

Notes

1 William I. Grossman, 'Notes on Masochism: A Discussion of the History and Development of a Psychoanalytic Concept', *Psychoanalytic Quarterly* 55 (1986): 380.
2 Renate Hauser, 'Krafft-Ebing's Psychological Understanding of Sexual Behaviour', in *Sexual Knowledge, Sexual Science*, ed. Roy Porter and Mikuláš Teich (Cambridge: Cambridge University Press, 1994), 210–227.
3 See Alison Moore, 'Rethinking Gendered Perversion and Degeneration in Visions of Sadism and Masochism, 1886–1930', *Journal of the History of Sexuality* 18 (2009): 138–157.
4 Sigmund Freud, 'The Economic Problem of Masochism' [1924], in *Essential Papers on Masochism*, ed. Margaret Ann Fitzpatrick Henry (New York: New York University Press, 1995), 274–285.
5 Freud, 'The Economic Problem', 278–279.
6 Gilles Deleuze, 'From Sacher-Masoch to Masochism' [1961], trans. Christian Kerslake, *Angelaki: Journal of the Theoretical Humanities* 9, No. 1 (2004): 125–133.
7 Deleuze, 'Coldness and Cruelty' [1967], in Gilles Deleuze and Leopold von Sacher-Masoch, *Masochism: "Coldness and Cruelty" and "Venus in Firs"* (New York: Zone Books, 1991), 9–138. See Erika Gaudlitz, 'Libidinal Symptomatology in Deleuze's *Masochism—Coldness and Cruelty*', *Deleuze Studies* 9 (2015): 1–24.
8 Nick Mansfield, *Masochism: The Art of Power* (Westport, CT: Praeger, 1997), ix, who considers the sublime to be the specific aesthetic mode of masochism.
9 Theodor Reik, *Masochism in Modern Man* (New York: Farrar, Straus & Co., 1941), 197–211.
10 Kaja Silverman, *Male Subjectivity at the Margins* (London: Routledge, 1992), 189.
11 Suzanne R. Stewart, *Sublime Surrender: Male Masochism at the Fin-de-siècle* (Ithaca, NY: Cornell University Press, 1998), 8.
12 Rita Felski, 'The Counterdiscourse of the Feminine in Three Texts by Wilde, Huysmans and Sacher-Masoch", *Proceedings of the Modern Language Association* 106 (1991): 1094–1105. On Wilde and sentimentalism see Eve Kosofsky Sedgwick, *Epistemology of the Closet*, updated edition with a new introduction (Berkeley, CA: University of California Press, 2008).
13 On ambiguities between the transgressive and conservative in masochism see Mansfield, *Masochism*, x–xi.
14 See Roland Dollinger, 'The Self-Inflicted Suffering of Young Werther: An Example of Masochism in the 18th-Century', in *One Hundred Years of Masochism: Literary Texts, Social and Cultural Contexts*, ed. Michael C. Fink and Carl Niekerk (Amsterdam: Rodopi, 2000), 91–108.
15 Richard von Krafft-Ebing, *Psychopathia Sexualis*, trans. of 12th edition by F.J. Rebman (New York: Physicians and Surgeons Book Co., 1924), 11–12, 144–151. See also Andrea K. Henderson, *Romanticism and the Painful Pleasures of Modern Life* (Cambridge: Cambridge University Press, 2008). The classic text is Mario Praz, *The Romantic Agony* (London: Oxford University Press, 1933).
16 Freud, '"A Child is Being Beaten": A Contribution to the Study of the Origin of Sexual Perversions' [1919], *The Standard Edition of the Complete Psychological Works of Sigmund Freud*, ed. James Strachey, Vol. 17, *An Infantile Neurosis and Other Works* (London: Hogarth, 1955), 175–204.
17 Lacan's rather scattered discussions of masochism similarly emphasise its literariness. See David Sigler, '"Read Mr. Sacher-Masoch": The Literariness of Masochism in the Philosophy of Jacques Lacan and Gilles Deleuze', *Criticism* 53 (2011): 189–212.

18 Mariane Noble, *The Masochistic Pleasures of Sentimental Literature* (Princeton, NJ: Princeton University Press, 2000), especially 62–85.
19 Laura Hinton, *The Perverse Gaze of Sympathy: Sadomasochistic Sentiments from 'Clarissa' to 'Rescue 911'* (New York: SUNY Press, 1999), 7.
20 Roland Barthes, *A Lover's Discourse: Fragments*, trans. Richard Howard, with an introduction by Wayne Koestenbaum (New York: Hill & Wang, 2010), 175–180.
21 See Jonathan Greenberg, *Modernism, Satire, and the Novel* (Cambridge: Cambridge University Press, 2011); Howard W. Fulweiler, *'Here a Captive Heart Busted': Studies in the Sentimental Journey of Modern Literature* (New York: Fordham University Press, 1993); Jennifer A. Williamson, *Twentieth-Century Sentimentalism* (New Brunswick: Rutgers University Press, 2014); James Chandler, *An Archaeology of Sympathy: The Sentimental Mode in Literature and Cinema* (Chicago, IL: Chicago University Press, 2013).
22 James Joyce, *Ulysses* (London: Penguin Classics, 2000).
23 Jay Michael Dickson, 'Defining the Sentimentalist in *Ulysses*', *James Joyce Quarterly* 44 (2006): 19–37.
24 Carl Jung, '*Ulysses*: A Monologue' [1932] in *The Spirit in Man, Art and Literature*, trans. R.E.C. Hull (London: Ark, 1984), 109–134. Thanks to Christopher Wintle for pointing out this source. On masochism in *Ulysses* see Frances L. Restuccia, 'Molly in Furs: Deleuzian/Masochian Masochism in the Writing of James Joyce', *NOVEL: A Forum on Fiction* 18 (1985): 101–116, who, after Deleuze's emphasis that masochism stems from literature, compares masochism's formal patterns with formal artistic patterns; see also Mansfield, *Masochism*, 43–50.
25 Roland Barthes, *Camera Lucida: Reflections on Photography*, trans. Richard Howard (London: Vintage, 2000), 21.
26 *Ibid.*, 70.
27 For a wide critique and commentary see Michael Fried, 'Barthes's Punctum', *Critical Inquiry* 31 (2005): 539–574.
28 Koestenbaum, 'Foreward' to Barthes, *A Lover's Discourse*. For a masochistic reading of *A Lover's Discourse* see Mansfield, *Masochism*, 76–83.
29 Barthes, 'Loving Schumann', in *The Responsibility of Forms: Critical Essays on Music, Art and Representation*, trans. Richard Howard (New York: Hill & Wang, 1985), 296.
30 Barthes, 'Rasch', in *The Responsibility of Forms*, 299–312.
31 Melina Esse, 'Rossini's Noisy Bodies', *Cambridge Opera Journal* 21, No. 1 (2009): 27–64.
32 Melina Esse, 'Performing Sentiment; or, How to Do Things with Tears', *Women and Music: A Journal of Gender and Culture* 14 (2010): 1–21. See also Elisabeth Le Guin, '"One says that one weeps, but one does not weep": *Sensible*, Grotesque, and Mechanical Embodiments in Boccherini's Chamber Music', *Journal of the American Musicological Society* 65 (2002): 207–254.
33 Schumann cited in *Schumann on Music*, trans. and ed. Henry Pleasants (New York: Dover, 1988), 114, 129–130. See Andreas Ballstaedt, 'Chopin as "Salon Composer" in Nineteenth-Century German Criticism', in *Chopin Studies*, ed. John Rink and Jim Samson (Cambridge: Cambridge University Press, 1994), 18–34.
34 Charles Rosen, *The Romantic Generation* (New York: HarperCollins, 1995), 383–385, 395–399.
35 Friedrich Niecks, 'Critical Excursions: Schumann', *The Musical Times* 22, No. 464 (October 1881): 498–499. Niecks's excoriating 'excursions' are contemporaneous with Nietzsche's famously scathing criticisms of Schumann. But as recent commentators have revealed, Schumann's creative relationship with

sentimentality runs productively throughout his career. See Jon W. Finson, 'At the Interstice between "Popular" and "Classical": Schumann's *Poems of Queen Mary Stuart* and European Sentimentality at Midcentury', in *Rethinking Schumann*, ed. Roe-Min Kok and Laura Tunbridge (Oxford: Oxford University Press, 2011), 69–87, and Holly Watkins, 'The Floral Poetics of Schumann's *Blumenstück*, Op. 19', *19th-Century Music* 36, No. 1 (2012): 24–45.

36 For the philosopher François Noudelmann, the sentimental landscape that Barthes associated with music certainly belongs to romanticism. *The Philosopher's Touch: Sartre, Nietzsche and Barthes at the Piano*, trans. Brian J. Reilly (New York: Columbia University Press, 2012), 112.
37 Kevin Kopelson, *Beethoven's Kiss: Pianism, Perversion, and the Mastery of Desire* (Stanford, CA: Stanford University Press, 1996), 4, 19–21 (emphasis in the original).
38 Andrew Brown, 'Subject and Counter-Subject: Some Notes on Barthes and Schumann', *Dalhousie French Studies* 34 (1996): 50.
39 Peter Ostwald, *Schumann: Music and Madness* (London: Gollancz, 1985), 27.
40 Michelle Elizabeth Yael Braunschweig, 'Biographical Listening: Intimacy, Madness, and the Music of Robert Schumann' (PhD dissertation, University of California, Berkeley, 2013): 31, 43–50.
41 Braunschweig, 'Biographical Listening', 74.
42 Jacques Mauger, 'Listening to Schumann: My Suffering, His Pain', *Canadian Journal of Psychoanalysis* 19 (2011), 214.
43 Mauger, 'Listening to Schumann', 215. Mauger is indebted to the classic work of Elaine Scarry who argues that pain, unlike other interior states, is not 'for' or 'of'; it destroys language ("Argh!") and this explains the rarity of representations of pain in art; by contrast psychological suffering does have referential content. Representations of it in art can seem almost ubiquitous or habitual, and artists who express this most powerfully raised as 'the most authentic class of sufferers'. *The Body in Pain: The Making and Unmaking of the World* (Oxford: Oxford University Press, 1985).
44 'Loving Schumann', 296.
45 Ian Buchanan, *Deleuzism: A Metacommentary* (Durham, NC: Duke, 2000) 101–103.
46 Deleuze, 'Re-presentation of Masoch', in *Essays Critical and Clinical*, trans. Daniel W. Smith and Michael A. Greco (New York: Verso, 1998), 53–55.
47 Lawrence Kramer, 'Rethinking Schumann's *Carnaval*: Identity, Meaning and the Social Order', in *Musical Meaning: Toward a Critical History* (Berkeley, CA: University of California Press, 2001), 100–132.
48 On the gendered reception of Chopin's nocturnes see Jeffery Kallberg, 'The Harmony of the Tea Table: Gender and Ideology in the Piano Nocturne', in *Chopin at the Boundaries* (Cambridge, MA: Harvard University Press, 1998), 30–61.
49 See Robert Solomon, 'On Kitsch and Sentimentality', *The Journal of Aesthetics and Art Criticism* 49 (1991): 1–14.
50 Elizabeth Maddock Dillon, 'Sentimental Aesthetics', *American Literature* 76, No. 3 (2004): 495–523.
51 Noudelmann points to two registers—the beat and the caress—the divided eroticism of the body; right hand is soft and pleasure, the left hand 'pricks' and 'beats'; *The Philosopher's Touch*, 137.
52 Slavoj Žižek, *The Plague of Fantasies* (London: Verso, 1997), 198.
53 Richard Leppert, *The Sight of Sound: Music, Representation and the History of the Body* (Berkeley, CA: University of California Press, 1993), 230–233.
54 For commentary see Dorothy Kosinski, 'The Gaze of Fernand Khnopff', *Notes in the History of Art* 11 (1992): 33.

55 Anne Leonard, 'Picturing Listening in the Late Nineteenth Century', *The Art Bulletin* 89 (2007): 266–286.
56 Rosen, *The Romantic Generation*, 368.
57 Jonathan Bellman, 'Frédéric Chopin, Antoine de Kontski and the *Carezzando* Touch', *Early Music* 29, No. 3 (2001): 398–407.
58 See Kallberg, 'The Harmony of the Tea Table'.
59 John Daverio, *Robert Schumann* (Oxford: Oxford University Press, 1997), 149. Anna M. Burton explores the psychoanalytic importance of the idealised images of Clara in 'Robert Schumann and Clara Wieck—A Creative Partnership', in *Psychoanalytic Explorations in Music*, ed. Stuart Feder, Richard L. Karmel and George H. Pollock (Madison, CT: International Universities Press, 1990), 441–463.
60 Peter F. Ostwald, 'Florestan, Eusebius, Clara, and Schumann's Right Hand', *19th-Century Music* 4 (1980): 31.
61 Mauger, 'Listening to Schumann'; Michel Schneider, *La tombée du jour* (Paris: Seuil, 1989)
62 See Buchanan, *Deleuzism*, 112; Deleuze, 'Re-presentation of Masoch', 55.

Bibliography

Abbate, Carolyn. *Unsung Voices: Opera and Musical Narrative in the Nineteenth Century*. Princeton, NJ: Princeton University Press, 1991.

Abrams, David M. 'Freud and Max Graf: On the Psychoanalysis of Music.' In *Psychoanalytic Explorations in Music: Second Series*. Edited by Stuart Feder, Richard L. Karmel, and George H. Pollock, 279–308. Madison, CT: International Universities Press, 1993.

Adorno, Theodor W. 'Sociology and Psychology' [1955]. *New Left Review* 1, no. 46 (1967): 67–97.

Adorno, Theodor W. *Mahler: A Musical Physiognomy*. Translated by Edmund Jephcott. Chicago, IL: University of Chicago Press, 1992/1960.

Adorno, Theodor W. 'On the Fetish-Character in Music and the Regression of Listening' [1938]. In *Essays on Music*. Edited by Richard Leppert. Translated by Susan H. Gillespie, 288–317. Berkeley and Los Angeles: University of California Press, 2002.

Adorno, Theodor W. *Philosophy of New Music*. Edited and translated by Robert Hullot-Kentor. Minneapolis: University of Minnesota Press, 2006/1946.

Agamben, Giorgio. *State of Exception*. Translated by Kevin Attell. Stanford, CA: Stanford University Press, 2005.

Agawu, Kofi. *Representing African Music: Postcolonial Notes, Queries, Positions*. New York and London: Routledge, 2003.

Aigen, Kenneth. 'In Defense of Beauty: A Role for the Aesthetic in Music Therapy Theory: Part I: The Development of Aesthetic Theory in Music Therapy.' *Nordic Journal of Music Therapy* 16, no. 2 (2007): 112–28.

Alvin, Juliette. *Music Therapy*. London: Hutchinson, 1974.

Anderson, Lorin. 'Freud, Nietzsche.' *Salmagundi* 47/48 (1980): 3–29.

Anzieu, Didier. *The Skin Ego*. Translated by Chris Turner. New Haven, CT and London: Yale University Press, 1989.

Ashby, Arved. 'Introduction.' In *The Pleasure of Modernist Music: Listening, Meaning, Intention, Ideology*. Edited by Arved Ashby, 1–19. Rochester, NY: University of Rochester Press, 2004.

Atton, Chris. 'Listening to "Difficult Albums": Specialist Music Fans and the Popular Avant-Garde.' *Popular Music* 31, no. 3 (2012): 347–61.

Auner, Joseph. *A Schoenberg Reader: Documents of a Life*. New Haven, CT: Yale University Press, 2003.

Austin, Diane S. 'The Role of Improvised Music in Psychodynamic Music Therapy with Adults.' *Music Therapy* 14, no. 1 (1996): 29–43.

Bibliography

Bailey, Robert. 'The Structure of the "Ring" and Its Evolution.' *19th-Century Music* 1, no. 1 (1977): 48–61.

Bailey, Robert (ed). *Richard Wagner, Prelude and Transfiguration from 'Tristan and Isolde'*. New York: W.W. Norton, 1985.

Ballstaedt, Andreas. 'Chopin as "Salon Composer" in Nineteenth-Century German Criticism.' In *Chopin Studies*. Edited by John Rink and Jim Samson, 18–34. Cambridge: Cambridge University Press, 1994.

Bard-Schwarz, David. *Listening Subjects: Music, Culture, Psychoanalysis*. Durham, NC and London: Duke University Press, 1997.

Bard-Schwarz, David. *An Introduction to Electronic Art through the Teachings of Jacques Lacan: Strangest Thing*. London and New York: Routledge, 2014.

Barthes, Roland. *Image-Music-Text*. Translated by Stephen Heath. New York: Hill and Wang, 1977.

Barthes, Roland. *The Responsibility of Forms: Critical Essays on Music, Art and Representation*. Translated by Richard Howard. New York: Hill & Wang, 1985.

Barthes, Roland. *Camera Lucida: Reflections on Photography*. Translated by Richard Howard. London: Vintage, 2000.

Barthes, Roland. *A Lover's Discourse: Fragments*. Translated by Richard Howard. New York: Hill & Wang, 2010.

Battan, Carrie. 'Past Peak.' *New Yorker*, November 9, 2015. Available at www.newyorker.com/magazine/2015/11/09/past-peak.

Beach, David. 'Schubert's Experiments with Sonata Form: Formal-Tonal Design versus Underlying Structure.' *Music Theory Spectrum* 15, no. 1 (1993): 1–18.

Beach, David. 'Modal Mixture and Schubert's Harmonic Practice.' *Journal of Music Theory* 42, no. 1 (1998): 73–100.

Beardsworth, Sara. *Julia Kristeva*. Binghamton, NY: SUNY University Press, 2004.

Beauchemin, Maude, Berta González-Frankenberger, Julie Trembley, Phetsamone Vannasing, Eduardo Martínez-Montes, Pascal Belin, et al. 'Mother and Stranger: An Electrophysiological Study of Voice Processing in Newborns.' *Cerebral Cortex* 21, no. 8 (2011): 1705–11.

Bellman, Jonathan. 'Frédéric Chopin, Antoine de Kontski and the *Carezzando* Touch.' *Early Music* 29, no. 3 (2001): 398–407.

Bent, Ian. 'The Problem of Harmonic Dualism: A Translation and Commentary.' In *The Oxford Handbook of Neo-Riemannian Theories*. Edited by Edward Gollin and Alexander Rehding, 167–93. New York: Oxford University Press, 2011.

Biancorosso, Giorgio. 'Whose Phenomenology of Music? David Huron's Theory of Expectation.' *Music and Letters* 89, no. 3 (2008): 396–404.

Biddle, Ian. 'Listening, Consciousness, and the Charm of the Universal: What It Feels Like for a Lacanian.' In *Music and Consciousness: Philosophical, Psychological, and Cultural Perspectives*. Edited by David Clarke and Eric Clarke, 65–77. Oxford: Oxford University Press, 2011.

Biddle, Ian. 'Opera's Unconscious, or What Men Don't Say.' In *Masculinity in Opera: Gender, History, and the New Musicology*. Edited by Philip Purvis, 197–215. New York and London: Routledge, 2013.

Bigand, Emmanuel, Bénédicte Poulin, Barbara Tillmann, François Madurell, and Daniel A. D'Adamo. 'Sensory versus Cognitive Components in Harmonic Priming.' *Journal of Experimental Psychology: Human Perception and Performance* 29, no. 1 (2003): 159–71.

Braunschweig, Michelle Elizabeth Yael. 'Biographical Listening: Intimacy, Madness, and the Music of Robert Schumann.' PhD dissertation, University of California, Berkeley, 2013.

Breazeale, Daniel. 'Check or Checkmate? On the Finitude of the Fichtean Self.' In *The Modern Subject: Conception of the Self in Classical German Philosophy*. Edited by Karl Ameriks and Dieter Sturma, 87–114. Albany: State University of New York, 1995.

Brendel, Alfred. 'Form and Psychology in Beethoven's Piano Sonatas.' In *Musical Thoughts and Afterthoughts*. Princeton, NJ: Princeton University Press, 1976.

Bronfen, Elisabeth. 'Extimate Violence. Shakespeare's Night World.' www.bronfen.info/writing/writing-2006/extimate-violence-shakespeare-s-night-world. Accessed 14 October, 2016.

Brooks, Peter. 'The Idea of a Psychoanalytic Literary Criticism.' In *Discourse in Psychoanalysis and Literature*. Edited by Shlomith Rimmon-Kenan, 1–18. London: Methuen, 1987.

Brower, Candace. 'Paradoxes of Pitch Space.' *Music Analysis* 27, no. 1 (2008): 51–106.

Brown, Andrew. 'Subject and Counter-Subject: Some Notes on Barthes and Schumann.' *Dalhousie French Studies* 34 (1996): 35–66.

Brown, Julie. 'Understanding Schoenberg as Christ.' In *The Oxford Handbook of the New Cultural History of Music*. Edited by Jane Fulcher, 117–62. Oxford: Oxford University Press, 2011.

Brown, Sandra. 'Some Thoughts on Music, Therapy, and Music Therapy: A Response to Elaine Streeter's "Finding a Balance between Psychological Thinking and Musical Awareness in Music Therapy Theory—A Psychoanalytic Perspective".' *British Journal of Music Therapy* 13, no. 2 (1999): 63–71.

Brown, Sandra. '"Hullo Object! I Destroyed You!".' In *The Handbook of Music Therapy*. Edited by Leslie Bunt and Sarah Hoskyns, 84–96. Hove: Brunner-Routledge, 2002.

Brunner, Christoph. 'The Sound Culture of Dubstep in London.' In *Musical Performance and the Changing City: Post-Industrial Contexts in Europe and the United States*. Edited by Fabian Holt and Carsten Wergin, 256–70. New York: Routledge, 2013.

Buchanan, Ian. *Deleuzism: A Metacommentary*. Durham, NC: Duke University Press, 2000.

Burnham, Scott. 'Method and Motivation in Hugo Riemann's History of Harmonic Theory.' *Music Theory Spectrum* 14, no. 1 (1992): 1–14.

Burnham, Scott. *Beethoven Hero*. Princeton, NJ: Princeton University Press, 1995.

Burstein, Poundie. 'Lyricism, Structure, and Gender in Schubert's G Major String Quartet.' *The Musical Quarterly* 81, no. 1 (1997): 51–63.

Burton, Anna M. 'Robert Schumann and Clara Wieck—A Creative Partnership.' In *Psychoanalytic Explorations in Music*. Edited by Stuart Feder, Richard L. Karmel, and George H. Pollock, 441–63. Madison, CT: International Universities Press, 1990.

Cambor, C. Glenn, Gerald M. Lisowitz, and Miles D. Miller. 'Creative Jazz Musicians: A Clinical Study.' *Psychiatry* 25 (1962): 1–15.

Caramanica, Jon. 'No More Kid Stuff for Taylor Swift.' *New York Times*, October 24, 2012. Available at www.nytimes.com/2012/10/28/arts/music/no-more-kid-stuff-for-taylor-swift.html?_r=1.

Carpenter, Alexander. 'Schoenberg's Vienna, Freud's Vienna: Re-examining the Connections between the Monodrama *Erwartung* and the Early History of Psychoanalysis.' *The Musical Quarterly* 93, no. 1 (2010): 144–81.

Carpenter, Alexander. '"This Beastly Science...": On the Reception of Psychoanalysis by the Composers of the Second Viennese School, 1908–1923.' *International Forum of Psychoanalysis* 24, no. 4 (2015): 243–54.

Chandler, James. *An Archaeology of Sympathy: The Sentimental Mode in Literature and Cinema*. Chicago, IL: Chicago University Press, 2013.

Chion, Michel. *La voix au cinema*. Paris: Cahiers du cinema, 1952.

Clark, Suzannah. *Analyzing Schubert*. Cambridge: Cambridge University Press, 2011.

Clark, Suzannah. 'On the Imagination of Tone in Schubert's *Liedesend* (D473), *Trost* (D523), and *Gretchens Bitte* (D564).' In *The Oxford Handbook of Neo-Riemannian Theories*. Edited by Edward Gollin and Alexander Rehding, 294–321. New York: Oxford University Press, 2011.

Clarke, David. 'Elvis and Darmstadt, or: Twentieth-Century Music and the Politics of Cultural Pluralism.' *Twentieth-Century Music* 4, no. 1 (2007): 3–45.

Clarke, Eric. *Ways of Listening: An Ecological Approach to the Perception of Musical Listening*. Oxford: Oxford University Press, 2005.

Cohn, Richard. 'Introduction to Neo-Riemannian Theory: A Survey and a Historical Perspective.' *Journal of Music Theory* 42, no. 2 (1998): 167–80.

Cohn, Richard. 'As Wonderful as Star Clusters: Instruments for Gazing at Tonality in Schubert.' *19th-century Music* 22, no. 3 (1999): 213–32.

Cohn, Richard. 'Tonal Pitch Space and the (Neo-)Riemannian *Tonnetz*.' In *The Oxford Handbook of Neo-Riemannian Theories*. Edited by Edward Gollin and Alexander Rehding, 322–50. New York: Oxford University Press, 2011.

Cohn, Richard. *Audacious Euphony: Chromatic Harmony and the Triad's Second Nature*. Oxford: Oxford University Press, 2012.

Colombo, Daria. 'Freud and His Circle.' In *Textbook of Psychoanalysis*, 2nd edition. Edited by Glen Gabbard, Bonnie Litowitz, and Paul Williams, 1–17. Washington, DC: American Psychiatric Publishing, 2012.

Cone, Edward T. 'Schubert's Promissory Note: An Exercise in Musical Hermeneutics.' *19th-Century Music* 5, no. 3 (1982): 233–41.

Coriat, Isador H. 'Some Aspects of a Psychoanalytic Interpretation of Music.' *The Psychoanalytic Review* 32 (1945): 408–18.

Covach, John. 'The Zwölftonspiel of Josef Matthias Hauer.' *Journal of Music theory* 35, no. 1 (1992): 149–84.

Covach, John. 'Hauer, Josef Mattias.' *Oxford Music Online*. Available at www.oxfordmusiconline.com/subscriber/article/grove/music/12544. Accessed May 10, 2016.

Culler, Jonathan. *Ferdinand de Saussure*. Ithaca, NY: Cornell University Press, 1986.

Currie, James R. 'Music after All.' *Journal of the American Musicological Society* 62, no. 1 (2009): 145–203.

Dahlhaus, Carl. *Foundations of Music History*. Translated by J.B. Robinson, Cambridge: Cambridge University Press, 1983.

Dahlhaus, Carl. 'Sonata Form in Schubert: The First Movement of the G-Major String Quartet, Op. 161 (D. 887).' In *Schubert: Critical and Analytical Studies*. Edited by Walter Frisch, 1–12. Translated by Thilo Reinhard. Lincoln: University of Nebraska Press, 1986.

Dahlhaus, Carl. 'Structure and Expression in the Music of Scriabin'. In *Schoenberg and the New Music*, 201–209. Translated by Derrick Puffett and Alfred Clayton. Cambridge: Cambridge University Press, 1987.

Darnley-Smith, Rachel. 'Improvisation as Transcendent Function: The Role of the Unconscious and Jung's Active Imagination in Twentieth Century Music Therapy.' (In Review.)

Darnley-Smith, Rachel. 'Music Therapy with Elderly Adults.' In *Music Therapy and Group Work: Sound Company*. Edited by Alison Davies and Eleanor Richards, 77–89. London: Jessica Kingsley, 2002.

Darnley-Smith, Rachel, 'What Is the Music of Music Therapy?: An Enquiry into the Aesthetics of Clinical Improvisation'. PhD dissertation, Durham University, 2013. Available at http://etheses.dur.ac.uk/6975.

Darnley-Smith, Rachel and Helen M. Patey. *Music Therapy*. London: Sage Publications Ltd, 2003.

Daverio, John. *Robert Schumann*. Oxford: Oxford University Press, 1997.

Dean, Tim. 'Art as Symptom: Žižek and the Ethics of Psychoanalytic Criticism.' *Diacritics* 32, no. 2 (2002): 21–41.

Dehing, Jef. 'The Transcendent Function.' *Journal of Analytical Psychology* 38, no. 3 (1993): 221–35.

Deleuze, Gilles. *Essays Critical and Clinical*. Translated by Daniel W. Smith and Michael A. Greco. New York: Verso, 1998.

Deleuze, Gilles. 'From Sacher-Masoch to Masochism' [1961], translated by Christian Kerslake. *Angelaki: Journal of the Theoretical Humanities* 9, no. 1 (2004): 125–33.

Deleuze, Gilles and Félix Guattari. *Anti-Oedipus*. Translated by Robert Hurley, Mark Seem and Helen R. Lane. London: Continuum, 2004.

Deleuze, Gilles and Leopold von Sacher-Masoch. *Masochism: "Coldness and Cruelty" and "Venus in Furs"*. Translated by Jean McNeil. New York: Zone Books, 1991.

Derrida, Jacques. *Of Grammatology*. Translated by Gayatri Chakravorty Spivak. Baltimore, MD: Johns Hopkins University Press, 2013.

Dickson, Jay Michael. 'Defining the Sentimentalist in *Ulysses*'. *James Joyce Quarterly* 44, no. 1 (2006): 19–37.

Dillon, Elizabeth Maddock. 'Sentimental Aesthetics'. *American Literature* 76, no. 3 (2004): 495–523.

Dobbins, Amanda. 'Taylor Swift's Version of Dubstep Is a Little Different Than Regular Dubstep.' *Vulture*, October 9, 2012. Available at www.vulture.com/2012/10/here-is-taylor-swifts-version-of-dubstep.html.

Dolar, Mladen. *A Voice and Nothing More*. Cambridge, MA and London: MIT Press, 2006.

Dollinger, Roland. 'The Self-Inflicted Suffering of Young Werther: An Example of Masochism in the 18th-Century.' In *One Hundred Years of Masochism: Literary Texts, Social and Cultural Contexts*. Edited by Michael C. Fink and Carl Niekerk, 91–108. Amsterdam: Rodopi, 2000.

Downes, Stephen. *The Muse as Eros: Music, Erotic Fantasy, and Male Creativity in the Romantic and Modern Imagination*. Aldershot and Burlington, VT: Ashgate, 2006.

Ehrenzweig, Anton. *The Psycho-Analysis of Artistic Vision and Hearing: An Introduction to a Theory of Unconscious Perception*. London: Routledge and Kegan Paul Ltd, 1953.

Ellmann, Maud (ed). *Psychoanalytic Literary Criticism*. London: Longman, 1994.
Engebretsen, Nora. 'Neo-Riemannian Perspectives on the *Harmonieschritte*, with a Translation of Riemann's *Systematik der Harmonieschritte*.' In *The Oxford Handbook of Neo-Riemannian Theories*. Edited by Edward Gollin and Alexander Rehding, 353–81. New York: Oxford University Press, 2011.
Eschen, Johannes Th. *Analytical Music Therapy*. London: Jessica Kingsley Publishers, 2002.
Esse, Melina. 'Rossini's Noisy Bodies.' *Cambridge Opera Journal* 21, no. 1 (2009): 27–64.
Esse, Melina. 'Performing Sentiment; or, How to Do Things with Tears.' *Women and Music: A Journal of Gender and Culture* 14 (2010): 1–21.
Evans, Dylan. *An Introductory Dictionary of Lacanian Psychoanalysis*. London and New York: Routledge, 2006/1996.
Falck, Robert. 'Marie Pappenheim, Schoenberg, and the *Studien über Hysterie*.' In *German Literature and Music: An Aesthetic Fusion, 1890–1989*. Edited by Claus Reschke and Howard Pollack, 131–45. Symposium on Literature and the Arts, Houston, 1989. Munich: Fink, 1992.
Feder, Stuart, Richard L. Karmel, and George H. Pollock. *Psychoanalytic Explorations in Music: Second Series*. Madison, CT: International Universities Press, 1993.
Felski, Rita. 'The Counterdiscourse of the Feminine in Three Texts by Wilde, Huysmans and Sacher-Masoch.' *Proceedings of the Modern Language Association* 106 (1991): 1094–105.
Fichte, Johann Gottlieb. 'Review of Aenesidemus.' In *Fichte: Early Philosophical Writings*. Translated and edited by Daniel Breazeale, 59–77. Ithaca, NY: Cornell University Press, 1988.
Finson, Jon W. 'At the Interstice between "Popular" and "Classical": Schumann's *Poems of Queen Mary Stuart* and European Sentimentality at Midcentury.' In *Rethinking Schumann*. Edited by Roe-Min Kok and Laura Tunbridge, 69–87. Oxford: Oxford University Press, 2011.
Fisk, Charles. 'What Schubert's Last Sonata Might Hold.' In *Music and Meaning*. Edited by Jennifer Robinson, 179–200. Ithaca, NY: Cornell University Press, 1997.
Foster, Hal, Rosalind Krauss, Yve-Alain Bois, and Benjamin H.D. Buchloch. *Art Since 1900: Modernism, Antimodernism, Postmodernism*. London: Thames and Hudson, 2004.
Freud, Sigmund. *The Standard Edition of the Complete Psychological Works of Sigmund Freud*. Edited by James Strachey, Vol. 5, *The Interpretation of Dreams*. London: Hogarth Press and the Institute of Psycho-Analysis, 1953.
Freud, Sigmund. '"A Child is Being Beaten": A Contribution to the Study of the Origin of Sexual Perversions' [1919]. In *The Standard Edition of the Complete Psychological Works of Sigmund Freud*. Edited by James Strachey. Vol. 17, *An Infantile Neurosis and Other Works*, 175–204. London: Hogarth, 1955.
Freud, Sigmund. 'The Unconscious'. In *The Standard Edition of the Complete Psychological Works of Sigmund Freud*, Vol. 14, *On the History of the Psycho-Analytic Movement, Papers on Metapsychology and Other Works*, 159–215. Translated by James Strachey. London: The Hogarth Press, 1957.
Freud, Sigmund. *The Standard Edition of the Complete Psychological Works of Sigmund Freud*. Edited by James Strachey. Vol. 9, *Jensen's 'Gradiva' and Other Works*. London: Hogarth Press and the Institute of Psycho-Analysis, 1959.

Freud, Sigmund. *Beyond the Pleasure Principle*. Edited and translated by James Strachey. New York: W.W. Norton, 1961.
Freud, Sigmund. *Leonardo da Vinci and a Memory of His Childhood*. Edited by James Strachey. Translated by Alan Tyson. New York and London: W.W. Norton and Company, 1961.
Freud, Sigmund. *The Standard Edition of the Complete Psychological Works of Sigmund Freud*. Edited by James Strachey. Vol. 19, *The Ego and the Id and Other Works*. London: Hogarth Press and the Institute of Psycho-Analysis, 1961.
Freud, Sigmund. *The Standard Edition of the Complete Psychological Works of Sigmund Freud*. Edited by James Strachey. Vol. 16, *Introductory Lectures on Psychoanalysis*. London: Hogarth Press and the Institute of Psycho-Analysis, 1963.
Freud, Sigmund. 'Observations on Transference Love.' In *The Freud Reader*. Edited by Peter Gay, 378–86. London: Vintage, 1995.
Freud, Sigmund. 'The Economic Problem of Masochism' [1924]. In *Essential Papers on Masochism*. Edited by Margaret Ann Fitzpatrick Henry, 274–85. New York: New York University Press, 1995.
Freud, Sigmund. *Totem and Taboo*. London and New York: Routledge, 2001.
Fried, Michael. 'Barthes's Punctum.' *Critical Inquiry* 31 (2005): 539–74.
Frisch, Walter. '"You Must Remember This": Memory and Structure in Schubert's String Quartet in G Major, D. 887.' *The Musical Quarterly* 84, no. 4 (2000): 582–603.
Frith, Simon. *Performing Rites*. Oxford: University of Oxford Press, 1996.
Fulweiler, Howard W. *'Here a Captive Heart Busted': Studies in the Sentimental Journey of Modern Literature*. New York: Fordham University Press, 1993.
Gabriel, Markus and Slavoj Žižek. *Mythology, Madness and Laughter: Subjectivity in German Idealism*. London: Continuum, 2009.
Gaudlitz, Erika. 'Libidinal Symptomatology in Deleuze's *Masochism—Coldness and Cruelty*.' *Deleuze Studies* 9 (2015): 1–24.
Gay, Peter. *Freud: A Life for Our Time*. New York: W. W. Norton, 2006.
Gillett, Judy. 'The Problem of Schubert's G Major String Quartet (D. 887).' *Music Review* 35 (1974): 281–92.
Gingerich, John. 'Remembrance and Consciousness in Schubert's C-Major String Quintet.' *The Musical Quarterly* 84, no. 4 (2000): 619–34.
Gödde, Günter. 'Freud and Nineteenth-Century Philosophical Sources on the Unconscious.' In *Thinking the Unconscious: Nineteenth-Century German Thought*. Edited by Angus Nicholls and Martin Liebscher, 261–86. Cambridge: Cambridge University Press, 2010.
Goldstein, Martin and Inge Goldstein. *The Experience of Science: An Interdisciplinary Approach*. New York: Plenum, 1984.
Gollin, Edward. 'Some Aspects of Three-Dimensional "Tonnetze".' *Journal of Music Theory* 42, no. 2 (1998): 195–206.
Gollin, Edward and Alexander Rehding. 'The Reception of Hugo Riemann's Music Theory'. In *The Oxford Handbook of Neo-Riemannian Theories*. Edited by Edward Gollin and Alexander Rehding, 3–54. New York: Oxford University Press, 2011.
Gorrell, Lorraine. *Discordant Melody: Alexander Zemlinsky, His Songs, and the Second Viennese School*. Westport, CT: Greenwood Press, 2002.
Graham, Stephen. *Sounds of the Underground: A Cultural, Political and Aesthetic Mapping of Underground and Fringe Music*. Ann Arbor: University of Michigan Press, 2016.

Graham, Stephen. '(Un)Popular Avant Gardes: Underground Popular Music and the Avant-Garde.' *Perspectives of New Music* 48, no. 2 (2010): 5–20.

Grazian, David. 'Digital Underground: Musical Spaces and Microscenes in the Post-Industrial City'. In *Musical Performance and the Changing City: Post-Industrial Contexts in Europe and the United States*. Edited by Fabian Holt and Carsten Wergin, 127–51. New York: Routledge, 2013.

Greenberg, Jonathan. *Modernism, Satire, and the Novel*. Cambridge: Cambridge University Press, 2011.

Gregg, Melissa and Gregory J. Seigworth (eds). *The Affect Theory Reader*. Durham, NC and London: Duke University Press, 2010.

Griffiths, Dai. 'The High Analysis of Low Music.' *Music Analysis* 18, no. 3 (1999): 389–435.

Grossman, William I. 'Notes on Masochism: A Discussion of the History and Development of a Psychoanalytic Concept.' *Psychoanalytic Quarterly* 55 (1986): 379–413.

Guyer, Paul. 'Kant, Immanuel.' In *Routledge Encyclopedia of Philosophy*. Edited by Edward Craig. London: Routledge, 2004. Available at www.rep.routledge.com/article/DB047SECT12. Accessed 14 May, 2011.

Hailey, Christopher. *Franz Schrecker 1878–1934: A Cultural Biography*. Cambridge: Cambridge University Press, 1993.

Hanslick, Eduard. *On the Musically Beautiful: A Contribution towards the Revision of the Aesthetics of Music*. Translated by Geoffrey Payzant. Indianapolis, IN: Hackett Publishing, 1986.

Harper-Scott, J.P.E. *The Quilting Points of Musical Modernism: Revolution, Reaction, and William Walton*. Cambridge and New York: Cambridge University Press, 2012.

Harper-Scott, J.P.E. 'Britten and the Deadlock of Identity Politics.' In *Masculinity in Opera*. Edited by Philip Purvis, 144–66. New York and Abingdon: Routledge, 2013.

Harris, Keith. 'Trace Taylor Swift's Country to Pop Transformation in 5 Songs.' *Rolling Stone*, September 9, 2014. Available at www.rollingstone.com/music/lists/taylor-swift-country-pop-transformation-20140909/we-are-never-ever-getting-back-together-2012-20140909.

Harrison, Daniel. *Harmonic Function in Chromatic Music: A Renewed Dualist Theory and an Account of Its Precedents*. Chicago, IL: University of Chicago Press, 1994.

Harrison, Daniel. 'Three Short Essays on Neo-Riemannian Theory.' In *The Oxford Handbook of Neo-Riemannian Theories*. Edited by Edward Gollin and Alexander Rehding, 548–78. New York: Oxford University Press, 2011.

Hauser, Renate. 'Krafft-Ebing's Psychological Understanding of Sexual Behaviour.' In *Sexual Knowledge, Sexual Science*. Edited by Roy Porter and Mikuláš Teich, 210–27. Cambridge: Cambridge University Press, 1994.

Heidegger, Martin. *Being and Time*. Translated by John Macquarrie and Edward Robinson. 7th Edition. Oxford: Blackwell Publishing, 2002.

Henderson, Andrea K. *Romanticism and the Painful Pleasures of Modern Life*. Cambridge: Cambridge University Press, 2008.

Hepokoski, James and Warren Darcy. *Elements of Sonata Theory: Norms, Types and Deformations in the Late-Eighteenth-Century Sonata*. Oxford: Oxford University Press, 2006.

Hinton, Laura. *The Perverse Gaze of Sympathy: Sadomasochistic Sentiments from 'Clarissa' to 'Rescue 911'*. New York: SUNY Press, 1999.
Hitchcock, Dorinda Hawk. 'The Influence of Jung's Psychology on the Therapeutic Use of Music.' *Journal of British Music Therapy* 1, no. 2 (1987): 17–21.
Hitschmann, Edward. 'Franz Schubert's Greif and Love' [1915]. *American Imago* 7 (1950): 67–76.
Hoffman, Justin. 'Listening with Two Ears: Conflicting Perceptions of Space in Tonal Music.' PhD dissertation, Columbia University, 2011.
Hogan, Marc. 'Hear Taylor Swift's Dubstep-Tinged "I Knew You Were Trouble".' *Spin*, October 9, 2012. Available at www.spin.com/2012/10/taylor-swift-i-knew-you-were-trouble-dubstep/.
Hostinský, Otakar. *Die Lehre von de musikalischen Klängen. Ein Beitrag zur aesthetischen Begründung der Harmonielehre*. Prag: Altenburg, 1879.
Huron, David. *Sweet Anticipation: Music and the Psychology of Expectation*. Harvard, MA: MIT Press, 2008.
Huyssen, Andreas. *After the Great Divide: Modernism, Mass Culture, Postmodernism*. Bloomington: Indiana University Press, 1986.
Hyer, Brian. 'Tonal Intuitions in "Tristan und Isolde".' PhD dissertation, Yale University, 1989.
Hyer, Brian. 'What Is a Function?' In *The Oxford Handbook of Neo-Riemannian Theories*. Edited by Edward Gollin and Alexander Rehding, 92–139. New York: Oxford University Press, 2011.
Inwood, Michael J. *A Heidegger Dictionary*. Oxford and Malden, MA: Blackwell Publishers Limited, 1999.
Isbister, J.N. *Freud: An Introduction to His Life and Work*. Cambridge: Polity Press, 1988.
Jameson, Fredric. *A Singular Modernity: Essay on the Ontology of the Present*. New York and London: Verso, 2002.
Jarman-Ivens, Freya. *Queer Voices: Technologies, Vocalities, and the Musical Flaw*. New York: Palgrave Macmillan, 2011.
Johnson, Bruce and Martin Cloonan. *The Dark Side of the Tune: Popular Music and Violence*. Burlington, VT: Ashgate, 2008.
Johnson, Julian. *Mahler's Voices: Expression and Irony in the Songs and Symphonies*. New York and Oxford: Oxford University Press, 2009.
Joyce, James. *Ulysses*. London: Penguin Classics, 2000.
Jung, Carl G. 'On the Relation of Analytical Psychology to Poetry.' In *The Collected Works*, Vol. 15, *The Spirit in Man, Art and Literature*. Edited and translated by Gerhard Adler and R.F.C. Hull, 65–83. London: Routledge Keegan and Paul, 1966.
Jung, Carl G. 'The Transcendent Function.' In *The Collected Works*, Vol. 8, *The Structure and Dynamics of the Psyche*. Edited by Herbert Read, Michael Fordham, and Gerhard Adler. Translated by R.F.C. Hull, 67–91. 2nd edition. London: Routledge Keegan and Paul, 1969.
Jung, Carl G. 'Definitions.' In *The Collected Works*, Vol. 6, *Psychological Types*. Translated by R.F.C. Hull and H.G. Baynes, 16th edition. Hove, East Sussex and New York, NY: Routledge Keegan and Paul, 1971.
Jung, Carl G. *Memories, Dreams, Reflections*. Edited by Aniela Jaffé. Translated by Richard Winston and Clara Winston. London: Collins/Font Paperbacks, 1983.

Jung, Carl G. '*Ulysses*: A Monologue' [1932]. In *The Spirit in Man, Art and Literature*, 109–34. Edited by Herbert Read, Michael Fordham, and Gerhard Adler. Translated by R.E.C. Hull. London: Ark, 1984.

Jung, Carl G. and Joan Chodorow. *Jung on Active Imagination: Key Readings Selected and Introduced by Joan Chodorow*. London: Routledge, 1997.

Juslin, Patrik N. and Daniel Västfjäll. 'Emotional Responses to Music: The Need to Consider Underlying Mechanisms.' *Behavioral and Brain Sci*ences 31 (2008): 559–621.

Kallberg, Jeffrey. *Chopin at the Boundaries*. Cambridge, MA: Harvard University Press, 1998.

Kangas, Ryan R. 'Mourning, Remembrance, and Mahler's "Resurrection".' *19th-Century Music* 36, no. 1 (2012): 58–83.

Kassabian, Anahid. *Ubiquitous Listening: Affect, Attention, and Distributed Subjectivity*. Berkeley and Los Angeles: University of California Press, 2013.

Kinderman, William and Harald Krebs (eds). *The Second Practice of Nineteenth-Century Tonality*. Lincoln: University of Nebraska Press, 1996.

Klein, Melanie. 'Infantile Anxiety-Situations Reflected in a Work of Art and in the Creative Impulse.' *International Journal of Psychoanalysis* 10 (1929): 436–43.

Klein, Michael L. *Music and the Crises of the Modern Subject*. Bloomington: Indiana University Press, 2015.

Klumpenhouwer, Henry. 'Late Capitalism, Late Marxism and the Study of Music.' *Music Analysis* 20, no. 3 (2001): 367–405.

Kohut, Heinz and Sigmund Levarie. 'On the Enjoyment of Listening to Music.' *Psychoanalytic Quarterly* 19 (1950): 64–87.

Kohut, Heinz. 'Observations on the Psychological Functions of Music' [1957]. In *Psychoanalytic Explorations in Music*. Edited by Stuart Feder, Richard L. Karmel, and George H. Pollock, 21–38. Madison, CT: International Universities Press, 1990.

Kopelson, Kevin. *Beethoven's Kiss: Pianism, Perversion, and the Mastery of Desire*. Stanford, CA: Stanford University Press, 1996.

Kopp, David. *Chromatic Transformations in Nineteenth-Century Music*. Cambridge: Cambridge University Press, 2002.

Kosinski, Dorothy. 'The Gaze of Fernand Khnopff.' *Notes in the History of Art* 11 (1992): 26–33.

Krafft-Ebing, Richard von. *Psychopathia Sexualis*. Translation of 12th edition by F.J. Rebman. New York: Physicians and Surgeons Book Co., 1924.

Kramer, Lawrence. *Music as Cultural Practice, 1800–1900*. Berkeley: University of California Press, 1990.

Kramer, Lawrence. *After the Lovedeath: Sexual Violence and the Making of Culture*. Berkley and Los Angeles: University of California Press, 1997.

Kramer, Lawrence. *Musical Meaning: Toward a Critical History*. Berkeley: University of California Press, 2002.

Kramer, Lawrence. *Opera and Modern Culture: Wagner and Strauss*. Berkeley, Los Angeles, and London: University of California Press, 2004.

Kramer, Lawrence. 'Chopin's Subjects: A Prelude.' *19th-Century Music* 35 no. 3, 2012: (unpaginated foreword).

Krims, Adam. 'Marxist Music Analysis without Adorno.' In *Analyzing Popular Music*. Edited by Allan Moore, 131–57. Cambridge and New York: Cambridge University Press, 2003.

Kristeva, Julia. *Revolution in Poetic Language.* Translated by Margaret Waller. New York: Columbia University Press, 1984.
Kristeva, Julia. *The Kristeva Reader.* Edited by Toril Moi. New York: Columbia University Press, 1986.
Kurth, Ernst. *Romantische Harmonik und ihre Krise in Wagners 'Tristan'.* Bern and Leipzig: Max Hesses Verlag, 1920.
Kurth, Ernst. *Musikpsychologie.* Berlin: Max Hesse, 1931.
Lacan, Jacques. *The Seminar of Jacques Lacan: Book I: Freud's Papers on Technique 1953–1954.* Edited by Jacques-Allain Miller. Translated by John Forrester. New York and London: W.W. Norton and Company, 1991.
Lacan, Jacques. *The Seminar of Jacques Lacan: Book II: The Ego in Freud's Theory and in the Technique of Psychoanalysis 1954–1955.* Edited by Jacques-Alain Miller. Translated by Sylvana Tomaselli, with notes by John Forrester. New York: Norton, 1991.
Lacan, Jacques. *The Seminar of Jacques Lacan, Book III: The Psychoses.* Edited by Jacques-Alain Miller. London and New York: Norton, 1997.
Lacan, Jacques. *Seminar XI: The Four Fundamental Concepts of Psychoanalysis.* Translated by Jacques-Alain Miller. London: Vintage, 1998.
Lacan, Jacques. *Seminar XI: The Four Fundamental Concepts of Psychoanalysis.* Edited by Jacques-Alain Miller. Translated by Alan Sheridan. London and New York: Routledge, 1998.
Lacan, Jacques. *Écrits: a Selection.* Translated by Alan Sheridan. London: Tavistock Publications, 2004.
Lacan, Jacques. *Écrits: The First Complete Edition in English.* Translated by Bruce Fink in collaboration with Héloïse Fink and Russell Grigg. London and New York: W.W. Norton, 2006.
Lacan, Jacques. *The Seminar of Jacques Lacan, Book VII: The Ethics of Psychoanalysis.* Edited by Jacques-Alain Miller. Translated by Dennis Porter. London and New York: Routledge, 2008.
Lachmann, Gary. *Jung the Mystic: The Esoteric Dimensions of Jung's Life and Teaching.* New York: Penguin, 2010.
Land, Nick. *The Thirst for Annihilation: Georges Bataille and Virulent Nihilism (an Essay in Atheistic Religion).* London: Routledge, 1992.
Lecourt, Édith. 'The Musical Envelope.' In *Psychic Envelopes.* Edited by Didier Anzieu, 211–35. London: Karnac Books, 1990.
Le Guin, Elisabeth. '"One Says That One Weeps, but One Does Not Weep": *Sensible*, Grotesque, and Mechanical Embodiments in Boccherini's Chamber Music.' *Journal of the American Musicological Society* 65 (2002): 207–54.
Lendvai, Ernő. *Béla Bartók: An Analysis of His Music.* London: Kahn & Averill, 1971.
Lendvai, Ernő. *Symmetries of Music: An Introduction to the Semantics of Music.* Edited by Miklós Szabo and Milós Mohay. Kecskemét: Kodály Institute, 1993.
Leonard, Anne. 'Picturing Listening in the Late Nineteenth Century.' *The Art Bulletin* 89 (2007): 266–86.
Leppert, Richard. *The Sight of Sound: Music, Representation and the History of the Body.* Berkeley: University of California Press, 1993.
Lerdahl, Fred. *Tonal Pitch Space.* Oxford: Oxford University Press, 2001.
Levinson, Jerrold. *Music in the Moment.* Ithaca, NY: Cornell University Press, 1997.
Levinson, Jerrold. 'Concatenationism, Architectonicism, and the Appreciation of Music.' *Revue Internationale de Philosophie*, no. 238 (2006): 505–14.

Lewin, David. 'On Generalized Intervals and Transformations.' *Journal of Music Theory* 24, no. 2 (1980): 243–51.
Lewin, David. *Studies in Music with Text*. New York and London: Oxford University Press, 2006.
Leys, Ruth. 'The Turn to Affect: A Critique.' *Critical Inquiry* 37 (2011): 434–72.
Lyotard, Jean-François. *Libidinal Economy*. London: Continuum, 2004.
MacDonald, Malcolm. *Schoenberg*. Oxford: Oxford University Press, 2008.
Mak, Su Yin. 'Schubert's Sonata Forms and the Poetics of the Lyric.' *The Journal of Musicology* 23, no. 9 (2006): 263–306.
Malawey, Victoria. 'Musical Emergence in Björk's *Medúlla*.' *Journal of the Royal Musical Association* 136, no. 1 (2011): 141–80.
Malloch, Stephen and Colwyn Trevarthen. *Communicative Musicality: Exploring the Basis of Human Companionship*. Oxford: Oxford University Press, 2009.
Mansfield, Nick. *Masochism: The Art of Power*. Westport, CT: Praeger, 1997.
Margolis, Norman M. 'A Theory on the Psychology of Jazz.' *American Imago* 11 (1954): 263–91.
Marston, Nicholas. 'Schubert's Homecoming.' *Journal of the Royal Musical Association* 125, no. 2 (2000): 248–70.
Mauger, Jacques. 'Listening to Schumann: My Suffering, His Pain'. *Canadian Journal of Psychoanalysis* 19 (2011): 212–19.
McClary, Susan. 'Constructions of Subjectivity in Schubert's Music.' In *Queering the Pitch: The New Gay and Lesbian Musicology*. Edited by Philip Brett, Elizabeth Wood, and Gary C. Thomas, 205–34. London: Routledge, 1994.
McGuire, William and Richard Francis Carrington Hull (eds). *C.G. Jung Speaking: Interviews and Encounter*. London: Picador, 1980.
McKay, Elizabeth N. *Franz Schubert*. Oxford: Oxford University Press, 1996.
Merton, Robert. *Sociological Ambivalence and Other Essays*. New York: Free Press, 1976.
Meyer, Leonard. *Music and Emotion*. Chicago, IL: University of Chicago Press, 1956.
Minagawa-Kawai, Yasuyo, Sunao Matsuoka, Ippeita Dan, Nozomi Naoi, Katsuki Nakamura, and Shozo Kojima. 'Prefrontal Activation Associated with Social Attachment: Facial-Emotion Recognition in Mothers and Infants.' *Cerebral Cortex* 19, no. 2 (2009): 284–92.
Monahan, Seth. 'Voice-Leading Energetics in Wagner's "*Tristan* Idiom".' *Music Analysis* 35, no. 2 (2016): 171–232.
Montani, Angelo. 'Psychoanalysis of Music.' *The Psychoanalytic Review* 32 (1945): 225–27.
Moore, Alison. 'Rethinking Gendered Perversion and Degeneration in Visions of Sadism and Masochism, 1886–1930.' *Journal of the History of Sexuality* 18 (2009): 138–57.
Moore, Allan F. 'Jethro Tull and the Case for Modernism in Mass Culture.' In *Analyzing Popular Music*. Edited by Allan F. Moore, 158–72. Cambridge and New York: Cambridge University Press, 2003.
Mosonyi, Desiderius. 'Die Irrationalen Grundlagen der Musik.' *Imago* 21 (1935): 207–26.
Nagel, Julie Jaffee. *Melodies of the Mind: Connections between Psychoanalysis and Music*. London: Routledge, 2013.

Nagel, Julie Jaffee and Samuel Bradshaw. 'Coda: Psychoanalysis and Music in the Psyche and Society.' *International Journal of Applied Psychoanalytic Studies* 10, no. 2 (2013): 147–51.

Nagel, Thomas. *The View from Nowhere*. Oxford: Oxford University Press, 1989.

Nass, Martin L. 'Some Considerations of a Psychoanalytic Interpretation of Music' [1971]. In *Psychoanalytic Explorations in Music*. Edited by Stuart Feder, Richard L. Karmel, and George H. Pollock, 39–48. Madison, CT: International Universities Press, 1990.

Nattiez, Jean-Jacques. 'The Concepts of Plot and Seriation Process in Music Analysis.' Translated by Catherine Dale. *Music Analysis* 4, no. 1/2 (1985): 107–18.

Nattiez, Jean-Jacques. *Music and Discourse: Toward a Semiology of Music*. Translated by Carolyn Abbate. Princeton, NJ: Princeton University Press, 1990.

Negus, Keith. 'Narrative Time and the Popular Song.' *Popular Music and Society* 35, no. 4 (2012): 483–500.

Nettl, Bruno. 'Infant Musical Development and Primitive Music.' *Southwestern Journal of Anthropology* 12 (1956): 87–91.

Nettl, Bruno. *The Study of Ethnomusicology: Thirty One Issues and Concepts*, new edition. Champaign: University of Illinois Press, 2005.

Niecks, Friedrich. 'Critical Excursions: Schumann.' *The Musical Times* 22, no. 464 (1881): 498–501.

Nietzsche, Friedrich W. *The Birth of Tragedy, and The Case of Wagner*. Translated by Walter Kaufmann. New York: Vintage, 1967.

Noble, Mariane. *The Masochistic Pleasures of Sentimental Literature*. Princeton, NJ: Princeton University Press, 2000.

Noudelmann, François. *The Philosopher's Touch: Sartre, Nietzsche and Barthes at the Piano*. Translated by Brian J. Reilly. New York: Columbia University Press, 2012.

Noy, Pinchas. 'The Psychodynamics of Music—Part 1.' *Journal of Music Therapy* 3, no. 4 (1966): 126–34.

Noy, Pinchas. 'The Psychodynamics of Music—Part 2.' *Journal of Music Therapy* 4, no. 1 (1967): 7–23.

Noy, Pinchas. 'The Psychodynamics of Music—Part 3.' *Journal of Music Therapy* 4, no. 2 (1967): 45–51.

Noy, Pinchas. 'The Psychodynamics of Music—Part 4.' *Journal of Music Therapy* 4, no. 3 (1967): 81–94.

Noy, Pinchas. 'The Psychodynamics of Music—Part 5.' *Journal of Music Therapy* 4, no. 4 (1967): 117–25.

Noy, Pinchas. 'How Music Conveys Emotions.' In *Psychoanalytic Explorations in Music: Second Series*. Edited by Stuart Feder, Richard L. Karmel, and George H. Pollock, 125–49. Madison, CT: International Universities Press, 1993.

Ostwald, Peter. 'Florestan, Eusebius, Clara, and Schumann's Right Hand.' *19th-Century Music* 4, no. 1 (1980): 17–31.

Ostwald, Peter. *Schumann: Music and Madness*. London: Gollancz, 1985.

Pavlicevic, Mercédès. 'Dynamic Interplay in Clinical Improvisation.' *Journal of British Music Therapy* 4, no. 2 (1990): 5–9.

Pavlicevic, Mercédès and Gary Ansdell. 'Between Communicative Musicality and Collaborative Musicing: A Perspective from Community Music Therapy.' In *Communicative Musicality: Exploring the Basis of Human Companionship*. Edited by Stephen Malloch and Colwyn Trevarthen, 357–76. Oxford: Oxford University Press, 2009.

Paynter, John. *Hear and Now: An Introduction to Modern Music in Schools*. London: Universal Edition, 1972.
Pesic, Peter. 'Schubert's Dream.' *19th-Century Music* 23, no. 2 (1999): 136–44.
Peters, Gary. *The Philosophy of Improvisation*. Chicago, IL and London: University of Chicago Press, 2009.
Pfeifer, Sigmund. 'Problems of the Psychology of Music in the Light of Psycho-Analysis. Part 1. Psychophysiology of Musical Sound.' *International Journal of Psychoanalysis* 3, no. 1 (1922): 127–30.
Poizat, Michel. *The Angel's Cry: Beyond the Pleasure Principle in Opera*. Translated by Arthur Denner. Ithaca, NY and London: Cornell University Press, 1992.
Pratt, Carroll C. 'Music as the Language of Emotion' [Lecture delivered 21 December 1950]. Washington, DC: The Library of Congress/The Louis Charles Elson Memorial Fund, 1952.
Praz, Mario. *The Romantic Agony*. London: Oxford University Press, 1933.
Priestley, Mary. *Music Therapy in Action*. London: Constable, 1975.
Priestley, Mary. 'Linking Sound and Symbol.' In *The Art and Science of Music Therapy: A Handbook*. Edited by Tony Wigram, Bruce Saperston, and Robert West, 129–38. Amsterdam: Harwood Academic Publishers, 1995.
Ramadanovic, Petar. 'No Place Like Ideology (On Slavoj Žižek): Is There a Difference between the Theory of Ideology and the Theory of Interpretation?' *Cultural Critique* 86 (2014): 119–38.
Rechardt, Eero. 'Experiencing Music.' *The Psychoanalytic Study of the Child* 42 (1987): 511–30.
Rehding, Alexander. *Hugo Riemann and the Birth of Modern Musical Thought*. Cambridge: Cambridge University Press, 2008.
Reich, Willi. 'Alban Berg's *Lulu*.' The *Musical Quarterly* 22 (1936): 383–401.
Reichardt, Sarah. *Composing the Modern Subject: Four String Quartets by Dmitri Shostakovich*. Aldershot: Ashgate, 2008.
Reik, Theodor. *Masochism in Modern Man*. New York: Farrar, Straus & Co., 1941.
Reik, Theodor. *Haunting Melody: Psychoanalytic Experience in Life and Music*. New York: Da Capo Press, 1983/1953.
Restuccia, Frances L. 'Molly in Furs: Deleuzian/Masochian Masochism in the Writing of James Joyce.' *NOVEL: A Forum on Fiction* 18 (1985): 101–16.
Reynolds, Simon. *Energy Flash: A Journey through Rave Music and Dance Culture*. London: Faber & Faber, 2012.
Riemann, Hugo. *Systematische Modulationslehre als Grundlage der musikalischen Formenlehre*. Hamburg: J. F. Richter, 1887.
Riemann, Hugo. *Vereinfachte Harmonielehre, oder die Lehre von den tonalen Funktionen der Akkorde*. London: Augener, 1893.
Rimmon-Kenan, Shlomith (ed). *Discourse in Psychoanalysis and Literature*. London: Methuen, 1987.
Rings, Steven. *Tonality and Transformation*. New York and Oxford: Oxford University Press, 2011.
Roazen, Paul. *Freud and His Followers*. New York: DaCapo Press, 1975.
Roberts, Randall. 'First Take: Taylor Swift Accents New Single with Hint of Dubstep.' *Los Angeles Times*, October 9, 2012. Available at http://articles.latimes.com/2012/oct/09/entertainment/la-et-ms-first-take-taylor-swift-accents-new-single-with-hint-of-dubstep-20121009.

Rodgers, Stephen. '"This Body that Beats": Roland Barthes and Robert Schumann's *Kreisleriana.*' *Indiana Theory Review* 18 (1997): 75–91.

Rose, Gilbert J. *Between Couch and Piano: Psychoanalysis, Music, Art and Neuroscience.* Hove and New York: Brunner-Routledge, 2004.

Rosen, Charles. *The Romantic Generation.* New York: HarperCollins, 1995.

Ross, Alex. *The Rest Is Noise.* New York: Picador, 2007.

Rusbridger, Richard. 'The Internal World of Don Giovanni.' *International Journal of Psychoanalysis* 89, no. 1 (2008): 181–94.

Samuels, Andrew, Bani Shorter, and Fred Plaut. *A Critical Dictionary of Jungian Analysis.* London and New York: Routledge, 1986.

Sautereig, Lutz D.H. 'Loss of Innocence: Albert Moll, Sigmund Freud and the Invention of Childhood Sexuality Around 1900.' *Medical History* 56, no. 2 (2012): 156–83.

Scarry, Elaine. *The Body in Pain: The Making and Unmaking of the World.* Oxford: Oxford University Press, 1985.

Schenker, Heinrich. 'Ihr Bild' in *Tonwille*, Vol. 1. Vienna: Universal, 1921.

Schenker, Heinrich. *Free Composition.* Translated by Ernst Oster. New York and London: Longman, 1979.

Scherer, Klaus R. 'Which Emotions Can Be Induced by Music? What Are the Underlying Mechanisms? And How Can We Measure Them?' *Journal of New Music Research* 33, no. 3 (2004): 239–51.

Scherzinger, Martin. 'Music, Corporate Power, and Unending War.' *Cultural Critique* 60 (2005): 23–67.

Schmalfeldt, Janet. *In the Process of Becoming: Analytic and Philosophical Perspectives on Form in Early Nineteenth-Century Music.* Oxford: Oxford University Press, 2011.

Schneider, Michel. *La tombée du jour.* Paris: Seuil, 1989.

Schoenberg, Arnold. *Style and Idea: Selected Writings of Arnold Schoenberg.* Edited by Leonard Stein. New York: St. Martin's Press, 1975.

Schoenberg, Arnold. *Letters.* Edited by Erwin Stein. Translated by Eithne Wilkins and Ernst Kaiser. Berkeley: University of California Press, 1987.

Schumann, Robert. *Schumann on Music.* Edited and translated by Henry Pleasants. New York: Dover, 1988.

Schwarz, David. *Listening Awry: Music and Alterity in German Culture.* Minneapolis and London: University of Minnesota Press, 2006.

Sedgwick, Eve Kosofsky. *Epistemology of the Closet.* Updated edition with a new introduction. Berkeley: University of California Press, 2008.

Shawn, Allen. *Arnold Schoenberg's Journey.* Cambridge, MA: Harvard University Press, 2002.

Sherry, Jay. *Carl Gustav Jung: Avant-Garde Conservative.* New York: Palgrave Macmillan, 2010.

Siciliano, Michael. 'Toggling Cycles, Hexatonic Systems, and Some Analysis of Early Atonal Music.' *Music Theory Spectrum* 27, no. 2 (2005): 221–48.

Siegel, Allen M. *Heinz Kohut and the Psychology of the Self.* London: Routledge, 1996.

Sigler, David. '"Read Mr. Sacher-Masoch": The Literariness of Masochism in the Philosophy of Jacques Lacan and Gilles Deleuze.' *Criticism* 53 (2011): 189–212.

Silverman, Kaja. *The Subject of Semiotics.* New York: Oxford University Press, 1983.

Silverman, Kaja. *Male Subjectivity at the Margins.* London: Routledge, 1992.

Simms, Bryan R. *The Atonal Music of Arnold Schoenberg, 1908–1923*. Oxford: Oxford University Press, 2000.

Skar, Patricia. 'The Goal as Process: Music and the Search for the Self.' *Journal of Analytical Psychology* 47, no. 4 (2002): 629–38.

Sly, Gordon. 'Schubert's Innovations in Sonata Form: Compositional Logic and Structural Interpretation.' *Journal of Music Theory* 45, no. 1 (2001): 119–50.

Smith, Kenneth. 'Lacan, Zemlinsky, and Der Zwerg: Mirror, Metaphor, and Fantasy.' *Perspectives of New Music* 48, no. 2 (2010): 78–113.

Smith, Kenneth. 'The Tonic Chord and Lacan's Object *a* in Selected Songs by Charles Ives.' *Journal of the Royal Musicological Association* 136, no. 2 (2011): 353–98.

Smith, Kenneth. *Skryabin, Philosophy and the Music of Desire*. Farnham and Burlington, VT: Ashgate, 2013.

Smith, Robert. *The Wounded Jung: Effects of Jung's Relationships on His Life and Work*. Evanston, IL: Northwestern University Press, 1997.

Soley, Gaye and Erin E. Hannon. 'Infants Prefer the Musical Meter of Their Own Culture: A Cross-Cultural Comparison.' *Developmental Psychology* 46 (2010): 286–92.

Solomon, Robert. 'On Kitsch and Sentimentality.' *The Journal of Aesthetics and Art Criticism* 49 (1991): 1–14.

Spicer, Mark. '(Ac)cumulative Form in Pop-Rock Music.' *Twentieth-Century Music* 1, no. 1 (2004): 29–64.

Spitz, Ellen Handler. 'Separation-Individuation in a Cycle of Songs: George Crumb's Ancient Voices of Children.' *The Psychoanalytic Study of the Child* 42 (1987): 531–43.

Springnether, Madalon. 'Reading Freud's Life.' In *Freud 2000*. Edited by Anthony Elliot, 139–68. New York: Routledge, 1998.

Steege, Benjamin. '"The Nature of Harmony": A Translation and Commentary.' In *The Oxford Handbook of Neo-Riemannian Theories*. Edited by Edward Gollin and Alexander Rehding, 55–91. New York: Oxford University Press, 2011.

Stein, Alexander. 'The Sound of Memory: Music an Acoustic Origins.' *American Imago* 64, no. 1 (2007): 59–85.

Stein, Alexander. 'Psychoanalysis and Music.' In *Textbook of Psychoanalysis*. Edited by Glen O. Gabbard, Bonnie E. Litowitz, and Paul Williams, 551–66. 2nd edition. Washington, DC and London: American Psychiatric Association, 2012.

Sterba, Richard. 'The Problem of Art in Freud's Writings.' *Psychoanalytic Quarterly* 9 (1940): 256–68.

Sterba, Richard. 'Toward the Problem of Musical Process.' *Psychoanalytic Review* 33 (1946): 37–43.

Sterba, Richard. 'Psychoanalysis and Music.' *American Imago* 22 (1965): 96–111.

Stewart, Allison. 'Taylor Swift's "Red" Is Another Winner, but She Needs to Start Acting Her Age". *Washington Post*, October 22, 2012. Available at www.washingtonpost.com/entertainment/music/taylor-swifts-red-is-another-winner-but-she-needs-to-start-acting-her-age/2012/10/22/af79a2fe-1a1e-11e2-ad4a-e5a958b60a1e_story.html.

Stewart, Suzanne R. *Sublime Surrender: Male Masochism at the Fin-de-siècle*. Ithaca, NY: Cornell University Press, 1998.

Subotnik, Rose Rosengard. *Deconstructive Variations: Music and Reason in Western Society*. Minneapolis and London: University of Minnesota Press, 1995.

Sullivan, Paul. *Remixology: Tracing the Dub Diaspora.* London: Reaktion Books, 2014.
Sulloway, Frank. *Freud: Biologist of the Mind.* New York: Basic Books, 1979.
Taylor, Paul. *Žižek and the Media.* Cambridge: Polity Press, 2010.
Taylor, Timothy D. *The Sounds of Capitalism: Advertising, Music, and the Conquest of Culture.* Chicago, IL and London: Chicago University Press, 2012.
Tilly, Margaret. 'The Therapy of Music.' In *C.G. Jung Speaking: Interviews and Encounter.* Edited by William McGuire and Richard Francis Carrington Hull, 261–63. London: Picador, 1980.
Tolbert, Elizabeth. 'Untying the Music/Language Knot.' In *Music, Sensation, and Sensuality.* Edited by Linda Phyllis Austern, 77–83. London: Routledge, 2002.
Trehub, Sandra E. and Erin E. Hannon. 'Conventional Rhythms Enhance Infants' and Adults' Perception of Music.' *Cortex* 45 (2009): 110–18.
Treitler, Leo. 'Reflections on the Communication of Affect and Idea through Music.' In *Psychoanalytic Explorations in Music: Second Series.* Edited by Stuart Feder, Richard L. Karmel, and George H. Pollock, 43–62. Madison, CT: International Universities Press, 1993.
Trevarthen, Colwyn and Stephen Malloch. 'The Dance of Wellbeing: Defining the Musical Therapeutic Effect.' *Nordisk Tidsskrift for Musikkterapi* 9, no. 2 (2000): 3–17.
Truscott, Harold. 'Schubert's String Quartet in G Major.' *Music Review* 20 (1959): 119–45.
Tyler, Helen M. 'The Music Therapy Profession in Modern Britain.' In *Music as Medicine: The History of Music Therapy Since Antiquity.* Edited by Peregrine Horden, 375–93. Aldershot: Ashgate, 2000.
Tymoczko, Dmitri. *A Geometry of Music: Harmony and Counterpoint in the Extended Common Practice.* New York and Oxford: Oxford University Press, 2011.
Wason, Robert W. Elizabeth West Marvin, and Hugo Riemann. 'Riemann's "Ideen zu Einer 'Lehre von den Tonvorstellungen'": An Annotated Translation.' *Journal of Music Theory* 36, no. 1 (1992): 69–79.
Watkins, Holly. 'Slavoj Žižek: Responding from the Void.' *Contemporary Music Review* 31, no. 5/6 (2012): 449–60.
Watkins, Holly. 'The Floral Poetics of Schumann's *Blumenstück*, Op. 19.' *19th-Century Music* 36, no. 1 (2012): 24–45.
Watson, Tessa. 'Music Therapy with Adults with Learning Disabilities.' In *The Handbook of Music Therapy.* Edited by Leslie Bunt and Sarah Hoskyns, 97–114. Hove: Brunner-Routledge, 2002.
Webster, James. 'Schubert's Sonata Form and Brahms's First Maturity.' *19th-Century Music* 2, no. 1 (1978/1979): 18–35.
Wickes, Lewis. 'Schoenberg, *Erwartung*, and the Reception of Psychoanalysis in Musical Circles in Vienna until 1910/1911.' *Studies in Music* 23 (1989): 88–106.
Wildgans, Friedrich. *Anton Webern.* Translated by E. T. Roberts and H. Searle. London: Calder & Boyars, 1966.
Williamson, Jennifer A. *Twentieth-Century Sentimentalism.* New Brunswick, NJ: Rutgers University Press, 2014.
Wilson, Samuel. 'Building an Instrument, Building an Instrumentalist: Helmut Lachenmann's *Serynade*.' *Contemporary Music Review* 32, no. 5 (2013): 425–36.
Wilson, Samuel. 'After Beethoven, after Hegel: Legacies of Selfhood in Schnittke's String Quartet No. 4.' *International Review of the Aesthetics and Sociology of Music* 45, no. 2 (2014): 311–34.

200 Bibliography

Wilson, Samuel. 'Valentin Silvestrov and the Symphonic Monument in Ruins.' In *Transformations of Musical Modernism*. Edited by Julian Johnson and Erling E. Guldbrandsen, 201–20. Cambridge: Cambridge University Press, 2015.

Winter, Robert, Maurice J. E. Brown, and Eric Sams. 'Schubert, Franz (Peter).' In *The New Grove Dictionary of Music and Musicians* 22, (2001): 655–729.

Wintle, Christopher. 'Webern's Lyric Character.' In *Webern Studies*. Edited by Kathryn Bailey, 229–63. Cambridge: Cambridge University Press, 1996.

Wollenberg, Susan. *Schubert's Fingerprints: Studies in the Instrumental Works*. Farnham: Ashgate, 2011.

Yates, Sybille. 'Some Aspects of Time Difficulties and Their Relation to Music.' *International Journal of Psychoanalysis* 16, no. 3 (1935): 341–54.

Žižek, Slavoj. *Looking Awry: An Introduction to Jacques Lacan through Popular Culture*. Cambridge, MA: MIT Press, 1991.

Žižek, Slavoj. *The Metastases of Enjoyment: Six Essays on Women and Causality*. London: Verso, 1994.

Žižek, Slavoj. '"There Is No Sexual Relationship": Wagner as a Lacanian.' *New German Critique*, no. 69 (1996): 7–35.

Žižek, Slavoj. *The Plague of Fantasies*. London: Verso, 1997.

Žižek, Slavoj. *Enjoy Your Symptom*. New York and London: Taylor & Francis, 2001.

Žižek, Slavoj. *How to Read Lacan*. London: Granta Books, 2006.

Žižek, Slavoj. *The Sublime Object of Ideology*. London: Verso, 2008.

Žižek, Slavoj. *Violence*. London: Profile Books, 2008.

Zoller, Guther. 'Original Duplicity: The Ideal and the Real in Fichte's Transcendental Theory of the Subject.' In *The Modern Subject: Conception of the Self in Classical German Philosophy*. Edited by Karl Ameriks and Dieter Sturma, 115–30. Albany: State University of New York, 1995.

Index

12-tone method 51–2

acousmatic voice 38
acoustic gaze 39–45
active fantasies 136–7
active listeners 158
acts of identification: fulfillment and representation 126–31; Freud and Schoenberg 62; identified with/identifiable as 124–6; transubjective focus 132
Adler, Alfred 58–9
aesthetic diversity: art-making 142–5
affordance: musical listening 153–4
Agamben, Giorgio: zoe and bios 38
Anzieu, Didier 37, 39
apostates: Freud 58–9; Schoenberg 60–1
applied psychoanalytic thinking 120
art-making: aesthetic diversity 142–5; formal *versus* therapeutic 145–6; music therapy 140–2; transcendent function 137–40
aspects of subjectivity 124
axis system 70–2

Barthes, Roland: *Camera Lucida* 169; 'The Grain of the Voice' 25–9; punctum 164
bass drop 107–8
bios 38
body: non-articulate sounds 35–7; vocal signification and 27–9
Brooks, Peter 120

Camera Lucida 169
chess automation device 32–3
chords: axis system 70–2; hearing functions 69–70; metaphors and metonymy 73–5; static 68–9; static minor-third related 68–9
Clarke, Eric: affordance 153–4
Coldness and Cruelty 166

communicating through voice: emotion 30–2; meaning 27–9
concatenation: musical listening 153
conscious: active *versus* passive fantasies 136–7; understanding the unconscious in conscious form 137–40
contemporary music therapy 140–2
cries triggering pleasure in opera 30–2

de-acousmatization 38
Deleuze, Gilles: *Coldness and Cruelty* 166; desire 77, 80
desire: Lacan's graph of desire 92–4; locating in musical text 94–7; music theory 66–8; teleological 77
developing mind 8–12
Dolar, Mladen 32–9
dubstep 104–5; bass drop 107–8; mixing with pop music 110–11; pleasures 109–10

early childhood: sound 2–3
'The Economic Problem of Masochism' 165
E.D.M. (electronic dance music) 104–5
Ehrenzweig, Anton 7–8, 14
Eisler, Hanns 60–1
emotions: communicating through voice 30–2
energetics: tonal 66–8
enjoyment *see* pleasure
expectation process of musical listening 155

fantasies: active *versus* passive 136–7; Lacan's graph of desire 92–4; locating desire in musical text 94–7
feminine: sentimentalism 167
fictional subjects 122–3

fictive subjects 123; acts of identification 125
Fisher-Dieskau, Dietrich: phenosong 27–9
fluidity of pop music 112
followers: Freud 58–9; Schoenberg 60–1
formal art-making 145–6
free art-making *see* art-making
Freud, Sigmund: apostates 58–9; 'The Economic Problem of Masochism' 165; Id-Ego-Superego model 52–3; 'Leonardo da Vinci and A Memory of His Childhood' 121; obsessions with priority 55–6; Oedipus 53, 59, 80, 129–30, 165; pleasure principle 29; "vulgar" Freudianism 6
Freud and Schoenberg parallels: disciples and apostates 58–62; Moses inspiration 62–3; priority and originality 54–8; structural models 50–4; superficial similarities 49–50
fulfillment of subjects 126–31

genosong: phenosong differences 27–9
genotext 25–6
genres: universalizing 6–7
Graf, Max: study of Richard Wagner 121
'The Grain of the Voice' 25–9
graph of desire: Schubert's sonata form 92–4
Guildhall School of Music and Drama in London 140

Haeuer, Josef Matthias 56–7
haunting melodies 121–2
Hitschmann, Edward: study of Franz Schubert 121
Hostinský, Otakar: *Tonnetz* 66–7
Huron, David: expectation 155

Id-Ego-Superego model 52–3
identifiable as subjects 124–6
identified with subjects 124–6
'Ihr bild' 40–5
'I Knew You Were Trouble' 104–11; dubstep 104–5; reviews of dubstep incorporation 109; turning point of Swift's career 111; violent imagery 110–11
imaginary silence 39
Imaginary-Symbolic tonal function 75–6
individuals as subjects of study 121
infantile sexuality 3, 9, 13, 55–6

Jones, Ernest 55, 130
Jung, Carl 58–9; active *versus* passive fantasies 136–7; transcendent function *see* transcendent function

Kohut, Heinz 4
Krafft-Ebing, Richard von 165
Krenek, Ernst 60
Kris, Ernst 3, 124
Kristeva, Julia 25–7, 125–6; genotext 25–6; phenotext 26–7

Lacan, Jacques: fantasy 4, 84–97; graph of desire 92–4; gaze 40–1, 45; metaphor formula 73; metonym formula 73; objet petit a 2, 33–9, 76–7
Lendvai, Ernö: axis system 70–2
'Leonardo da Vinci and A Memory of His Childhood' 121
Levinson, Jerrold: concatenation 153
"LFO rape" (low-frequency oscillator riffs) 105
listening to music: affordance 153–4; concatenation 153; expectation 155; opera cries triggering pleasure 30–2; resistance 155–7; symbolic listening 158–60
locating desire in musical text 94–7
low-frequency oscillator riffs ("LFO rape") 105
Lulu's death in *Lulu* 30–1

Marie's death in *Wozzeck* 30–1
marketization of pop music 112–13
masochism 164–6; 'Chopin' 173–8; Schumann 171–3; sentimentalism 167–71
Masochism in Modern Man 166
mastery: oceanic feeling 4–6
melodies: haunting 121–2
metaphors 73–5
metonym formula 73
metonymy 74–5
modernism: bass drop 107–8; definition 100; dubstep 104–5; fluidity of pop music 112; mixing dubstep with pop 110–11; musical language 102–4; pleasures of dubstep 109–10; resistance 112–13; representation 7; sentimentalism 168; shock value 108–9; Taylor Swift's 'I Knew You Were Trouble' 104–11; underground music 105–7

Moll, Albert 55–6
Moses inspiration 62–3
musical language: modernism 102–4
musically trained *versus* untrained analysis 152–3
musical subjects 123–4
music therapy: aesthetic diversity 142–5; formal *versus* therapeutic art-making 145–6; transcendent function 140–2

negative therapeutic reaction 97
neo-Riemannian theory: hearing functions 69–70; Imaginary-Symbolic tonal function 75–6; Lendvai's axis system 70–2; metaphors 73–5; static minor-third related chords 68–9; teleological desire 77; tonal energetics 66–8
non-articulate body sounds 35–7

objective violence 100–1; subjective violence becoming part of 111
object voice 32–9; acousmatic 38; bare life and political life 38; non-articulate body sounds 35–7; repetitive patterns 33–5; silence 38–9
oceanic feeling 4–6, 12, 39, 126
opera: cries triggering pleasure in listeners 30–2

pain *versus* suffering 173
Panzera, Charles: genosong 27–9
parallels between Schoenberg and Freud: disciples and apostates 58–62; Moses inspiration 62–3; priority and originality 54–8; structural models 50–4; superficial similarities 49–50
particularity of a music focus 7
passive fantasies 136–7
phenosong: genosong differences 27–9
phenotext 26–7
pleasure: dubstep 109–10; opera cries 30–2; resistant listening 155–7
pleasure principle 29
Poizat, Michel 29–32
pop music: bass drop 107–8; dubstep 104–6; fluidity 112; 'I Knew You Were Trouble' 104–11; mixing dubstep with pop 110–11; musical language 102–4; pleasure in dubstep 109–10; resistance 112–13; shock value 108–9; underground 105–7
post-linguistic utterances 37
pre-linguistic utterances 37

Priestley, Mary 139
primitive aspects 8–10
priority and originality: Freud 55–6; Schoenberg 56–8
psychobiographies 121
psychological processes of musical listening: affordance 153–4; concatenation 153; expectation 155; musically trained *versus* untrained adults 152–3; resistance 155–7; symbolic listening 158–60
punctum 164

Reik, Theodor 8, 121–2, 124, 128; *Masochism in Modern Man* 166
repetitive voice patterns 33–5
representation of subjects 126–31
resistance: musical listening 155–7; pop music 112–13
rhythm 5, 8, 13–14, 26, 108, 125, 141–2, 144

Schoenberg, Arnold: 12-tone method 51–2; apostates 60–1; conflicts with Webern 61–2; priority and originality 56–8
Schoenberg and Freud parallels: disciples and apostates 58–62; Moses inspiration 62–3; priority and originality 54–8; structural models 50–4; superficial similarities 49–50
Schubert, Franz: 'Der Doppelgänger' 33–5; Hitschmann's study 121; 'Ihr Bild' 40–5; Lacan's graph of desire 92–4; locating desire in musical text 94–7; mental health 86; old-style evaluation 84; tonal symbolic order 86–91
Schumann, Robert: sentimentalism 171–3
self-positing 156
sentimentalism: 'Chopin' 173–8; masochism 167–71; Schumann 171–3
shock value in modernism 108–9
shofar sound 38
signifying functions 73
silence 38–9
sonata theory: Lacan's graph of desire 92–4; locating desire in musical text 94–7; old-style evaluation 84; tonal symbolic order 86–91
sonogram comparisons: phenosong/ genosong 27–9

sound: early childhood 2–3; God/shofar 38
speaking machines 32–3
static minor-third related chords 68–9
Sterba, Richard 2–4, 9, 13–15, 129
structural models of Schoenberg and Freud 50–4; 12-tone method 51–2; Id-Ego-Superego model 52–3
styles: universalizing 6–7
subjective violence 100–1; bass drop 107–8; becoming part of objective violence 111; E.D.M. 105
subjects 119–20; aspects of subjectivity 124; fictional 122–3; fulfillment and representation 126–31; identified with/identifiable as 124–6; individuals 121; musical 123–4; tangible 120–2; transubjective 132
sublimation 120–1
suffering *versus* pain 173
Swift, Taylor: 'I Knew You Were Trouble' 104–11
symbolic listening 158–60
symbolic silence 38–9

tangible subjects 120–2; acts of identification 124–5
teleological desire 77
therapeutic art-making 145–6
tonal energetics 66–8
tonal function: energetic 66–8; Imaginary-Symbolic 75–6; Lendvai's axis system 70–2; magnetic 69–70; metaphors and metonymy 73–5; static 68–9; symbolic order of Schubert 86–91; teleological desire 77
Tonnetz 66–7

transcendent function: aesthetic diversity in art-making 142–5; formal *versus* therapeutic aesthetic 145–6; music therapy 140–2; understanding the unconscious through art-making 137–40
transubjective focus of subjects 132
Tristan & Isolde 16, 67, 75, 78–9, 131

unconscious: active *versus* passive fantasies 136–7; understanding through art-making 137–40
underground music 105–7
universalizing genres/styles 6–7

violence: bass drop 107–8; E.D.M. 105; mixing dubstep with pop music 110–11; objective 100–1; subjective 100–1; subjective becoming part of objective violence 111
voice: acoustic gaze 39–45; communicating emotion 30–2; communicating meaning 27–9; object voice 32–9

Wagner, Richard: Graf's study 121; harmony 74, 88, 93; hysteria 75; *Tristan & Isolde* 16, 67, 75, 78–9, 131; *Parsifal* 31
Webern conflicts with Schoenberg 61–2
Weill, Kurt 60
Wozzeck 30–1

Žižek, Slavoj 75, 85, 96–7, 100–3, 112, 157
zoe 38